APA PUBLICATIONS
Part of the Langenscheidt Publishing Group

INSIGHT GUIDE
CORSICA

Editorial
Edited by
Clare Griffiths
Editorial Director
Brian Bell

Distribution
UK & Ireland
GeoCenter International Ltd
The Viables Centre, Harrow Way
Basingstoke, Hants RG22 4BJ
Fax: (44) 1256 817988

United States
Langenscheidt Publishers, Inc.
46–35 54th Road, Maspeth, NY 11378
Fax: 1 (718) 784 0640

Canada
Thomas Allen & Son Ltd
390 Steelcase Road East
Markham, Ontario L3R 1G2
Fax: (1) 905 475 6747

Australia
Universal Publishing
1 Waterloo Road
Macquarie Park, NSW 2113
Fax: (61) 2 9888 9074

New Zealand
Hema Maps New Zealand Ltd (HNZ)
Unit D, 24 Ra ORA Drive
East Tamaki, Auckland
Fax: (64) 9 273 6479

Worldwide
**Apa Publications GmbH & Co.
Verlag KG (Singapore branch)**
38 Joo Koon Road, Singapore 628990
Tel: (65) 6865 1600. Fax: (65) 6861 6438

Printing
Insight Print Services (Pte) Ltd
38 Joo Koon Road, Singapore 628990
Tel: (65) 6865 1600. Fax: (65) 6861 6438

©2004 Apa Publications GmbH & Co.
Verlag KG (Singapore branch)
All Rights Reserved

First Edition 1990
Fourth Edition 2004

CONTACTING THE EDITORS

www.insightguides.com

ABOUT THIS BOOK

This guidebook combines the interests and enthusiasms of two of the world's best-known information providers: Insight Guides, whose titles have set the standard for visual travel guides since 1970, and Discovery Channel, the world's premier source of nonfiction television programming.

The editors of Insight Guides provide both practical advice and general understanding about a destination's history, culture, institutions and people. Discovery Channel and its website, www.discovery.com, help millions of viewers explore their world from the comfort of their own home and encourage them to explore it first hand.

Insight Guide: Corsica is structured to convey an understanding of the island and its people as well as to guide readers through its sights and activities:

◆ The **Features** section, indicated by a yellow bar at the top of each page, covers the natural and cultural history of Corsica in a series of informative essays.

◆ The main **Places** section, indicated by a blue bar, is a complete guide to all the sights and areas worth visiting. Places of special interest are coordinated by number with the maps.

◆ The **Travel Tips** listings section, with an orange bar, provides a handy point of reference for information on travel, hotels, shops, restaurants, language and more. Information may be located quickly using the index printed on the back cover flap, which also serves as a handy bookmark.

EXPLORE YOUR WORLD®

The contributors

To capture the diverse richness of an island such as Corsica takes a guide book that can reflect its beauty and describe its idiosyncrasies and charms. Why, ever since antiquity, has Corsica been regarded as "the island of beauty" while being rough and wild at the same time? And the Corsicans? Are they really the taciturn, melancholic individuals as portrayed in the 19th century, whose tempers are unleashed in acts of blood revenge or vendetta? Or is their character better epitomised by their proud love of freedom and limitless hospitality?

These are just some of the questions examined by this book, which provides a vivid picture of the stunning landscape and reveals the enduring culture of the people who were close to Samuel Johnson's heart when he wrote: "Empty my head of Corsica! Empty it of honour, empty it of humanity, empty it of friendship, empty it of piety."

This latest edition of the book was supervised in Insight Guides' London office by **Clare Griffiths**. It builds upon the first edition of the guide, edited by **Jutta Schütz** who assembled a team of writers which included **Dr Alphons Schauseil, Richard S Moulijn, Dr Hartmut Lücke, Ilse Tubbesing, Heidemarie Karin Geiss, Ruth Merten, Dr Gerhard H. Oberzill, Anita Back** and **Gert Hirner**.

The updater for this edition was **David Abram** who first visited the island about 16 years ago during the sabbatical year of a French degree. Abram discovered Corsica's hiking potential when he came across some waymarks and followed them for two days until wild pigs finished off his supplies. Since then he's walked extensively in The Himalayas, Europe and North America but still regards Corsica as a benchmark trekking destination.

Along with thoroughly revising and updating the book Abrams contributed new essays on the Corsican language and the island's fascinating traditional music. In the Places section he wrote new chapters for the Alta Rocca and the beautiful area south of Corte.

Many of the images in this book are the work of photographers **Pete Bennett, János Stekovics** and **Michael Gotin**. Picture research was by **Hilary Genin**. Proofreading and indexing were by **Penny Phenix**, and **Sylvia Suddes** undertook an overall check.

Map Legend

━ ━ ‥ ━	International Boundary
━ ━ ━ ━	Département Boundary
━ • ━ • ━	National Park/Reserve
━ ━ ━ ━	Ferry Route
✈ ✈	Airport: International/ Regional
🚌	Bus Station
❶	Tourist Information
✉	Post Office
✝ † ⛪	Church/Ruins
†	Monastery
☾	Mosque
✡	Synagogue
🏰 🏯	Castle/Ruins
🏠	Mansion/Stately home
∴	Archaeological Site
∩	Cave
⚐	Statue/Monument
★	Place of Interest

The main places of interest in the Places section are coordinated by number with a full-colour map (e.g. ❶), and a symbol at the top of every right-hand page tells you where to find the map.

INSIGHT GUIDE
CORSICA

CONTENTS

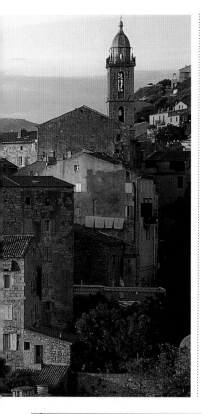

Sartène at dusk.

Travel Tips

Places

CORSICA THE BEAUTIFUL

With two-thirds of Corsica given over to national park, there's more to the island than its beautiful beaches

When the Ancient Greeks arrived here in the 6th century BC they called Corsica *Kalliste*, "the beautiful". The chances are that they were inspired to this epithet even before they landed on the shore. Certainly, the visitor approaching the island by sea today, particularly from the north or west, can feel nothing but a sense of awe at the sheer magnificence of the landscape as it rises steeply from the coast and only stops at the gleaming mountain summits as high as 2,500 metres (8,000 ft) above. Viewed from the railings of a ship, such grandeur is bound to entice all but the most fanatical of beach-goers to set out and explore.

While much of the coast is indeed very beautiful, it is in the interior that the true drama of Corsica unfolds: in the towering peaks, in the unfathomable gorges, the weird rock formations, green valleys, blue glacial lakes, dark forests and lonely mountain villages. It is also in the interior that many of the historic treasures of the island – the menhir statues with their mysterious expressions, the old Genoese bridges, the Romanesque chapels and Pisan churches – are to be found. They are monuments in stone to a long and eventful past, which has not only witnessed the grief and suffering caused by centuries of foreign occupation, but has also seen the development of a strong sense of identity among the islanders. Despite the vicissitudes of history and the problems of the modern world, this identity has endured, as have many of the customs and traditions that surround it.

Despite the fact that some Corsicans have in the past resorted to violence as a means of expressing their disenchantment with certain modern developments, the vast majority of the islanders accept and welcome the fact that tourism now plays such an important role in the local economy. The Corsicans are a warm and friendly people and receive their guests with courteous dignity. Even back in the 18th century, when the War of Independence against the Genoese was raging, the Scottish man of letters James Boswell could only find positive things to say about the island and its inhabitants. "I had got upon a rock in Corsica and jumped into the middle of life", he wrote. Visitors who wish to discover the island and all its wonders for themselves, rather than simply lying on the beach, can be sure to experience a similar sensation. ❑

PRECEDING PAGES: Calvi, Corsica's hallmark resort, framed by the blue of the gulf; at the foot of Monte Castello, the village of Cervione is dominated by the spire of St Marie et St Érasme; the crystal clear waters and fine sand of a beach on the Cap d' Asciaio.
LEFT: a view of the beautiful Vallée de la Restonica.

Decisive Dates

MEGALITHIC CULTURE

6,000 BC First humans settle in Corsica.

4,000 BC The first *castelli* are built on the island.

3,500 BC Construction of stone megaliths (burial places and temples) containing buried coffins.

3,000–3,500 BC The Torréen fortresses *(torre)* are built.

2,500 BC First dolmen (stone tables) are built.

2,000 BC Phallus-shaped menhirs (long stones) slowly start to be given on human features.

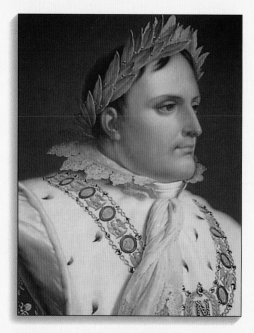

GREEKS, ROMANS AND SARACENS

500 BC Start of the Greek colonisation of Corsica.

565 BC Greeks (Phocaeans) found the city of Alalia.

259 BC Roman conquest and Alalia (Aléria) falls

221 BC Corsica and Sardinia are amalgamated to form a single Roman province.

181–172 BC Unsuccessful Corsi revolts against the Romans. Half of the native population die, while the survivors withdraw to the interior.

AD 100 Christianity arrives on the island.

456 The Vandals invade and destroy Aléria.

534 Byzantine Emperor Justinian I defeats the Vandals.

700 The Moors (Saracens) repeatedly terrorise the island – right into the 15th century.

RULE FROM PISA

754 In what became known as the Donation of Pépin, Pépin the Younger vows to hand over Corsica to Pope Stephen II.

774 Charlemagne presents Corsica to the Vatican.

1016 The Vatican entrusts Pisa with administration of the island.

1077 Pope Gregory VII grants Corsica to Pisa.

1133 Pope Innocent II divides Corsica between Genoa and Pisa.

1268 The Genoese found Calvi.

1288 Pisa is defeated.

FIVE CENTURIES UNDER THE GENOESE

1297 The Pope makes James II, King of Aragon, new custodian of the island.

1358 Rebellious peasants lay siege to the castles of their feudal landlords in northern Corsica.

1376 Arrigo della Rocca asks the Aragonese to support the rebellion.

1380 The Genoese found Bastia.

1420 Bonifacio, founded in 828 by the Tuscan count of the same name, withstands the King of Aragon's siege.

1453 The city-republic of Genoa cedes administration of the island to the Bank of St George.

1553 Corsica is occupied by the French for the first time, under the rule of Henri II.

1569 Genoa reconquers Corsica.

1640–70 Religious revival

1652 Genoa buys the island back from the Bank of St George and continues to fight Corsican freedom fighters under Alfonso Corso.

THE STRUGGLE FOR INDEPENDENCE

1729 Revolt of Corte and peasants.

1736 Baron von Neuhof of Germany offers military help to overthrow the Genoese and is crowned King Theodore I.

1746 Giampietor Gaffori becomes leader and wins back most of the island from the Genoese. He is later murdered.

1755 Pasquale Paoli is appointed national leader in the Castignaccia.

1762 The Moor's head with the white headband is chosen as the island's official symbol.

1765 The University of Corte opens

1769 The defeat of Corsicans near Ponte Nuevo. Pasquale Paoli goes into exile. Napoleon is born in Ajaccio.

1789 Corsica is part of the French Empire.

1790 Paoli returns from London exile and appeals to the English for help.

1794–6 Intervention by the British leads to Corsica ruled by an English viceroy.

1807 Death of Pasquale Paoli in England.

THE QUEST FOR AUTONOMY

1827 Opening of the Ajaccio–Bastia road.

1830 First steamship sails from Ajaccio to Bastia.

1855–70 Corsican blood feuds and the repression of banditry.

1910–20 5–6,000 people emigrate a year.

1914–18 During World War I, 30,000 Corsicans die for France.

1942 Corsica is occupied by Fascist Italy.

1943 Liberation of Corsica.

1955–62 Around 17,500 French colonials from North Africa are presented with land on Corsica.

1963 Corsican students on the mainland found the Union Corse l'Avenir. Among its aims is to establish an independent university for Corsica and the compulsory teaching of the Corsican language and its history in all schools.

1967 Front Régionaliste Corse (FRC) and the Azzione per la Rinascita Corsa (ARC) are formed. The ARC founds the Arritti (Upright) publication. The ARC demands the creation of an elected Corsican national assembly and voices demands for complete self-determination.

1975 Wine scandal exposed by the ARC. Two *gendarmes* are killed during an occupation by autonomists.

1976 The Front de Libération National de la Corse (FNLC) is formed, under which all existing underground organisations are amalgamated. A wave of terrorist attacks begin, with the aim of liberating Corsica.

1977 Formation of the Unione di u Populu Corsu (UPC) which distances itself from any armed action.

1981 University of Corte reopens.

1982 Corsica receives a special regional statute without any real rights.

1991 Regional autonomy law is passed.

1992 Statute extended with a regional executive. The nationalists receive 25 percent of the vote in the regional elections.

1998 Eight Corsicans are arrested in connection with the assassination of Claude Erignac, the senior French official on Corsica. Chief suspect, Yvan Colonna, a leading figure in the seperatist movement, goes into hiding. A parliamentary fact-finding committee find evidence of misappropriation and squandering of public funds.

1999 Start of the so-called "Processus Matignon" – a package of devolutionary measures proposed in exchange for an end to paramilitary violence on the island.

THE 21ST CENTURY

2000 François Santoni. a prominent nationalist leader is shot dead. Fellow dissident, Jean-Michel Rossi, publishes a whistle-blowing book on the island's paramilitary movement, revealing the extent

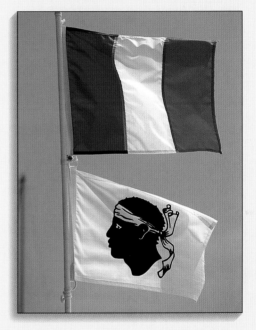

to which it had been corrupted by organised crime. He is also murdered.

2002 End of the "Processus Matignon" as a government crack-down on the island begins. Announcement that Corsica is to be treated the same as any other French regions lobbying for greater devolution.

2003 Five days before the referendum on limited autonomy for Corsica, France announces the arrest of Yvan Colonna, wanted in connection with the murder of Claude Erignac in 1998. In a 60 percent turnout, the referendum to create a new regional assembly is rejected by just 2,000 votes. On the night of the vote four villas owned by French mainlanders are bombed and for now the status quo remains. ❏

PRECEDING PAGES: a mural depicting a soldier of the regiment of the "Royal Corse" in the Musée a Bandera.

LEFT: a portrait of Napoleon Bonaparte.

RIGHT: the French flag (top) and the Corsican Moor's head flag (below).

MEGALITHIC CULTURE AND THE TORRÉENS

Corsica's prehistoric era has only recently been intensively studied, revealing a dramatic and rich early culture

Arriving on Corsica, the visitor is greeted by the blank gaze of the menhirs, the enigmatic stelae populating the island landscape either singly or in groups. They bear secret, almost eerie witness to the passage of the millennia, so that the observer wonders why it took so long for archaeologists to start their investigations into these fascinating megalithic monuments.

The first reference in the Western world to these man-made monuments will be found in Prosper Mérimée's *Notes d'un Voyage en Corse*, published in 1840. The celebrated author, who was the Inspector General of Historic Monuments in France at the time, confessed that "the island's early history is veiled in a dense cloak of mystery."

This state of ignorance was to continue for more than a century, for until a few decades ago archaeologists expected little joy from a serious investigation of Corsica, an island notorious for the forbidding nature of both its terrain and inhabitants. It was not until 1954 that the French archaeologist Roger Grosjean, inspired by his teacher, Abbé Breuil, began to shed a very different light on the island's early history.

Stone-Age culture

Even during the centuries before Greek invaders brought their civilization to these shores, Corsica was hardly a refuge of primitive goatherds. It was the home of a sophisticated culture able to construct monuments with a clear religious purpose. In this respect, Corsica can match its Mediterranean neighbour Sardinia as well as Sicily, Malta and the Balearic Islands of Mallorca and Menorca. Many of these ancient stones were appropriated across the intervening millennia to build houses or walls surrounding the fields, or were weathered away or overgrown by the *macchia*. Nonethe-

less, Grosjean was successful in shedding considerable light on their origins.

The first settlers, who were "primitive" hunter-gatherers and fishermen, probably reached the island during the 7th millennium BC,

towards the end of the Mesolithic era. They arrived via Elba from Liguria, the North Italian region surrounding Genoa. A second wave of immigrants with a knowledge of agriculture and cattle farming descended about 1,000 years later, at the beginning of the Neolithic era. The original inhabitants of Corsica knew how to make simple clay pots, examples of which have been radiocarbon dated to some 7,500 years ago.

Cardium ceramics of this type, named after the mollusc used to create the dominant dot-like pattern, can be found all over the Mediterranean area, suggesting that trade and cultural exchange across the sea was already taking place.

LEFT: anthropomorphic menhirs are unique to Corsica.
RIGHT: the central monument at Filitosa.

Early village life

As far as historians can tell, living conditions during these early years of Corsican history must have been almost idyllic. Those of the inhabitants who no longer dwelt in caves or sought shelter under overhanging cliffs lived in open, unfortified villages. During the winter months their sheep grazed the lower plains; in summer they were driven up to the higher mountain pastures, a custom maintained to this day with the practice of transhumance. The women wove cloth on simple looms. The hard materials required to make arrowheads and tools did not occur naturally on the island: it is for "big" and "stone", defines this characteristic practice of the early island inhabitants.

For many years it was believed that the origins of these monumental constructions, which seem to embody their builders' longing for permanence, were to be found in the Eastern Mediterranean. However, research has shown that the megaliths of Brittany are at least a 1,000 years older than the earliest pyramids of Egypt. Moreover, the largest concentration of "big stones" is to be found in the Western Mediterranean and along the European Atlantic coast (Carnac, Stonehenge, Jutland, etc). For this reason it seems more likely that the practice

thought that the early settlers brought in flint and obsidian from neighbouring Sardinia, which was as yet uninhabited.

And yet, man shall not live by bread alone. He fears the powers of nature, sees them as the manifestation of a superior being, questions his own origins and the purpose of his existence and speculates over the possibility of life after death. Such preoccupations lead to ancestor worship and reverence for the dead, including the construction of burial places and temples. The ancient Corsicans were no exception in this respect. From about 3,500 BC the erection of megaliths became more widespread. The word, derived from the Greek developed independently within the continent. But that doesn't exclude the possibility that it had its origins in the worship of the great Earth Mother and other deities, which had been practised in the Aegean and Asia Minor for thousands of years.

Stone coffin cult

Archaeologists distinguish three periods of megalithic culture in Corsica. Previously, the placing of modest burial gifts in the grave beside the deceased had been customary. During the middle of the 4th millennium BC, under the influence of new trends (possibly a new wave of immigrants), the new practice of burying the dead in stone chambers came to be widely accepted. The sarcophagi were constructed of single, precisely hewn stone slabs, which were set into the ground and covered by a mound of earth (tumulus). Entire cemeteries, or necropolises, containing stone tombs of this kind are to be found near Porto-Vecchio and in the Sartenais.

Standing sentinel over the graves would be found one or two so-called menhirs or druid stones. These are simple upright monuments, almost always of granite, which, because of their frequent occurrence in Brittany, take their name from the Breton words *men* ("stone") and *hir* ("long").

The second period of megalithic culture on Corsica is characterised by a change in burial customs. From about the middle of the 3rd millennium the stone coffins were no longer buried but simply placed directly on the ground, although they continued to be covered by a tumulus. After the mound of earth had been eroded by wind and weather over a period of time, the constructions thus exposed came to resemble stone tables. They were also given a Breton name: *dolmen*, or "stone table". The finest example, discovered by the 19th-century French novelist Prosper Mérimée, is the dolmen at Fontanaccia in the Cauria region. During the earliest period of megalithic culture the druid stones were scarcely more than 1–2 metres (3–6 ft) high, and were unadorned. During this later phase, however, they doubled in size. They continued to flank single tumuli or were positioned in rows known as *alignements*, or parallel avenues of stones. In contrast to the discoveries in Brittany, where the rows of menhirs were clearly aligned in accordance with various astronomic criteria, nearly all such rows on Corsica follow a north–south direction. However, this does not rule out the possibility that mystic cult concepts existed here as well.

Stelae with faces

The third phase of megalithic culture can be distinguished from about 2,000 BC. The phallus-shaped menhir of earlier times, looking for all the world like a fertility symbol, slowly

started to take on human features. A head and shoulders gradually emerged from the stone column, later developing a mask-like face with eyes, ears, a nose and a mouth. Then ribs and clothing became discernible; later still, the figures were depicted with weapons and occasionally with arms.

In order to make them more lifelike, the statues were probably originally painted with blood-coloured haematite or ochre. These anthropomorphic stelae were positioned facing eastwards, towards the rising sun. Maybe it was hoped that the resurrection of the dead would also come from that direction.

Do the stone images we see today actually portray the deceased person? Perhaps they represent some glorified ancestors, or possibly the swords and daggers indicate some protective function.

Perhaps they are even enemies conquered by the deceased, who have thus been banished or forced into obedience beyond the grave? One riddle gives way to another, each as insoluble as the last. What cannot be disputed, however, is that these Corsican monuments represent the first large-sized sculptures in the Western hemisphere, constructed centuries before analogous works were created by the Greeks or the Etruscans. Most of these expressive,

LEFT: stone coffins were placed above ground during the second period of Megalithic culture.
RIGHT: a well-preserved dolmen at Fontanaccia in the Cauria region.

humanoid menhirs are to be found in Filitosa in the southwest of the island.

The legend of the Torréens

By the middle of the 2nd millenium BC this early culture had reached its climax. After that, it fell into an abrupt decline. Until the late 1980s scientists believed that this collapse was caused by an invasion of a belligerent foreign people whose arrival marked the beginning of the end of the Stone Age. Unlike the existing inhabitants, the new arrivals had the advantage of bronze weapons. It is still uncertain where these new immigrants came from and what they

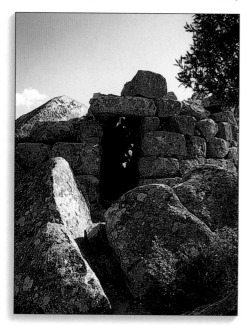

were called in their own language. The archaeologist Roger Grosjean called them Torreani – Torréens in French – after the *torre* or towers which they were thought to have introduced to the island.

Historians believed the first Torréens landed about 1,500–1,200 BC on the Gulf of Porto Vecchio in the south of the island. Some of the tower-like buildings in the surrounding plain, such as those found at Torre and Tappa, were considered to be among their earliest constructions. Their architecture and traces of ashes and fire suggested that the place-name Torre was used for sites that served as crematoria, and possibly for human burnt

offerings as well. Only later, according to this theory, did the Torréens advance towards the interior, where they inevitably came into conflict with the Corsi.

These original inhabitants defended their positions with determination, but ultimately their stone weapons proved no match for the bronze swords and daggers of the newcomers. The Torréens completely destroyed the Stone-Age settlers' villages and the defeated Corsi withdrew to the northernmost regions of the island.

The latest theory

Current research now suggests that there were probably no such representatives of a foreign, superior culture as the Torréens at all. The long-running theory was based on a belief that the Torréens brought to the island the metallic weapons that are shown on the Paladini, the armed menhir-statues, and that it was these same foreigners who constructed Cyclopean citadels such as Araghju on a rock ledge near Porto-Vecchio. They also apparently transformed the peaceful peasant village of Filitosa into a *Castellu*, using demolished menhirs to reinforce their walls.

All those rather convincing theories broke down in the 1980s when archaeologists made new discoveries. In Terrina, close to the area later inhabited by Etruscans, Greeks and Romans on the plateau of Alalia (now Aléria), they detected not only a copper pit but also moulds for shaping metals to produce exactly the kind of daggers and swords that can be seen on the Paladini menhirs.

With the help of the Carbon 14 dating method, this early civilization can be traced to around 3,500–3,000 BC. That is at least 1,500 years before the Torréens are supposed to have arrived. These dating tests showed conclusively that the so-called Torréen fortresses were built during this period.

The Corsican word *torre* is still used to describe both smaller constructions and part of the bigger *castelli*, however, so the term Torréen is still thought to be appropriate and it continues to be widely used to describe this later period. ❑

LEFT AND RIGHT: the entrance and stairs to the Torréen place of worship at Torre, just north of Porto-Vecchio.

GREEKS, ROMANS AND SARACENS

Corsica has been fought over, occupied and colonised for millennia,
and these conflicts have given the island its unique identity

The symbol of the Moor's head was first used by the Aragonese kings to celebrate the victory over the Moors in the 13th century. On the island itself the Moor has a deeper significance: for centuries he has been the symbol of the island's independence after long years of foreign rule. That the Corsicans should have been faced with a perpetual struggle throughout their turbulent history was due in no small part to their island's attractive location as a trading post in the Mediterranean.

The arrival of the Phocaeans

The Greek colonisation of Corsica began in the 6th century BC, as Herodotus, the celebrated historian, relates. When Harpagus, the King of the Medes, besieged the town of Phocaea in Asia Minor, its citizens were faced with the alternatives of surrender or flight. They chose the latter. Since the Greeks living in Phocaea were a seafaring nation, their escape route was also clear: the sea. After a long voyage they finally landed on the east coast of Corsica (Greek: *Kyrnos*), where they were welcomed by the Greek colony already on the island. In 565 BC they founded together the town of Alalia, later known to the Romans as Aléria. Legend has it that their choice of a new home was determined by an oracle.

Since the Greeks were canny and experienced merchants, they were able to make a living from a flourishing trade in copper, lead, silver and iron. They extracted the raw materials from the island interior, especially from Mercuri, Conca and Venaco, transporting the ores to Alalia for smelting. The resulting highly-prized metals were then exported by ship. The Greeks built most of their sailing vessels themselves, from materials found in the forests of Corsica: wood, wax and resin. A nation of experienced mariners, they brought the requisite skills with them from their homeland.

LEFT: the excavations at Aléria.
RIGHT: part of a mosaic floor in the Roman settlement of Mariana, to the south of present-day Bastia.

Alalia as a trading centre

The processing of metals was not the only avenue to prosperity open to the commercially-minded Greeks. On the fertile coastal plains in the east of the island, formed by the alluvial deposits from the River Tavignano, they grew grapes for wine, as well as olive trees and cere-

als. A small proportion of the harvest served the citizens' own needs and the remainder was exported. A further source of income was provided by the bounty of the sea: salted fish, prepared with salt from the salt marshes along the coast.

Within a short space of time Alalia had become an important commercial centre and staging post on the way to the Greek settlement on the mainland at Massilia (Marseille). Archaeological finds such as the fine Greek vases, today on view in the Jérôme Carcopino Museum in Aléria, provide evidence of the lively trading activity which must have gone on here, as well as reflecting the high standard of living at the time. The clay used for the domestic utensils came from the Casabianda Plateau.

But the Phocaeans, whose ambition it was to gain control over the entire Tyrrhenian Sea, were not permitted to enjoy their wealth for long. Not only did they fail to establish good relationships with the native population, the Corsi, who had retreated to the island interior, they also attacked and robbed their neighbours, the Etruscans and Carthaginians, who retaliated in 535 BC by sending over a combined invasion fleet.

Although the Phocaeans carried the day in the ensuing naval battle of Alalia, it was really

only a Pyrrhic victory. Having lost most of their ships and sustained heavy casualties, they decided to transfer their capital to Massalia, retaining Alalia solely as a mercantile link with their new colonies in southern Italy, as well as with Greece, Carthage, Gaul, Sicily and Spain.

A sample of what the Greeks left behind them can be seen today in the museum in Aléria. They also bequeathed the island its most popular and enduring epithet: *Kalliste* – "The Beautiful".

A Roman colony

Invaders of Corsica always arrived on the east coast, not only because landings here were much easier than on the rocky western shores, but also because of the relative proximity of the long Italian shore. In successive waves of settlement the Etruscans and Carthaginians now took advantage of the island's rich resources. Before long, however, Corsica was to become a bone of contention once more.

The next significant date was 259 BC, when Corsica attracted the attention of the Roman consul, Lucius Cornelius Scipio. He recognised its favourable location as a trading post in the Mediterranean.

It was in that year, during the course of the First Punic War waged by the Romans against the Carthaginians (264–241 BC), that Scipio conquered Alalia. From this point onwards the town was known by its present name, Aléria. By 230 BC the entire east coast of the island was firmly under Roman rule. The Romans took over their predecessors' profitable sources of income, but on a much larger scale than before. The agricultural hinterland was extended, and everything was better organised – to match the dimensions of the Roman Empire. They also established oyster farms, which soon became a highly profitable business. The wealthy Romans on the mainland were fond of banquets at which it was considered fashionable to serve one's guests molluscs from the coast of the island colony. The oysters were packed in jars of brine and transported to the cities of the mainland.

The enslavement of the Corsi

The Romans had more difficulty bringing the island interior under their sway, for here they encountered the obstinate resistance of the native Corsi, who lived in a state of perpetual rebellion against their oppressors. After a series of successful military campaigns against the indigenous population, the Romans finally forced them to pay high tribute. Corsican prisoners were compelled to work for their new masters in the quarries, mines and fields. Corsican slaves were also popular on the mainland because their tough constitution and strong physique made them suitable for arduous manual work. In view of the continuous building projects throughout the length and breadth of the vast empire, they were in constant demand.

In 221 BC Corsica and Sardinia were amalgamated to form a single Roman province. On

Corsica itself the only towns the Romans colonised were Aléria and Mariana, named after its founder, Marius, an uncle of Julius Caesar, and lying to the south of what is now the town of Bastia.

Between 181 and 172 BC the forces of occupation yet again overdid their exploitation of the Corsi, repeatedly raising taxes and the tribute due in cork, honey and wax as well as the customs duties payable on the rivers and harbours. The local inhabitants revolted but they had no chance against the legions sent from Rome; over half the island's native population perished. The remainder, totalling some 30,000

urban countenance as a result of the construction of a triumphal arch and forum as well as an aqueduct, baths and a harbour for civilian and naval vessels.

On a walk around the archaeological site of Aléria, the prosperity of the Romans can best be appreciated by a study of the *Balneum*, a vast bathing complex. It included changing cabins, several swimming pools and tanks for cold, warm and hot water. The ground was warmed by underfloor heating; the boilers were fuelled with wood from the island interior. Nor were economies made when it came to the fittings and decorations of the

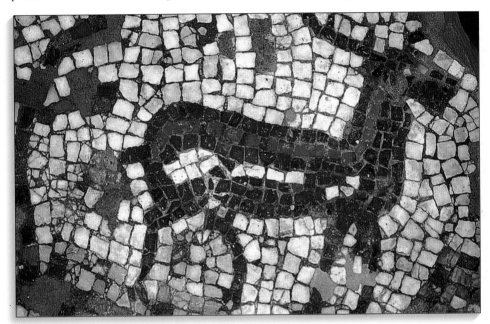

souls, did what their descendants were to do time and again throughout the island's turbulent history: they withdrew to the interior, where they went into hiding in the forests. They lived simply, relying on the resources nature had to offer them.

Urban luxury

Now known as "Colonia Julia", Aléria became the Romans' capital on the island, with a population of some 30,000. The town acquired an

LEFT: the bust of a Roman noblewoman.
ABOVE: mosaic detail from Mariana, named after its founder Marius, an uncle of Julius Caesar.

houses, which included a number of fine mosaics.

Many of the consumer goods the Romans used, such as their fine glazed ceramics, were locally produced, and Aléria developed into a centre of light industry. There were, for example, cloth dyers' and craftsmen's studios and firms specialising in the preservation of fish.

Until the 6th century the Romans acquired most of the agricultural produce they required from their colony at Mariana, which formed the centre of the Roman territory in the north of the island.

The early church complex at Mariana testifies to Rome's first attempts at converting the island to Christianity during the 3rd century; in the first instance this, like the Roman colonisation, was restricted primarily to the coastal areas. The first four bishoprics on Corsica, apart from Mariana, were at Nebbio, Aléria, Sagone and Ajaccio. The earliest Christian engravings found on the island – in Aléria – date from this period: the symbolic *olla* and the fish.

When the Western Roman Empire slowly declined into collapse during the 4th and 5th centuries, the Church took over the administrative tasks of the Roman governors. The governmental boundaries were redrawn, later forming the parishes (*pieve*).

The Moor with the headband

Aléria's fate was sealed in the 5th century AD. From AD 410 to 430 the town was stricken by a raging fire, followed by malaria epidemics. In AD 456 the Vandals invaded the island and destroyed the town completely. This Germanic tribe had left their home in the Danube Valley to invade Gaul, and subsequently crossed into Spain and conquered Roman Africa before sacking Rome itself in AD 455.

They restored Carthage and made it the capital of their empire. But the reputation of the Vandals is not based on what they did, but how they did it: they laid waste to practically everything they came across. Such was their cruelty that in the 18th century a French bishop coined the term "Vandalism" to mean wanton destruction.

During the following centuries the island was plagued by a succession of fresh invasions, by the Goths, the Byzantines and the Langobards. The 9th century saw the beginning of the conquest of Corsica by the Saracens or Moors – a reign of terror which was to last for more than 200 years.

The Saracens proved to be even crueller masters than the Vandals. They conquered the coastal regions, expelling or killing the inhabitants of Aléria and Mariana and preventing the continued spread of Christianity. As during the Roman occupation, the Corsicans retreated to the forests of the interior. The legacy of the years of Moorish rule can be found today in Campo dei Mori, Morosaglia and Campomoro.

Corsican folk history has kept alive the memory of a Roman nobleman, Ugo della Colonna, as a popular resistance leader. He had fallen out of favour with Pope Stephen IV and was able to save his honour by winning Aléria back from the Moors in a knightly duel, by finally routing the Saracen king Nugalon in the Battle of Mariana after a 20-year military campaign, and by forcing all pagan Corsicans to be baptised.

The Moor's head with the white headband, chosen as the island's official symbol on 24 November 1762, recalls to this day the final expulsion of the Saracens during the 11th century. No one seems to know, however, whether the Moor's head, portrayed on a white background, was depicted from the beginning with the headband as a symbol of the liberation of the fatherland, or whether the bandage originally covered one eye to symbolise the island's slavery.

It is claimed that the great Corsican patriot Pasquale Paoli was responsible for placing the headband in its present position on the Moor's brow. Whatever its origin, the pirate-like Moor epitomises even today the stubborn resistance to foreign rule which fills the heart of every nationalistic Corsican. ❏

LEFT: early Christian reliefs on the 12th-century church of Santa Maria Assunta in Canari.
RIGHT: the head of a bearded Neptune in the mosaic floor of the baptistry in Mariana.

RULE FROM PISA

The Pisan period of rule produced some interesting cultural developments, but it was made unstable by political rivalry with Genoa

In 754, in what became known as the Donation of Pépin, Pépin the Younger – whom later historians adorned with the less-than-flattering title of "The Short" – had vowed to hand over the land to Pope Stephen II. This promise of a gift of territory was to form the basis of the Papal States which still exist in

had settled on Corsica some time previously from Tuscany, but to all intents and purposes they were able to do exactly as they thought fit. In any case, the rival clans lived in a state of perpetual feud, which they carried on amidst much bloodshed and suffering on the part of the ordinary people.

rudimentary form. By so doing Pépin wanted to return the favour of the curia, which had acknowledged him as King of the Franks. Among the lands which fell to the Holy See as part of this barter was the island of Corsica.

But Rome was far away, and so by and large the island was left to its own devices. It was not until the rival naval powers of Pisa and Genoa formed an alliance to drive out the marauding pirate fleet of the Saracens, in order to protect their own trading interests, that noblemen from Tuscany and Liguria appeared on the scene to appropriate parts of the island for themselves. The new feudal lords paid lip service to the authority of the Malaspinas, who

The island's chronicles record in favourable terms the deeds of only one of these local lords, Count Arrigo Bel Messer, who ruled around AD 1000. However, his attempt to replace the intolerable anarchy with law and order came to an abrupt end under the dagger thrusts of hired assassins; his seven young sons were also put to death, by drowning. After the death of the "Good Count" the island inhabitants lamented: "Lord Bel Messer was killed by a murderer's curse: And the state of Corsica goes from bad to worse."

The seeds of new strife were sown when some of the Ligurian noblemen acknowledged the suzerainty of the bishops of Genoa, whereupon the Tuscan lords swore their allegiance to their fellow-countryman, Pope Gregory VII.

The Pope intervenes

In Pope Gregory VII they acquired a belligerent henchman who at the time was embroiled in the Investiture Dispute with the German king, Henry IV. The quarrel concerned whether the right to appoint bishops lay with the Papal mitre or the Crown, and ended in Henry's famous submission as a humble penitent in Canossa. Gregory VII, a native of Tuscany, made use of his territorial advantage and in 1077 awarded Corsica in feoff to Bishop Landolfe of Pisa. It

nance of the Mediterranean area was inevitable. In 1099 the citizens of Pisa took part in the First Crusade to liberate the Holy City of Jerusalem from the rule of the "infidel" Muslims, taking ample advantage of the opportunity to gather up a vast hoard of oriental treasures. But in the Levant they were also exposed to new artistic influences, which they combined with the architectural tradition of Lombardy in the construction of magnificent buildings which have earned a special chapter in the history of art under the rubric "Pisan style".

The wealth acquired by fair means or foul by the soldiers, ship owners and traders strength-

was a sinecure which was subsequently to slip out of the hands of the Church once more.

Eastern influence

Thanks to its favourable location on a broad, fertile plain near the place where the River Arno flows into the Ligurian Sea, by the early Middle Ages Pisa had already grown into a prosperous port and trading centre. Its ensuing rivalry with Genoa and Venice for the domi-

LEFT: San Michele de Murato, one of Corisica's best examples of Pisan Romanesque architecture.
ABOVE: ornate doorway and exterior of the Pisan Romanesque church of La Trintá, at Aregno.

ened the political influence of the middle classes. Full of self-confidence, the Pisans (like the citizens of other northern Italian cities) were no longer prepared to permit decisions to be made for them from the pulpit. They gradually took over responsibility for their own fate. The aristocracy (of wealth) elected from its midst councillors *(signori)* and invested them, under the direction of a *podestà* or leader, with political authority within the state. The role of the bishop was restricted to spiritual affairs. And so Corsica acquired a secular government.

"The Pisans ruled wisely, justly and peacefully", wrote the chronicler Giovanni della Grossa, admittedly some 200 years later. He described them as "by and large beloved of the populace". In any case, the rule of law and order returned to the island; under Pisan protection the Corsicans summoned up the courage to return to the coastal plains, which had been depopulated by pirates and marauding knights. An economic boom was set in motion, accompanied by the construction of more than 300 churches to ensure the eternal salvation of the citizens. By contrast, the Pisans left behind relatively few secular buildings. Some historians have attributed to them the square watchtowers, claiming that only the round ones are Genoese, but this theory is now obsolete.

Even though artists from the mainland were called in to assist the local stonemasons, masons and painters, the result was always relatively modest.

And yet, Pisa's influence is still unmistakable today, especially on the north of the island, in the regions around Nebbio, the Castagniccia and the Balagne. As in the parent city, the Corsican churches of this era are characterised by careful craftsmanship of the fine building materials and polychrome masonry. In Sisco and Brando on Cap Corse they quarried marble blocks, and these were placed in alternate narrow and wide layers in the church of La Canon-

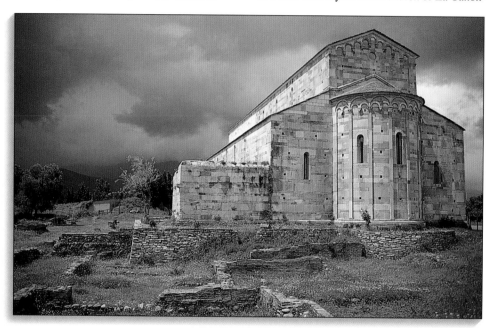

Romanesque simplicity

Today many of the churches on Corsica dating from the Pisan era, built in a style corresponding to the Romanesque, lie in ruins or have completely disappeared. The visitor should not expect architectural wonders of those buildings which have survived.

If you associate Pisa with the Piazza dei Miracoli, bordered by masterly examples of Western architecture, from the Baptistry and the Cathedral to the famous Leaning Tower, and expect to find something similar on Corsica, you are bound to be disappointed. It is important to remember that Corsica has always been regarded as the back of beyond.

ica, which stands on the site of the Roman settlement of Mariana near the airport at Bastia. Santa Maria Assunta, which is modelled in both style and material on La Canonica, stands sentinel above Saint-Florent on the north coast of the island. In the Bevinco Valley, the master builders who created San Michele de Murato (in the mountains southwest of Bastia) discovered dark-green serpentine and whitish limestone, which they combined with pink and yellow slabs to produce what Prosper Mérimée described as the "most elegant church on the island".

Only exceptionally is it found – as in the examples cited above – that the Corsican churches built during the Pisan era take the form of substantial triple-naved basilicas. Most are unadorned small churches or chapels with a single nave; despite their harmonious proportions they are more rustic than elegant, and blend perfectly with the bucolic landscape.

In many cases the roofs of the Pisan-style churches on Corsica consisted merely of wood or *teghie*, slabs of natural stone. At first the ornamentation was very simple, consisting of nothing more elaborate than geometric patterns. Representation of figures only came later; the finest examples of these, too, will be found in the places of worship listed above.

Lions and fabulous creatures gaze down from the façades and capitals, alongside rams' heads and serpents, lambs bearing crosses and wolves baring their teeth. Here and there you will also spot mysterious "manikins", like those on the church of the Holy Trinity in Aregno. In Murato there is an unusual portrayal of the Temptation of Eve.

Half-and-half is no answer

The period during which Pisa was able to enjoy undisturbed its island colony was to last for less than 50 years. Genoa was prepared to go to any lengths to wrest the prize from its strongest competitor, even resorting to bribing the Roman curia. In fact, all six dioceses on Corsica were transferred to the Ligurian Republic, an act which provoked open hostility – even on the island itself – between the rival maritime powers. Innocent II saw the solution to the dispute in terms of a Solomonic judgment; in 1133 he divided Corsica, permitting the northern dioceses of Accia, Mariana and Nebbio to remain under Genoese control whilst transferring those in the south – Ajaccio, Aléria and Sagone – back to Pisa. It was an unhappy solution which brought no joy to any of the parties concerned.

The general consensus is that this decision by the "innocent" pope created a division on the island, the after-effects of which can be seen in some spheres to this day – for example, in the modern administrative districts within the Département Haute-Corse, which more or less corresponds to the boundaries laid down by the

---

LEFT: the austere church of La Canonica at Mariana.
RIGHT: the simple door decoration of the 9th-century chapel of Santa Reparata near Bonifacio.

former Genoese region, and the Corse du Sud area, which used to be Pisan. In fact, however, the "two Corsicas" existed long before that, for the differences have their foundations in the geology of the island. The main watershed runs in a northwest–southeasterly direction along the central mountain ridge.

In the 13th century, however, half the island remained under the jurisdiction of Pisa until, on 6 August 1284, a decisive battle was fought off the island of Meloria (near Livorno), during which the Genoese won a resounding victory. The Corsicans resisted their new masters – or at least, the supporters of Pisa did so – and the

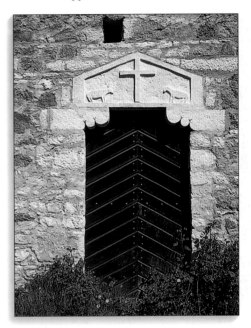

island produced its first freedom fighter: the rebel Rinucello della Rocca. In his capacity as the *Giudice* – the Judge – of Cinarca, he succeeded in making himself master of all Corsica, firstly in the name of Pisa, and then, having swapped sides, in the name of the Genoese. But when the latter finally defeated Pisa, he was captured through the treachery of one of his own men and had to spend the last seven years of his life festering in a Genoese dungeon.

The demise of this legendary *condottiere* put at least a symbolic end to the resistance, and the new power over the Western Mediterranean began its rule over Corsica, which was to last for almost 500 years. ❏

FIVE CENTURIES UNDER THE GENOESE

After defeating Pisa, Genoa consolidated its hold on the island, but its rule was opposed by local lords and was eventually lost to the French

Following its defeat, Pisa formally abandoned its claim to Corsica in 1288. The islanders promptly rose up against the Genoese, and they were not alone in their opposition; for financial as well as political reasons the Pope was not in favour of the new constellation. In 1297 Boniface VIII gave the King of Aragón, James II, both Corsica and Sardinia in feoff. The Ligurian Republic was not prepared to accept this; however, as it was involved in a dispute with Venice at the time, it was in no position to defend its colony properly. And so a sort of war by proxy came to pass: the belligerent feudal rulers of Corsica took up the cause of first one side and then the other, depending on which of them offered the better deal. In between times, they settled old scores. Once again the island was plunged into civil war and anarchy: epidemics on plague, malaria and famine also took their toll on the population. The unrest did not even stop short of the churches and monasteries, and many of the ruins in evidence today can be traced back to this turbulent era.

Revolts against the aristocracy

From 1358, rebellious peasants, tired of the perpetual family feuds, laid siege to the castles of their feudal lords throughout northern Corsica. Since most of the latter were Aragón sympathisers, Genoa felt obliged to support the revolt, which was led by a certain Sambucuccio d'Alando. He conquered large sections of the island; however, only in the northeast, *en decà des monts* – in the "land on this side of the mountains" – did he succeed in putting the noblemen to flight.

Their estates were handed over to the communities in return for the guarantee of free grazing rights for the herds of all villagers. That is why the land in question is known as *terra di commune/terre du commun*, whereas in the

southwest the *terra dei signori/terre des seigneurs* remained the property of the nobles until the French Revolution in 1789.

These "free" communities established a form of self-administration based on organisational

structures (*paese* and *pieve* – commune and parish) introduced under the Pisans. The "mayor" was theoretically chosen by election, but in practice the *caporali*, the heads of the leading families, were able to assert their will. It was not long before they, too, were drawn into alliances and feuds just like those they had witnessed amongst the nobility. And yet, the effects of this early democratisation are in evidence to this day. Whilst the *terra di commune* tends to think and vote on the left, the land beyond the mountains is regarded as right-wing and conservative.

Genoa was obliged to accept the liberties for which the citizens in the north had fought; its

LEFT: the Genoese watchtower at Porto, built in 1549.
RIGHT: Pope Boniface VIII, who gave Corsica to Aragón.

governor urgently needed allies against Aragón. For almost two centuries the Spanish refused to give up their official title to the island. They appear to have been helped in their claims by Arrigo della Rocca, a great-grandson of the same *Guidice* de Cinarca who had fought for Pisa against the Genoese. But no sooner had he landed on the island in 1376 than he forgot his orders and took possession of the disputed territory – not for Aragón, but for himself, subsequently having himself proclaimed Count of Corsica.

At the beginning of the 15th century King Alfonso V of Aragón tried to conquer Corsica the island nobility. On the contrary: each and every minor princeling laid claim to the office and title of Count of Corsica, and Genoa remained too weak to restore law and order. This was the unfortunate situation in 1453, when the city state let out the island to the Genoese Bank of St George, with which the miniature republic had run up massive debts over the past 50 years.

What was even more remarkable, within a short space of time the financial authorities were successful in achieving what neither governor nor viceroy had managed so far: they brought peace to the island. The governor sent by the bank, Antonio Spinola, used the stick-

once more, sending Arrigo's nephew Vincentello d'Istria. The latter ruled as viceroy in the name of the Spanish, building in the heart of the island the citadel at Corte. But when, in 1434, the Genoese managed to track down Vincentello, Aragonese intervention on the island came to an abrupt and bitter end. The viceroy was captured on the high seas, while attempting to escape, and publicly beheaded on the staircase in front of the Palace of Government in Genoa.

A bank as peacemaker

It goes without saying that such an occurrence did not put an end to the inglorious feuds between and-carrot method of overcoming the islanders' resistance. His methods were based on a canny mixture of threats, promises, blackmail and force. His task was made easier by the fact that by this stage the nobility had largely destroyed itself.

Genoese architecture

The atmosphere of security prevailing during the reign of "St George" encouraged economic development, and especially building. Along the coastline, within sight of each other, the bank had erected a chain of turretted watchtowers, the system of defence known as the *torregiana*. Within the towers a permanent watch was kept with the aim of preventing the perpetual pirate raids with which the island had been plagued for as long as anyone could remember. At the time there were several hundred of these vaguely conical constructions, between 12 and 17 metres (38–54 ft) high, with a diameter of some 7 metres (22 ft) and tapering slightly towards the top. Today, only about half a dozen remain intact.

As soon as the sail of a pirate ship appeared on the horizon, the sentinels on the watchtower platforms would light a bonfire and the citizens would flee into the hinterland. Even so, it was not possible to prevent the *turchi*, pre-

In some places on the island, the city of Genoa had begun a building programme even before it handed over the territory to St George. In contrast to their former rivals, the Pisans, who had constructed churches and chapels to the greater glory of God, the Genoese showed a more practical talent. Their main activity lay in the fortification of existing or newly founded towns around the coast. As early as 1195 the citadel of Bonifacio was completed; it was followed by that of Calvi in 1268, Bastia in 1380, and later by Saint-Florent, Ajaccio and Porto Vecchio.

A further example of the down-to-earth

dominantly North African Muslim pirates – Saracens or buccaneers from the Barbary coast – from landing. They set fire to farmsteads and drove away the cattle, raping the women and killing those inhabitants whom they did not carry off into slavery. In the middle of the 16th century, in Algeria alone, no fewer than 6,000 Corsican prisoners were sold on the slave markets or were already languishing in the homes of their various masters.

architectural approach of the Genoese merchants will be found on the island: their elegantly arched bridges. Although they, like the watchtowers, are also decaying rapidly, Corsican conservationists have so far shown few signs that they intend to preserve them.

It is a pity, because their design – usually incorporating a single, or more rarely a triple arch, with a characteristic central angled bend and widely spaced steps – are not only typical of the era, but also make an essential contribution to the charm of the island's landscape. Nowadays they are seldom used by anyone except the occasional riders on mules or, more recently, people on walking tours of the island.

LEFT: the Genoese Tour de l'Osse (Boone Tower) near Pietracorbara.
ABOVE: many of the dry-stone bridges built during the Genoese period are still in use today.

Sampiero Corso

Barely 50 km (30 miles) northeast of Ajaccio, perched above the Prunelli Valley, lies the scattered village of Bastelica. The little community's main claim to fame is "the most Corsican of Corsicans": in front of the church belonging to the Santo district is a martial bronze monument dedicated to the freedom fighter Sampiero Corso. With a battle-cry on his lips, he stands on his pedestal brandishing his dagger in the air with his right hand while his left rests on a shield bearing the family coat of arms complete

with lion. At his feet, relief pictures depict scenes from the hero's struggle against Genoa.

The son of a peasant family, Sampiero was born on 8 May 1498 in the hamlet of Dominicacci. An intelligent boy, he strove for higher things – an ambition always easier to achieve through a career in the army. Entering the pay of the Medici family as a *condottiere*, he led a band of mercenaries known as the "Black Band", and his reputation soon spread. He arrived at the French court in the retinue of Catherine of Medici, the wife of the Dauphin Henri de Perpignan, where he distinguished himself as brilliantly on the dance floor as on the battlefield. Always to be found in the front line, Sampiero was said to be "worth 10,000 soldiers".

In 1547, King Henri II promoted the distinguished warrior, who had even saved his monarch's life in battle, to the rank of General of the Corsican infantry. Cloaked in glory, Sampiero returned to his native island and, at the age of almost 50, married the 15-year-old Vannina d'Ornano, the daughter of Corsican rural aristocracy. Genoa, having followed the general's career with extreme suspicion, took advantage of the middle aged warhorse's moment of weakness to clap him in prison under a pretext. Only the intercession of King Henri brought about his release. Sampiero, offended that the Genoese should have ruined his honeymoon, took up the bitter fight to expel them from the island.

The general persuaded Henri II of France that it was strategically necessary to annex Corsica. The king responded by sending an expeditionary force under Marshal de Thermes; the fleet of the notorious buccaneer Dragut provided cover on the flank. Sampiero incited his people to rebellion, and within a short time they had driven the Genoese from the island. In 1557 Corsica was declared to be part of France. But the hero's jubilation was premature: two years later, for political reasons, Henri II returned his newly acquired province to Italy. From this point onwards, Sampiero fought for his island's independence without outside support.

But his ultimate downfall did not come in battle. Rightly or wrongly, Sampiero was convinced of the infidelity of his young wife. But hers was not a crime of passion: she had made a journey to Genoa and he accused her of establishing political contact with the enemy.

Beside himself with rage, the Corsican Othello set off in pursuit of the fleeing Vannina. Having caught up with her in Aix-en-Provence, he strangled her. The deed provided the scenario for a dramatic vendetta. Genoa offered a reward of 2,000 gold ducats, soon attracting the attention of members of the d'Ornano family who could well use the blood money. On 17 January 1567 Sampiero wandered into the ambush laid by Vannina's brothers near Eccia, not far from his birthplace.

For a century now a monument has marked the place where the Genoese cavalry surrounded the warrior and hacked him to pieces. His son Alfonso managed to escape with a handful of loyal followers. Sampiero's head was put on a spear and exhibited by the town gate of Ajaccio as a warning to the people. Corsica had acquired its first martyr. ❑

A French intermezzo

The relatively peaceful years during which Corsica was ruled by the Bank of St George came to an end in 1553, after the French king, Henri II, had taken a liking to the island. At the time he was engaged in a war against the Habsburg emperor, Charles V, whose allies included Genoa. Thus it was that the military campaign acquired, to all intents and purposes, a moral justification.

The advice to invade Corsica came from Henri's general Sampiero Corso *(see box story opposite)*, who was obsessed by the idea of rescuing his native island from the Genoese yoke. The military campaign was led by the French Marshal de Thermes, and supported by Muslim corsairs from Algeria, under the command of the notorious mercenary Torghud Ali Pasha, alias Dragut, with whom the "Grande Nation" had formed an alliance.

Apart from the fortified towns of Calvi and Bastia, the entire island was conquered by the new invaders; most of the resident Genoese were expelled. In 1557, Giordano Orsini, the French king's representative, declared at a public assembly in the mountain village of Vescovato that Corsica had been "assimilated under the throne of France."

Most of the local inhabitants cheered. However, two years later, to the boundless disappointment of Sampiero and his supporters, Henri II returned Corsica to the Genoese as part of the Treaty of Cateau-Cambrésis. In order to maintain the European balance of power, the French king abandoned all claim to his Italian territories.

Since the search for other allies proved fruitless, Corsica then rose up under Sampiero without foreign assistance. In order to quash the popular revolt more effectively, the city of Genoa bought the island back from the Bank of St George in 1652, simultaneously involving an entire armada of ships. Nonetheless, the powerful city republic was unable to conquer the badly equipped but intensely patriotic freedom fighters in a fair fight. Once again in the island's history, the fate of Corsica was to be decided by nothing more noble than treason and murder.

LEFT: Sampiero Corso was convinced that his young wife, Vannina d'Ornano, was a traitor.
RIGHT: the monument to Sampiero in Bastelica.

The island must suffer

Following the violent death of his father, Sampiero's eldest son, Alfonso, continued the underground struggle for two more years. He finally abandoned the cause, retreating to exile in France. The last pockets of resistance were gradually exterminated.

What was left of this once-prosperous country? In what condition was the island in the midst of these trials and tribulations? "By the end of Sampiero's rebellion the full extent of Corsica's misery was evident. The island had become a desert, its people decimated by war, enforced emigration – impoverished and run

wild" (Ferdinand Gregorovius, 1852). In spite of this, Genoa's sole interest in its newly repossessed colony lay in exploiting it to the full. The capital invested in the re-purchase of the island had to be shown to produce returns. One example of the endless ingenuity of the Genoese tax inspectors can be seen in the "weapons tax", payable by everyone bearing a firearm.

Since any self-respecting Corsican without a gun felt he had been deprived of his manliness, he gritted his teeth and paid up, thus helping to swell the state coffers by a tidy sum of money. It was some years later, during each of which up to 1,000 murders were registered, that the authorities banned the general carrying of weapons, having come to the conclusion that it might be counter-productive to the maintenance of public order. The inland revenue promptly found another taxable item to compensate for the loss of income: 12 soldi were levied annually on each Corsican hearth.

In order to put an end to at least the political quarrels, in 1571 Genoa granted Sampiero's followers a general amnesty. The *Statuti civili e criminali di Corsica* were passed – a series of binding clauses which formed the basis of a code of civil and criminal law. A tightly structured administration was to forge closer links between the island and the parent city. The

island was divided into 10 provinces and a total of 66 parishes *(pievi)*, each of which included up to 50 villages *(paesi)* entitled to hold public assemblies *(consultas)*.

A governor appointed by Genoa took up residence in Bastia; he in turn was represented by a deputy. Ajaccio, Bonifacio and Calvi were ruled by commissioners; commandants took over the island fortresses and administrators were appointed for the rural areas. A Council of Twelve, consisting of local residents, advised the governor and was entitled, with his permission, to present petitions to the Genoese senate on behalf of the *magistrato di Corsica*.

Corsica's "Golden Age"

To be fair to the Genoese it should be pointed out that they also built some churches, but they were few in number. Between 1270 and 1350 St Dominique's, the island's only Gothic church, was built in Bonifacio. The Renaissance never established a hold on Corsica and one of the few examples of the style will be found in the Cathedral of Ajaccio. Nonetheless, once the fortresses were secure and the opposition had been crushed, Corsica lived through some 150 years of virtual peace. The economy recovered, and even the building industry experienced a unique boom. It was during the baroque era that almost every village – at least in the more prosperous regions – received an appropriate place of worship. The best example is undoubtedly the church of St John the Baptist in La Porta, a hamlet with fewer than 500 inhabitants.

The external façades of the churches of Corsica's "Golden Age" often appear unadorned. Inside, however, they are magnificent. Gilt stucco, pompously ostentatious architecture, damask-lined walls with a wealth of pictures, turn them into an overwhelming experience. Some of the best-known examples are the church of Ste-Marie *(see page 200)* and the Oratoire de l'Imaculée Conception and the Chapelle Ste-Croix *(see pages 198–9 and 200)*. Local artists were mostly responsible for the wood carving (statues of saints, pulpits, choir stalls and scenes of the Cross); the paintings were mainly the work of Italians. In a number of instances entire altars and choir screens of polychrome marble were imported in their entirety from Liguria and merely assembled in situ by local craftsmen.

The beginning of the 18th century saw the rapid eclipse of Genoa's star. The maritime republic sank further and further into political and economic difficulties, trying as it did so to extract even higher taxes from Corsica. This pressure, combined with other unpopular measures such as allowing Greek refugees who had fled from Turkish invaders to settle in Cargèse, led to still greater discontent. This finally resulted in a war of independence which was to last for 40 years, and which was fought under a single watchword which was to prove impossible to ignore: Corsica for the Corsicans. ❏

LEFT: the distinctive Genoese style.
RIGHT: the Bastion de l'Etendard at Bonifacio.

THE STRUGGLE FOR INDEPENDENCE

New Genoese taxes triggered the Corsican's fight for independence, which lasted for 14 years until rule from France began

For many years Genoa had shamelessly exploited its island colony to the utmost. The poverty of the Corsicans and their hatred of their rulers grew ever greater, to the extent that in 1729 it only took a trivial cause of annoyance for armed resistance to break out. An old woman or an old man – the event is recorded differently by the various historical sources – reputedly owed the Genoese tax collector "half a sou" (a few pence). The Genoese official had no pity on the desperate poverty of the debtor and threatened punishment, possibly even execution.

Ferdinand Gregorovius describes how the old man ran around his village, "deliberating on this act of cruelty and talking to himself, as old men are wont to do. Other inhabitants met him, listening and forming a crowd by the wayside. The old man started to lament, then, passing over from his situation to that of the whole country, he roused his listeners to anger, describing to them the plight of the people and the tyranny of the Genoese, finally uttering the cry, 'Now it is time to put an end to our oppressors!'" The appeal spread like wildfire across the island as trumpets and alarm bells summoned the people to revolt against the forces of occupation.

Two Corsican noblemen were chosen by plebiscite to serve as generals at the head of the revolution. They tried initially to patch up the family feuds in order to be able to lead a united Corsican army into battle against the Genoese. In 1731 the rebellion was given official recognition by the legal assembly in Corte; even the Church began to see it as self-defence and released the islanders from their duties as subjects of Genoa.

Imperial intervention

By the time the Corsicans had already conquered a number of towns and were laying siege to the coastal fortresses of Bastia, Ajaccio

and Calvi, the city state of Genoa, by no means as powerful as it once had been, requested Emperor Charles VI to send them reinforcements. Within a short space of time, Austrian troops under the command of General Wachtendonck landed on the island. In desperation the Corsicans appealed to their countrymen living

on the mainland to return to join the fight. Many of them did so.

The Corsicans fought so bravely that the emperor was forced to send additional forces – a second army under the leadership of Prince Louis of Württemberg. But the Corsicans retreated to the mountains and embarked upon a guerilla warfare campaign against the invading troops, who had no knowledge of local conditions. In 1732 a peace was negotiated in which the Corsicans were promised an amnesty, tax exemption and the right to apply for public office.

Scarcely had the foreign troops withdrawn when Genoa violated the treaty and the fighting

LEFT: statue of Giampietro Gaffori in Corte.
RIGHT: Emperor Charles VI sent troops to Corsica.

resumed. In 1735 the Corsicans proclaimed the island's independence from Genoa during an assembly in Corte, granting themselves a democratic constitution. Since their emissaries to the courts of Europe found no allies, they placed their little nation under the protective care of the Virgin Mary.

A German baron becomes king

Genoa now resorted to a sea blockade. As the Corsicans' supplies dwindled to a desperately low level, help suddenly appeared from a most remarkable quarter. On 12 March 1736, Baron Theodor von Neuhoff of Westphalia anchored

cil of 24 men chosen by the people and by the Corsican parliament, which continued to retain legislative powers. King Theodore held court in the episcopal palace of Cervione in the Castagniccia where he did not merely enjoy the trappings of monarchy, but appears to have campaigned energetically on behalf of his island kingdom. Internally, he restored law and order, tried to revive trade and led a newly created Corsican army in a series of successful battles against the Genoese.

Nonetheless, after eight months it was plain that his extravagant promises were lacking in substance. The allied navy he had announced

off the coast of Aléria with a ship full of weapons, ammunition and other supplies. An adventurer and knight of fortune, he had not been entirely neglecting his own interests when, in searching for financiers to support his rescue plan, he used his connections not only to wealthy merchants, but to the royal courts of Europe. He wanted one prize: the throne of Corsica.

Having no alternative means of gaining their independence from Genoa, the Corsican leaders agreed to the deal. And so Corsica was actually declared a kingdom and the German nobleman was proclaimed king. However, the authority of Theodore I was limited by a coun-

failed to arrive, and the Corsicans' situation once more became acute. Theodore realised it was time for him to abandon his island. He claimed he had to visit the mainland in person to summon the tardy assistance. And indeed, Theodore did succeed in raising funds from all kinds of Corsica sympathisers, sending from time to time a relief ship with aid and instructions to stand firm.

Paris sends troops

Having observed the comings and goings initially with an air of amusement and scorn, Genoa gradually began to feel uneasy. Already heavily in debt, the city state raised further loans in order to buy in Swiss regiments. When even this failed to produce the longed-for breakthrough against the unruly Corsicans, the Genoese finally asked the French for support. In 1738 King Louis XV sent five regiments to bring the rebels under Italian sway.

At first the French commander, Count Boissieur, followed his instructions to negotiate with the Corsicans. But even after six months the latter were not prepared to surrender and to submit to the authority of the Genoese Republic. King Theodore next reentered the scene with three fully-laden ships flying the colours of the Netherlands. This

The negotiations with France and Genoa collapsed when the Corsicans were called upon again to put away their weapons and accept Genoan rule. Then they were defeated in battle by the French troops, who had received additional reinforcements, and their leader was sent into exile. Almost before the French had left the island, hostilities again flared up between the Corsicans and the Genoese.

This was the scenario in January 1743, when King Theodore made his third and final entrance into the Corsican theatre of war. Once more he had managed to find financiers for the Corsican cause, this time in England. And so

time he had been able to convince a number of Dutch merchants of the attractiveness of supporting Corsica. Now, however, it was the turn of the Corsican aristocracy whom he had generously adorned with the titles of count and baron, to refuse him their obedience, since they laid greater store by negotiations with France. The Dutch ships turned back when they found the situation too precarious; for Theodore the only alternative was to leave the island once more.

on this occasion he arrived with three English ships laden with military supplies. But the Corsicans would have no more truck with their monarch. He was forced to accept that his efforts had been in vain, and that his dream of a kingdom had vanished for ever. Disappointed, he retreated to England.

From Gaffori to Paoli

The Corsicans found their next tragic hero in Giampietro Gaffori, and his storming of the citadel in Corte has become a legend. In his distress, the Genoese military commander had Gaffori's young son kidnapped and held him over the fortress wall in order to stop the Cor-

LEFT: members of the Corsican clergy approved the declaration of war against Genoa.
ABOVE: sails before the Corsican coast rarely bode well.

King Theodore I

On 12 March 1736 a horn-like sound, echoed on shell trumpets from village to village, announced the arrival off the coast of Aléria of a ship flying the British flag. Fishermen, shepherds and peasants thronged together, even bringing their wives riding on mules to observe the island's leaders going on board to negotiate with a mysterious stranger. "A Spanish hat with a feather covered his head; tucked into his yellow silk belt were a pair of richly ornamented pistols and in his right hand he held a long sceptre." Thus he was

described by Ferdinand Gregorovius in his history of Corsica in 1852.

The theatrical entrée was not that of some oriental sultan; the gentleman clad as for an appearance in an operetta was in fact Baron Theodor von Neuhoff from Westphalia, who had just arrived from Tunis, where he had completed the preparations for his Corsica expedition. A few days later he was to be crowned King Theodore I of Corsica. Whether the idea was his own, or whether it was the reward for his efforts to secure the release of four leading Corsicans from a Genoese prison is a moot point.

What is certain, however, is that the local citizenry was confident that this outsider, free from involvement in the local family feuds, would be able to free them from the yoke of Genoese rule. The hereditary royal title was certain to give him the necessary authority, despite the fact that a wreath of bay and oak leaves had to serve instead of the unavailable gold crown. Alas, the Corsicans' hopes were not fulfilled; does that mean that they were the victims of a confidence trickster, a false baron? Who was this character, whose bizarre fate served not only as the subject for novels and an opera, but who is also mentioned by Theodor Heuss, amongst others, who sees him as a "marginal figure in history" in his book *The Shadow Conspiracy*?

"King" Theodore was born in 1694 as the son of a Westphalian nobleman in Metz. His father had quarrelled with his family following his marriage to a member of the bourgeoisie, and had subsequently enlisted in the French army. After his premature death his relatives showed their desire for reconciliation by providing a home for his widow and the two children, Theodor and Elisabeth. Amélie von Neuhoff later moved to Paris with her adolescent children, taking up a post as lady-in-waiting to Liselotte von der Pfalz. Theodor acquired the manners of court by serving her as page, and she subsequently arranged for him to undergo officers' training.

Theodor was, however, also attracted by the frivolous life at court. He had soon run up his first gambling debts and fell out of favour with Liselotte. For the rest of his life he was always on the move – at the court of Spain or England as a political agent in the service of Sweden, or fleeing from his creditors or from a marriage he had contracted in Spain with an Irish lady-in-waiting upon the insistence of influential patrons.

Theodor's involvement with Corsica revealed him to be a skilled negotiator with considerable powers of endurance. "He must have had a remarkable talent for gaining access to the most impossible funds, and for presenting himself to the world's leaders in such a way that they saw their own real interests reflected in his," wrote Theodor Heuss. Others describe him as a "brilliant tactician without fortune".

Living in exile in England, Theodor spent seven years in a debtors' prison and died shortly after his release in 1756. A memorial plaque in St Anne's Church in London, in whose cemetery he was buried in a pauper's grave, reads: "Fate gave him a kingdom, but it refused him bread". ❑

LEFT: Theodor von Neuhof was elected king in 1736 but was forced to flee a few months later.

sican attack. Another version of the story claims that it was Gaffori's wife who begged him to continue the siege regardless. In any case, Gaffori refused to allow himself to be intimidated by the fact that his son had been taken hostage, and went on to take the citadel. As if by a miracle, his son survived.

In 1746 a public assembly proclaimed Corsica's independence once more. Gaffori was elected the sole leader of the country. He succeeded in winning back almost the entire island; the Genoese governor finally had to instigate a conspiracy to get rid of him; Gaffori was murdered in 1753.

"run wild, unused to the rule of law and order, and torn apart by parties and blood feuds" – to quote Gregorovius again. For this reason, agriculture and industry as well as educational establishments were all in a parlous state.

A democratic constitution

While attempting in the first instance to reconcile warring families, Paoli also ordered vendetta murderers to be pilloried and hanged. The restoration of peace within the island's frontiers was, however, only the first phase in the development of a comprehensive national infrastructure. Paoli organised the administra-

The Corsicans had one more trump card to play. In 1755 they entrusted Pasquale Paoli with the task of bringing their struggle for independence to a successful conclusion. Paoli had grown up in exile in Naples, where he had gone in the company of his father, the Corsican general Hyacinto Paoli. The young Paoli had received an excellent humanistic education in Naples. And so his first measures were not the continuation of the war, but the alleviation of the deplorable state of affairs amongst the Corsicans themselves. He found his people

tion, creating – even before the French Revolution – a democratic system of government based on the traditional Corsican community principle of the *Terra del Commune*. He was also responsible for a progressive, liberal legal code and encouraged education by the construction of schools and the foundation of the university in Corte. Paoli was distrustful of professional soldiers and reduced the full-time army to a small force enlarged by the introduction of conscription.

The improvements in Corsica were noted with amazement and admiration throughout Europe. "If we take into account their progressive ideas, the self-government by the people,

ABOVE: the only crown "king" Theodore ever wore was the one on the coins he had minted.

the freedom of the citizens laid down on all sides by the law, their participation in national life, the public nature and simplicity of the administrative system, the people's courts, then we must admit that the state of Corsica was more humanely structured than any other of its century," commented Ferdinand Gregorovius. Famous intellectuals and rulers of the time also expressed their respect, including Jean-Jacques Rousseau and Frederick the Great of Prussia.

This did not mean that the conflict with what had once been the mighty sea power of Genoa was over once and for all. Assisted by French

troops, the Genoese continued to occupy a number of coastal fortresses. However, they were forced to concede that they were no longer a match for the freedom-loving and by now well-organised Corsicans. And so in 1768 they decided upon a tactical move: as part of the Treaty of Versailles they allowed their claims to the island to be purchased by the French. The latter showed no scruples when it came to agreeing to the deal, thus securing a strategically important outpost in the Mediterranean.

Sold and conquered

The Corsicans were not asked for their opinion; they simply formed part of the island's

"inventory" and were thus included in the sale agreement. Thus it came about that France was forced to put an end to the islanders' autonomy. A French fleet set sail, and the Corsicans summoned up all their reserves of strength to resist. In any case, the French victory was not won without considerable effort. In the Battle of Borgo the Corsicans showed once more that their militia, despite being inferior in numbers, was able to put to flight the well-trained French army. Even Corsican women, armed with swords and shotguns, took part in the fighting.

But how should the Corsicans assert themselves against a world power which could send unlimited troop reinforcements, whilst their own reserves – despite active support from English, German and Italian sympathisers – were bound to be exhausted some time? The Corsicans' only chance would have been official intervention by England, but the British government decided to maintain its position of neutrality.

The decisive battle took place at Ponte Nuovo on 9 May 1769. The Corsican forces were driven from the Golo Bridge into the defile and annihilated. Paoli abandoned the struggle and fled into exile in England. France took over control of the island. By an ironic stroke of fate, Napoleon Bonaparte was born in Ajaccio during the same year – a man destined to be crowned emperor, but who would not be prepared to give his native island its freedom once more.

In 1790, one year after the French Revolution broke out, Paoli again returned to Corsica. He was nominated as President by the National Assembly, an election acknowledged by Paris. When the French Revolution assumed violent proportions of which he did not approve, he asked England for protection. Between 1794 and 1796 Corsica was ruled by a British viceroy. In the final instance, however, the English abandoned the field in favour of the French. Paoli died in exile in England in 1807. His death did not, however, mark the end of the Corsican dream of self-determination and freedom. Today, after over 200 years of belonging to France, the desire for autonomy is as much alive as it ever was. ❑

LEFT: the second half of the 19th century saw poverty and malaria in many parts of the island.

Pasquale Paoli

Pasquale Paoli, revered by Corsicans as the "Father of the Fatherland", was born on 5 April 1724 in Morosaglia as the son of General Hyacinto Paoli. At the age of 15 he followed his father into exile in Naples, where he soon joined the local Corsican regiment. In 1745 he became a Freemason, thereby coming into contact with the train of thought underlying the European Enlightenment. The ideas were reinforced by his attendance at lectures in philosophy and national economy at the Academy of Naples. From 1752 he conducted a lively correspondence with residents of his native island, in the course of which he urged them to continue the struggle for freedom from Genoan rule. In 1755 he responded to the appeals of his compatriots to return to Corsica in order to serve as their leader.

His main service to his country was his achievement in transforming the "slovenly band of rebels", as the rest of Europe saw the Corsicans, into a state with an exemplary national structure. The Scottish travel writer James Boswell, who visited Corsica in 1765, regarded the Corsican government of the day as "the best model... ever to exist in the democratic tradition". In his book about the island, *Journal of a Tour to Corsica* (1768), Boswell reports on his first meeting with Paoli: "He is tall, strong and well-built; his features are handsome, with a free, open expression and a manly, noble bearing. He was in his fortieth year at the time, and was dressed in green and gold. He generally wore simple Corsican attire; only when appearing before the French did he believe that a little superficial glamour might help to give the government a more glittering appearance." Boswell relates that he was never still and that he only sat down to eat. The Scottish traveller reports that his conversations at table were instructive and entertaining.

The restless statesman felt little inclination to marry. Boswell comments that he was "married to his native land, and the Corsicans are his children". Indeed, he seems to have been the object of a real personality cult. Boswell experienced the thronging of a vast crowd whom Paoli's guards could not prevent from forcing its way into his room. But Paoli had only to tell them that he was not at that moment holding audience, and his supporters respectfully withdrew.

RIGHT: Pasquale Paoli, "Father of the Fatherland".

In a burst of self-criticism, Paoli later explained his own flight into exile in England after the defeat in the Battle of Ponte Nuovo as a lack of boldness in the way the war was conducted. Only the French Revolution some 20 years later summoned him back to Corsica. During the journey, he arrived in Paris for the first time on 3 April 1790. The French government had put a violent end to the liberal constitution of his people; now, on his entry into the capital, he was greeted with stately respect.

In Marseilles he was met by a Corsican delegation including the two Bonaparte brothers, Joseph and Napoleon. Once again, Paoli was able to take up this cause as the president of the National

Assembly. But the bloodthirsty excesses of the French Revolution repelled him. He broke with France once more, joining forces with England, the country which had given him asylum. Corsica spent a period of two years under the rule of an English viceroy. One might have expected this to be Paoli, but King George II decided to send Sir Gilbert Elliot.

The king requested the elderly Paoli to return to England, which he did for the last time in October 1795. Like Neuhoff, he died in London, at the age of 82. But 82 years later he was brought home again by his fellow Corsicans. He was finally laid to rest in the house in Morosaglia in which he had been born; today, it serves as a memorial to the Corsicans' patriotic struggle. ❏

THE QUEST FOR AUTONOMY

Corsican voters recently narrowly rejected a proposal for limited autonomy maintaining the status quo with mainland France

On a number of occasions during the course of Corsican history, the interests of the major European nations in the island's strategic position prompted them to take it by force. Until the 19th century the attempts of the various occupying powers to develop Corsica's economy failed due to a permanent lack of funds, the apathy of the native population towards economic matters, and the island's mountainous topography.

A life of self-determination

The remoteness of most of the mountainous and upland communities favoured their economic autonomy and political self-determination. This was evident even during the Middle Ages in the inhabitants' resistance not only to exploitation by the various invaders, but also to outside attempts at political influence. Every scheme aiming at the economic, political or religious subordination of the reputedly barbaric populace introduced by the missionaries of civilization from the mainland, was interpreted by the island's leaders to their own advantage and virtually never accepted by Corsican society as a whole. Thus, the largely autonomous Corsican regional culture was able to survive until well into the 19th century.

Only during the course of the industrial revolution was the island opened up as an export market for continental Europe. Initially, only the more densely populated coastal regions were encouraged to give up their economic independence and to face up to the unpredictability of economic crises in return for the chance of economic expansion.

The interior was able to preserve its stable symbiosis between agriculture and cattle farming until this was disrupted by entry into the world market, and finally superseded after World War I.

LEFT: students were the driving force behind the "Libertie" movement in the 1970s.
RIGHT: monument at Ponte Nuovo, site of the French victory over Pasquale Paoli.

The destruction of the rural social milieu caused by heavy losses in that war, and the temptations and economic opportunities offered by the culture of continental France, set in motion a pattern of development whose implications, both social and ecological, reach far beyond the control of those affected.

The winds of change

When, in 1909, the French president Georges Clémenceau drew public attention to the misery and deprivation on Corsica, his aim was not merely to reveal economic defects, but also to point to the steadily rising numbers of young Corsicans who were choosing to emigrate. Only pensioners and the elderly remained behind; the villages were decaying, the fields and hill terraces lay fallow and the island's industry was also in decline.

In principle, the situation is unchanged to this day. The Corsicans' main complaint, however, is that virtually no one seems to take their problems seriously, despite the fact that they have always fought with both word and deed for autonomy and independence.

After World War II, two striking political innovations did much to encourage the formation of regional movements in France. Firstly, in the Treaty of Evian (1962), Algeria was granted its independence. The treaty symbolised the victory of the right of self-determination over and above the principle of the indivisibility of the French Republic. Furthermore, the end of France's colonial policy marked the beginning of a new era, that of so-called internal colonisation. It aimed at an increased mobilisation of resources by means

the beginning, they were voiced only by an elite class of intellectuals and led to the establishment of various action groups. In 1963, Corsican students on the mainland founded the *Union Corse l'Avenir*, whose name was soon transformed into the *Union Nationale des Etudiants Corses*.

Among its decidedly left-wing aims was the establishment of an independent university for Corsica. The union's newspaper campaigned against the growing exodus from the island, which ran parallel to the immigration of foreigners, and against the centralised administration. It appealed to the population not to leave

of a specific regional policy, and was intended to balance the very real damage suffered by the French economy as a result of the loss of Algeria. This new concept of "economic regionalism" required not only a reform of the functions of the central bureaucracy on a national level, but also a political decentralisation.

Moderate demands

In recent times, new trends of this nature have accelerated the formation of regionalist tendencies on Corsica as well. In the initial phase, which lasted from 1962 to 1973, Corsican regionalism was marked above all by demands for economic and administrative privileges. At

the concern for their well-being to technocrats and profit-conscious businessmen, and voiced protests at the increasing land speculation on the east coast of the island. The union's cultural demands included the application of the so-called "Loi Deixonne", which lays down the compulsory teaching of the Corsican language and Corsican history in all schools.

The following year, the Corsican doctor Max Simeoni – with his brother Edmond the best-known propagandist of the Corsican people – founded the *Comité d'Etudes et de Défense des Intérêts de la Corse*, a committee whose aim was the protection of Corsican interests. Simeoni maintained that "Our opponents are the

State and its regime – not France, and not the French people, but colonialism in all its forms." The members of his association were traders and lower middle-class town dwellers, who demanded tax concessions to compensate for the cost of living on the island, which was higher than that on the mainland, as well as the repair of the roads and bridges damaged during World War II, subsidies for the costs of sea transport and the maintenance of the island's narrow-gauge railway.

In 1967 there was a split within the regionalist movement to form the *Front Régionaliste Corse* (FRC) and the *Azzione per la Rinascita*

of an elected Corsican national assembly with its own executive, and legislative, administrative and financial powers under the control of the French government.

The ARC's programme for the development of the island included the creation of a tourist infrastructure by means of the construction of new roads, ports, airports and sports stadiums, reforestation after forest fires, the maintenance of extensive grazing areas, the production of quality wines and the prevention of emigration by the retention of existing schools. It campaigned for the re-opening of the university in Corte and the foundation of institutes of agri-

Corsa (ARC). The latter founded the now-famous publication *Arritti* ("Upright"), which gained a respectable circulation amongst minor industrialists, artists and manual workers. After the division, whilst the FRC went into a decline with relatively few activities, the ARC was able to create a stable, tightly organised association. Since it saw Corsica's problems as institutional in origin, its initial reaction was to reject any idea of political affiliation. Its demands for an autonomous administration led to the creation

culture and tourism. The programme was obviously fed by the illusion that by means of state protection the island would gain sufficient freedom to develop its own economy. This idea corresponded in certain points with the intentions of the French government, but was only put into practice by the latter in a limited manner and at a remarkably slow rate.

And so, in this first phase, a radical minority within the ARC began to voice its demands for complete self-determination, *Auto-détermination*, on behalf of the Corsican people. At first little notice was taken, but later the first illegal moves on the part of the *Comité pour la Corse Indépendante* and the *Front Paysan Corse de*

LEFT: a demonstration for a "global solution".
ABOVE: the FLNC amalgamated all existing underground organisations in 1976.

la Libération began to attract public attention. Within this category belonged the *Ghjustizia Paolina*, formed on the occasion of the visit to Corsica by the French Prime Minister. Acts of "democratic terrorism" against banks, travel agencies, police stations, estate agents and public buildings were proclaimed.

Radical trends

During the second phase, which lasted from 1974 until 1980, the legal wing of the Corsican regionalist movement was successful in abandoning its intellectual isolation and winning over the support of the majority of islanders for its

demands for autonomy. This change of political affiliation was provoked in the first instance by means of protests at the pollution of Corsican coastal waters by thousands of tons of highly toxic industrial waste. Montedison, an Italian firm, deposited the refuse out at sea, but a proportion of it drifted onto the Corsican coast in the form of red sludge. Since the French government provided no support for the justifiable Corsican environmental protests which ensued, the campaign culminated in an attack on a ship belonging to the Italian firm concerned. While some members of the group ended up in mainland prisons, the irrevocable step from moderate regionalism to demands for radical autonomy was taken.

Lethal waste and legionnaires

The environmental scandal had been preceded by a massive wave of protest at the proposed construction of an underground atomic testing station on the island, and at the plan to sink atomic waste in the sea between the French mainland and Corsica. Adding to the tension was the stationing of French Foreign Legionnaires on the island following their withdrawal from Algeria. The troops were generally viewed as an army of occupation. Moreover, there was growing resistance to the sale of the Corsican coast to financial consortia from the French mainland, which went on to line their pockets with the vast proportion of the island's income from tourism. As far as the new holiday villages were concerned, virtually everything was imported from the mainland, from the building materials to the food supplies: even the staff were almost exclusively non-Corsican.

Thus Simeoni was speaking for many when he said: "The loveliest areas of Corsica were handed over to real estate speculators and industrial tourist agents, who now destroy the local hotel business, commandeer the beaches and mutilate the countryside without producing any real profit for the inhabitants."

Wine scandal

In 1975, public indignation reached its climax when the ARC uncovered a wine scandal, in which a mainland firm that marketed Corsican wine had apparently gone bankrupt, thereby causing the financial ruin of a large number of Corsican wine growers. The protest resulted in the violent occupation of the wine cellar of one of the fraudulent bankrupts by supporters of the ARC near Aléria, with the aim of withdrawing after holding a press conference to bring the matter to public notice.

The French Ministry of the Interior flew heavily armed *gardes mobiles* onto the island. During the course of the subsequent siege two policemen were shot dead and several of those occupying the building were injured. After they had been arrested the ARC was officially banned. Since the affair, Aléria has become the symbol for the continuing struggle for freedom. Many radical supporters of autonomy maintain that they merely represent the latest generation in the centuries-old tradition of Corsican freedom fighters. The event itself unleashed a wave of terrorist attacks by the *Fronte di Liberazione*

Naziunale di a Corsica (FLNC), under whose banner all existing underground organisations had amalgamated in 1976. Since then its members have continued to wage an illegal war to liberate Corsica. Their hero is Pasquale Paoli, who for 40 years fought bitterly against first the Genoese and then the French. They are inspired by the romantic dream of an independent island, with the right of self-determination for Corsicans within the framework of the French Republic.

Since no real concessions to those demands were made by a succession of governments, the underground militia intensified the battle

a few minutes each day every Corsican feels himself to be one of them". Explanations for this attitude range from personal pride in being a Corsican, to a matriarchal family tradition and strong village ties, which are still felt by the 95,000 Corsicans who live on the mainland as well as those in distant countries. All of them have a strong desire to cling to their roots.

The nationalist movement splits

A strong common insular identity mixed with a tendency to adopt opposing opinions – especially where internal politics are concerned – is deeply rooted in the Corsican character, so

against what it describe as "internal colonialism" by dynamiting illegally constructed villas or holiday villages and attacking such symbols of the state as tax administrations and Gendarmerie stations. Whenever supposed bombers land up in prison, even moderate islanders join the demand to release these self-styled patriots. Corsicans demonstrate a certain understanding for the terrorist actions, maintaining that, although the nationalists do not represent a significant percentage of the population, "for

LEFT: the paramilitaries continue their armed struggle for independence from France.

ABOVE: the male-dominated Corsican Assembly.

it was inevitable that the nationalist movement should split. Within the underground militia the more moderate part which condemned "unnecessary" violence, took on the name of FLNC *"canal authentique"* (authentic route), while the hardliners added *"storicu"* (historical). Both claimed to represent the original organisation.

A similar development took place in the legally constituted parties. The first to distance itself from any form of destruction and armed actions was the *Unione di u Populu Corsu* (UPC) which was founded in 1977 by Edmond and Max Simeoni, both doctors who had been imprisoned because of their participation in the Aléria disaster. Edmond became an independent symbol of national unity accepted by hard-liners, autonomists, independence seekers and even by some of the traditional "French" parties, while his brother Max was elected deputy of *Les Verts*, the ecologists, in the Strasbourg parliament where he could fight for the island on the European platform.

Both FLNC militias showed signs of reflection and declared themselves open to negotiate a political solution, but factions of their adherents continued the "armed combat" under the slogans of *"Resistenza"* or *"Fronte Ribellu"*. The Paris government obviously was interested in – and perhaps even pushed – this process of

self-destruction. In the mid-1990s the split had turned into a lethal feud. Supposed top figures of the underground were killed in an outburst of fratricidal violence. This tragic chapter was only brought to a close by spontaneous demonstrations of a non-political movement called "Women against violence".

A limited truce

A period of stocktaking followed. There were secret contacts between government agents and the underground which then declared, as so often before, a limited truce. It would have been helpful to ease the situation if an enlarged Regional Statute for Corsica had been adopted

with the preamble of the *"peuple corse partie intégrante du peuple français"* ("the Corsican people as an integral part of the French people"). Both the Regional and National Parliament voted for it, but the Constitutional Council rejected it as "not compatible with the principles of the French Republic". Then in February 1998 the "governor" of this Republic, the Préfet Claude Erignac, was shot dead on his way to a concert in Ajaccio. The indignation was unanimous. Politicians and the known underground groups condemned the killing and distanced themselves from the unknown murderers. The event changed the political context completely.

Missing millions

Préfet Erignac had stirred a nest of vipers. He had started to investigate the whereabouts of millions of subsidies that had been granted by the state, mostly just to calm down Corsican demands, but whose appropriation had never been effectively controlled. In a far-reaching action a considerable number of people in executive positions in both agricultural and financial institutions were put under arrest, as well as former and active nationalists.

In September 1998 a parliamentary fact-finding committee established a double complicity of both the Regional Assembly and the French State in the misappropriation and squandering of public money. This official report was received with satisfaction by all political groups. But the suspects were arrested in the presence of the Parisian media, sparking racist anti-Corsican insults. They were then held for a long time pending trial, without the right to meet a lawyer or relatives. This was not what Corsicans had expected from the government declaration to re-establish a legal status on the island.

As a reaction, one of the FLNA militia groups, A Cuncolta, added *"indipendentista"* to its name, leading to the dismissal of hundreds of members and a complete reshuffle of the nationalist scene. From prison François Santoni, a former high-ranking militant of the Cuncolta, declared that the assassins of Préfet Erignac might be former extremist nationalists, "but they acted as instruments of other interests."

By now there were about a dozen nationalist groups, both old and new, and the killers had not been brought to justice. Meanwhile Corsica was still waiting for the government to ratify the European Convention on minority languages, so Corsican could be a compulsory subject in island schools.

L'Affaire de la Paillote

The government clampdown, however, only intensified under the man dispatched by prime minister Lionel Jospin to replace the murdered Préfet Erignac. Bolstered by a dramatic swing in Corsican public opinion against the armed struggle, Bernard Bonnet tackled the island's corruption and violence head on, arresting prominent paramilitaries and gangland figures. But unbeknown to the general public, he and

Paillote" – had not only incriminated Bonnet himself, but also threatened to engulf Jospin.

With its Corsica policy in tatters and Bonnet behind bars (after a trial in which he attempted to lay the blame for the attack squarely on the PM), the Elysée Palace had to come up with a very bold initiative to break through the deadlock. This eventually came in December 1999 with the start of the so-called Processus Matignon – a package of devolutionary measures proposed in exchange for an end to paramilitary violence on the island. In essence, Matignon represented precisely what the majority of moderate nationalists had been demand-

the unit of crack police drafted in after the Érignac shooting also embarked on an undercover "dirty tricks" campaign designed to hit back at the FLNC's business interests. One such action – the burning down of an illegally constructed beach restaurant (paillote) near Ajaccio – went disastrously wrong. Items discovered by regular detectives amid the smouldering remains led them straight to Bonnet's elite squad. Its boss, Colonel Henri Mazares, was promptly arrested and within days the ensuing scandal – dubbed by the French press as "L'Affaire de la

LEFT: Edmond Simeoni, part-founder of the UPC.
ABOVE: separatist propaganda posters.

ing for years, and looked like it might well be the breakthrough everyone was hoping for. But the proposals went too far for those on the Gaullist side of Jospin's coalition cabinet, who feared that such concessions would only stir up resentment among other minorities within the Republic, and possibly lead to its eventual break up.

To placate Matignon's right-wing detractors, the PM began diluting some of its key elements – much to the annoyance of the Corsican negotiators. As the process floundered, news broke that one of the island's most prominent nationalist leaders, François Santoni, had been shot dead by gunmen. Former boss of A Cuncolta, the FLNC-Canal-Historique's political wing, Santoni had made international headlines when he and fellow dissident, Jean-Michel Rossi, published a whistle-blowing book on the island's paramilitary movement, revealing the extent to which it had been corrupted by organised crime. Since then he'd renounced violence and started a more moderate political wing committed to the peace process. But the dramatic revelations of the book, *Pour Solde de Tout Compte*, had been calculated to cause maximum damage to the FLNC and its mafia partners; thus it came as no surprise when first Rossi, and then Santoni, were murdered.

Opponents of the Processus Matignon seized upon the killings as proof of the folly of "talking to terrorists". When Gaullist home affairs minister, Jean Pierre Chevènement, resigned in protest at the government's policies, Jospin and his initiative seemed perilously exposed. The end of the road for Matignon eventually came with the defeat of Lionel Jospin in the presidential election of 2002, and the Supreme Court's ruling that the whole package was, in any case, "unconstitutional". One of the new prime minister, Jean-Pierre Raffarin's first acts was to dispatch his hard-line home affairs minister to the island. At a press conference in Ajaccio, Nicholas Sarkozy set out a new doc-

trine: that none of the concessions previously promised by Jospin's administration would be honoured and that Corsica would henceforth be treated in the same way as other French regions lobbying for greater devolution.

Instead, Sarkozy warned, the island was to be swamped by a huge number of police reinforcements. A major crackdown ensued in which roadblocks, raids and arrests netted a string of key convictions.

The paramilitaries responded with a characteristic salvo of bombings and machine-gun strafings of state buildings. Meanwhile, divisions among the nationalist politicians deepened. On the one side, moderates lined up behind Corsica Nazione head, Jean-Guy Talamoni, advocate of a pragmatic, "one-step-at-a-time" approach of squeezing concessions from the French government through negotiation. On the other, Santoni's arch rival, current Cuncolta chief Charles Pieri, rallied the hardliners, resolutely opposing the government's insistence that Corsica's problems should be resolved within the wider framework of regional devolution. Corsica, Pieri has always maintained, is special and requires correspondingly special treatment – a suggestion that Jospin accepted as a given, but which his right-wing successors regard as heresy.

Greater Autonomy Rejected

In an historic referendum on 7 July 2003, Corsicans narrowly voted to reject an offer for greater autonomy from France. It is assumed that the result will mean the continuation of the campaign for full independence from the mainland (four French holiday villas were bombed on the night of the vote). Opinion polls show that most Corsicans want to remain French. Given that 40 percent of islanders are French government employees, many may have concluded that without this economic motor Corsica would be left to support itself on tourism alone. It would seem that for now the status quo on Corsica will remain. At the same time four suspects, held in connection with the Préfet Erignac murder, were put on trial in Paris. In a bizzare twist, two days before the vote Yvan Colonna, the main suspect in the killing, was arrested after five years on the run. ❑

LEFT: limited autonomy was rejected in July 2003.
RIGHT: the nation debates the issue of autonomy.

Corsica Corsi

Corsi

FRANCS   MENSUEL D'INFORMATION • N° 8 - MAI 2000

Y A -T- IL UNE VIE APRÈS LA CLANDESTINITÉ ?

RÉFÉRENDUM

55 % des voix à la motion ZUCCARELLI

Les Corses favorables à la dissolution de l'Assemblée territoriale

GEOGRAPHY

From the mountain summits and ravines to the forests of the lower hills, to the beaches of the coast, Corsica offers an incredible diversity of scenery

Corsica has many faces and many names. Geographers tend to refer to it simply as *"Ile des Contrastes"*, while writers have fondly called it the *"Ile de Beauté"* and the tourist brochures often sing its praises as the "Queen of the Mediterranean islands". But no single phrase can provide sufficient description of an island with such a varied landscape and temperament as Corsica.

Approaching Corsica by boat, a visitor will at first have the impression of a single majestic mountain range jutting straight out of the sea. Although its topography is considerably more complicated than that, Corsica is indeed the most mountainous island in the Mediterranean; within only a few kilometres of the shore are landscapes of soaring peaks, dramatic gorges, rushing torrents and magnificent pine forests. The island extends from Cap Corse in the north to Capo Pertusato in the south, a distance of 183 km (114 miles), and from Capo Rosso to Alistro, its widest point, at 83 km (52 miles).

Mountainous backbone

Closer examination will reveal that the topography of Corsica resembles a skeleton. The backbone of the island is linked by more than 20 mountains over 2,000 metres (6,562 ft), including the impressive Monte Cinto (2,710 metres/8,891 ft), the island's highest peak. As the main watershed, this great ridge of mountains, often as little as 30 km (18 miles) from the coast, runs from the northwest to the southeast, dividing the island into two halves of approximately the same size: the western half called by the locals *"Au delà des monts"* (beyond the mountains, when looked at from the direction of the Italian peninsula) and the eastern half which they refer to as *"En deçà des monts"* (this side of the mountains).

PRECEDING PAGES: the jagged pinnacles of the Aiguilles de Bavella; the chalk cliffs of Bonifacio.
LEFT: the Aigle ("eagle") rock, Calanques de Piana.
RIGHT: Corsica is the most mountainous island in the Mediterranean.

The high mountains, which make up no less than 47 percent of the island's total area, are broken by only four passes: the Col de Vergio, Col de Vizzavona, Col de Verde and Col de Bavella. This geographical divide has always had a decisive role to play in the fortunes of the island and its inhabitants; all down the cen-

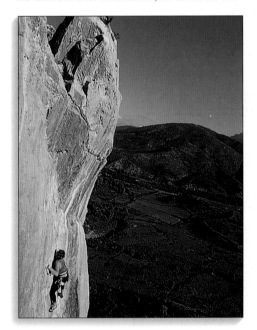

turies, when barely a road existed and the only means of transport was on foot or by mule, Corsica was virtually split into two separate entities. La Haute Corse and La Corse du Sud, the two French *départements* which make up the island today, roughly follow this ancient *En deça* and *Au delà* partition.

Corsica's mountain landscape is characterised by rugged peaks, jagged ridges, steep slopes and deep valleys – a paradise for mountaineers, hikers and skiers, rock-climbers and pony-trekkers. High corries and the rock formations left behind by moving glaciers are unmistakable evidence that the higher elevations of the island were subjected to the rigours of the Ice Age. Even in summer, patches of snow are still to be found at altitude. A number of mountain lakes, such as Lac Cinto, Lac Bellebone, Lac de Nino or Lac de Creno are further evidence of the glaciation that took place during the Pleistocene era.

Forests and mountains

Glacial activity ended at the milder altitudes of today's canyon-like river valleys. Classic examples of such ravines are the much-visited Scala di Santa Regina as well as the gorges of Restonica, Asco and Spelunca. This is also the level at which the forest begins, and Corsica possesses

coast to the east and west. They are separated by long valleys, such as the Filosorma, Sorru, Cinarca, Ornano and Tallona. Each of these is a cul-de-sac with no easy access to the neighbouring valleys. This inaccessibility has for centuries made them ideal sanctuaries for the local inhabitants, seeking refuge from conquerors or pirates from across the sea.

The geological make-up of the main mountain massif primarily consists of granite formed during the late Palaeozoic era about 350 million years ago. Since then the granite has been weathered into bizarre formations which can be seen up to a height of around 2,000 metres

some of the most beautiful forests of any Mediterranean island, indeed of anywhere in southern Europe. A particularly characteristic tree is the Laricio pine, which can grow to heights of more than 40 metres (130 ft). Large stands occur in the forests of Valdu Niellu, Barocaggia, Tartagine, Aitone and Vizzavona. Streams cascade between the trees. There are deep pools and waterfalls. And when the stone hut (*bergerie*) of a shepherd appears in a clearing, then the scenery of the mountain forest is complete. During the summer months the shepherds make their delicious curd cheese called *brocciu*.

From the main ridge of the island, countless subsidiary ridges descend like ribs down to the

(6,500 ft). Rock cavities are the most common feature, created by weathering of the lines of weakness in the rock structure which gradually gouged out the core of the crags. "Windows" to these caves were subsequently created when the elements broke through the rock faces.

Then there are rocky summits which rise steeply for several hundred metres above the level of the main mountain ridge. Because of their shape they are called "bell" mountains or "helmet" mountains. An impressive example can be found on Monte Tritorre near Guagno. A further natural wonder of a very special kind can be seen in the gigantic "rocking stones". Only the tips of these huge boulders actually rest on solid rock; they are balanced in perfect equilibrium despite the efforts of nature to topple them from their pedestals. A spectacular example is the Uomo di Cagna (Man of Cagna) near Sartène. The locals maintain that the outlines of the boulders resemble animal and human figures, and many of them are named accordingly. The granite crags of Les Calanques above the Gulf of Porto have also been worn into bizarre forms resembling animals.

Chestnut country

The mountains in the northeastern part of the island are generally much less rugged than this was submerged by a layer of Triassic and cretaceous formations consisting of limestone and conglomerates advancing from the east.

It used to be said that the inhabitants of this area nourished themselves from the "bread of the forest" and drank the "wine from the rocks". One only needs to take a stroll in the forest to understand why: edible chestnuts as far as the eye can see. Even in the height of summer the region looks fresh and green. Springs bubble forth from the limestone in abundance, a fact which has had a great influence on the settlement and cultivation of the area: this is the most densely populated part of the entire island.

those of the main central massif. The contours are more gentle and rounded and much of the area is covered by forest. The highest mountain in the area is Mont San Petrone (1,800 metres/5,905 ft). Most of the passes do not go any higher than about 550 metres (1,800 ft).

Geologically speaking, this area is younger than central and western Corsica and is composed of different rock types. Its base consists of a mantle of schist, a metamorphic crystalline rock. During the course of the Alpine orogenesis – the Tertiary period of mountain building –

LEFT: lush vegetation near Aullène.
ABOVE: chestnuts grow widely in the central zone.

A varied coast

Many tourists come to Corsica for its fantastic beaches. In fact there are three types of coast along the island's 1,000 km (over 600 miles) of shore: straight coast, gulf coast and cliffed coast. In the east, the mountains rise from a flat coastal belt of up to 12 km (7½ miles) in width which drops in a series of shallow terraces into the Tyrrhenian Sea. In the north, in the regions of Marana and Casinca, this is known as the Plain of Biguglia; in the south as the Plain of Aléria. In between, in the Tavagna and the Compoloro, the belt is narrower because the hills of the Castagniccia massif reach to within only 3 km (2 miles) of the shore. In a broad curve between Bastia and the Solenzara estuary 90 km (56 miles) to the south, this stretch of coast is characterised by fine, sandy beaches.

In the course of time, the two longest rivers on the island, the Golo and the Tavignano have transported vast amounts of material from the interior of the island. Arriving at the sea, the alluvium gets washed along the coast by the current and the waves. The sand bars and marshy lagoons so typical of this stretch of coast have been created from the resultant deposits. The sand bar to the north of the Golo estuary is more than 10 km (6 miles) long and forms a barrier between the sea and the Etang de

put in place and the area transformed into the largest intensively irrigated area of cultivation on Corsica, a development repeated in the rapid expansion of tourism on this side of the island.

Tourism booms along the sandy beaches of the east coast, but those with a taste for the dramatic should explore the north and west, where the coastline looks very different. The mostly granite formations provide for a constant fluctuation between sandy and rocky shore. Here, the subsidiary ridges of the west Corsican mountains often reach right down to the coast, where they then drop, often for hundreds of metres, straight into the sea. The gulfs of Porto,

Biguglia, the largest lagoon in Corsica, which is rich in fish. Such lagoons are also to be found along the southern coastal belt which begins around Alesani: Etang de Diane, Etang d'Urbino and Etang de Palo.

At one time, the coastal strip was virtually uninhabitable and deserted, not only because of the constant invasions from across the sea, but also because the marshlands provided excellent breeding grounds for the anopheles mosquito, a character that plagued the region right across the centuries, until its final irradication by DDT after World War II. Since then, drainage and irrigation systems, which were first established here by the Romans, have been

Sagone, Ajaccio and Valinco are separated from one another by broad peninsulas, with exposed rocky capes and outlying islands. These gulfs were created by tectonic forces when the land sank and submerged whole valleys, producing this typical indented coastline of *rias*. Apart from the larger sandy bays, the occasional sandy beach can also be found in among the rocky headlands, many of them can only be reached from the sea.

Spectacular cliffs

A very special wonder of nature is to be found along the stretch of coast around Bonifacio in the far south of the island. Gleaming white cliffs rise for up to 60 metres (200 ft) out of the sea, providing a magnificent contrast with the azure-blue waters of the Straits of Bonifacio. The cliffs are composed of thin layers of Miocene chalk, which, during the course of the millennia, have been eroded into the spectacular cliff forms that we see today. And the waves continue to loosen the rock, carry off the debris and gouge out caves along the lines of weakness. The constant undercutting has resulted in massive blocks of rock breaking away from the cliffs and landing in the water at their base, where the process of erosion is continued by the relentless pounding of the waves. The ero-

the areas around Bavella and Asco. The wild boar's (sanglier's) habitat is the *maquis* and the lower mountain forest areas where it eats acorns and chestnuts. Boars are widely hunted throughout the island during the winter but their numbers are maintained at about 30,000. The males, weighing in at about 80 kg (176 lbs), are fierce animals with short tusks which are used for rooting and grubbing. The Corsican red deer, recently reintroduced to the island, can be found in Quenza, from where they are released into the surrounding countryside.

Corsica's birdlife is spectacular, coastal areas are the habitat of seagulls, ospreys, cormorants

sive force of the sea has not only endowed this stretch of coast with marvellous cliffs, but also with underwater grottos that provide a paradise for divers and snorkellers.

Wildlife

Corsica is home to a number of endemic species. The mouflon, a short-fleeced sheep, has destinctive facial markings and the males have huge horns which become more coiled with age. A protected species since 1956, the 400 to 600 mouflon on the island are centred in

and the large bearded vulture. The mountains are home to the golden eagle, and kites, recognised by their forked tail, are often seen in the Parc Naturel Régional; woodpeckers live in the woods among the pine and cork oak trees. Hermann's tortoise, now extinct in the rest of Europe, live in the *maquis*. Two endemic species of lizard, the Tyrrhenian wall lizard and Bedriag's wall lizard can also be found along with the harmless Aesculapian snake. The sea has abundant fish, including grouper and bream while striped dolphin and porpoise can be seen offshore. There are also over 2,000 species of plants, 80 of which are endemic, which make up Corsica's *maquis* undergrowth. *(see page 71).* ❑

LEFT: a rocks dominate this part of the west coast.
ABOVE: the mountains provide some great walks.

THE MACCHIA

*Napoleon maintained that he could recognise Corsica from its smell alone,
an assertion with which many islanders and visitors would agree*

Vast expanses of trees and shrubs, covering hills and valleys as far as the eye can see; the sight is a familiar one to the traveller who has visited other regions surrounding the Mediterranean. But nowhere else does the evergreen undergrowth so completely characterise the landscape; nowhere else is the botanical palette so varied – and nowhere else is the vegetation so luxuriant and impenetrable as here on Corsica. More than half the island's surface area is covered by this scrubland. The islanders call it *macchia*, derived from the Corsican name for the rockrose *(mucchiu)*. The French name is *maquis*. Many species of plant growing in the scrubland of Corsica are only to be found here; since they are endemic, their generic name includes the epithet *corsicus*.

An impenetrable refuge

During World War II, French partisans hid from Italian and German troops in the thick undergrowth of the *macchia*. The scrubland gave them their name: the *maquisards*. During the war, the term Maquis was applied to any resistance organisation, but it clearly originated in Corsica where it took one Axis soldier to control two Corsicans, including women and children. Even in historic times the *macchia* was used as a refuge from Roman, Saracen and Genoan invaders. Last but not least, it offered many a Corsican protection when he needed to escape from his pursuers because he had perpetrated an act of *vendetta*, blood revenge.

The *macchia* consists of a dense undergrowth up to 3 metres (10 ft) high, of sclerophyllous shrubs; in general it is the result of the overuse and over-grazing of the island's holm-oak forests. On Corsica the scrubland consists of 12 main shrub types, the most typical of which are brier, arbutus (strawberry tree), myrtle, mastic and broom. Its composition varies according to altitude, site, rainfall, soil conditions and

---

LEFT: the cork oak has its bark removed every eight to ten years and made into cork stoppers.
RIGHT: the Corsican word for *maquis* is *macchia*.

degree of depredation. The various types of *macchia* are labelled according to the dominant species or combination of species. There are three main levels: the myrtle level (up to 200 metres/640 ft), the mastic level (200–600 metres/640–2,000 ft) and the arbutus-brier level (600–1,000 metres/2,000–3,200 ft).

Versatile plants

The scrubland of Corsica is seen at its most magnificent in spring. The shrubs are still bright green from the winter rains, and across the hillsides and valleys their blossoms extend in a sea of colours. Spring is also the best time of year to walk through this unique botanical garden.The brilliant golden yellow of the gorse gleams between the characteristic rockroses, filling the air with a sweet smell of honey. It attracts countless numbers of bees from the brightly coloured hives dotted throughout the scrubland, in which is produced the much praised local honey with its characteristic taste. The brier may grow taller than a man in places, its shoots adorned with tiny, white, bell-shaped flowers. Known in Corsican as *scopa*, the brier's twisted stems are used to carve the famous *bruyère* pipes. In shady spots grows the myrtle, whose scent carries over long distances. The stamens glisten decoratively against the white petals. The branches produce a fine aroma when burned; for this reason, they are often used to grill fish and tender meat. The leaves yield an aromatic oil which is used as a seasoning for sauces; from the resiny-tasting fruits is distilled *myrte*, the famous Corsican liqueur.

Not far away the bell-shaped blossoms of the arbutus can be seen, producing tempting-

native son, always maintained: "I would recognise Corsica with my eyes closed, from the scent alone." Before the dew falls and the dawn breaks, ethereal oils are exuded by the thorns, twigs, stems and sclerophyllous leaves, most of which are small to prevent excessive transpiration. Only in this manner can many plants survive the drought of the summer months.

From earliest times the *macchia* has served the Corsicans as a hunting ground, where they pursue wild boar, partridge, birds and – until recently – the mouflon. Today, the huntsmen mostly return without prey, for despite restrictions, poaching and shooting at anything that

looking bright red fruits in autumn. Although they are inedible when raw, they can be made into a delicious jelly, *gelée d'arbouses*. *Erbiglie* is the islanders' collective name for the herbs used to give their cuisine its unique flavour. Rosemary and marjoram both grow wild in the *macchia*, lemon balm can be found along the wayside, and various types of mint grow in the damper spots.

The many flowers blossoming under the thicket of shrubs help to round out the characteristic scent of the *macchia*. In the dry, hot summer months, when the shrubs are no longer in flower, the scent still lingers unforgettably. It explains why Napoleon, the island's most famous

moves have sadly decimated the game stocks. Nowadays, many regions of *macchia* have become a silent scrubland, where scarcely a bird can be heard singing. Of even greater ecological significance are the effects of the seasonal grazing by migrant flocks. In many places the continuous depredations of sheep and goats have resulted in the replacement of the typically lofty shrubs by semi-high and low-growing bushes.

The monstrous match

The blossoms and aromatic scents of the *macchia*, together with the many-faceted usefulness of a number of the plants, represent the sunny side of the situation. When the scrubland catches fire, however, tragedy strikes. Large areas are completely destroyed, villages temporarily cut off from the outside world, and even holiday complexes must sometimes be evacuated. An example is the huge fire that raged through the Vallée de la Restonica in the summer of 2000.

Why is the island so frequently plagued by fires of this kind? Corsican farmers maintain that shepherds are responsible for the vast infernos, by which they gain new pastures for their flocks of sheep and goats. Others point the finger at farmers who burn stubble to produce potash to improve soil quality; their fires can also burn out of control.The police and fire brigade, however, insist that, in most cases, political extremists use this method to draw attention to Corsican demands for independence. Also under suspicion are careless visitors; during a dry summer, a burning cigarette stub, or an incompletely extinguished camp fire, can set an entire region ablaze. As a consequence it is forbidden to light fires outside, except in controlled areas. Fires must also be reported to the fire brigade as soon as they are spotted.

It is seldom possible to pinpoint the culprit with certainty. What remains is a frightening record of destruction: in the last decades of the 20th century, an average of 5,000 hectares (12,000 acres) of shrubland caught fire each year – almost half the total area of *macchia* on the island. Decades later, the damage caused by fire can be seen like a scar across the countryside. There is no more vegetation, so during the next winter the rain will be able to erode the soil unhindered. Thus it is by no means certain that the dense undergrowth of the *macchia* will ever be able to re-establish itself in these areas again. It is usually replaced by a degenerated form of scrubland, the so-called *garigue*, which establishes itself on steep slopes where there have been repeated fires. One representative of this adaptation is the poisonous asphodill, which has large numbers of flower-bearing stems growing up to 1 metre (3 ft) high.

The dangers of fire

The typical vegetation of the *macchia* has developed a certain resistance to fire. Many species seem to possess an almost inexhaustible capacity for regeneration. Some are even largely resistant to fire: as soon as the autumn rains begin to fall, new shoots develop from buds at or near ground level which remained undamaged by the fire. In some cases, the roots send up new shoots but this young greenery is likely to provide nourishment for goats and sheep.

In the past, many islanders were strangely indifferent to the ravages of fire, as if they were unavoidable, but this attitude has changed among some sections of the population as Corsicans begin to regard the protection of their environment as an aspect of national pride. It would be a tragedy if the *macchia*, linked so closely to the Corsican lifestyle were to be completely

destroyed and replaced by a sterile wilderness. The Désert des Agriates, between St-Florent and the mouth of the Ostriconi River, 30 km (19 miles) of *maquis* so scorched that it resembles a moonscape, is a reminder of this possibility.

Until the local administration succeeds in improving measures against the catastrophic fires and over-grazing, there is little chance that conservation laws for the preservation of the unique Corsican scrubland, for example the creation of a national park, will provide effective protection. The nearby Mediterranean coastal regions of Italy and Spain provide plenty of examples of the tragic fate awaiting the *macchia* if they should fail. ❑

LEFT: lush *maquis* vegetation.
RIGHT: the barbary fig is part of the cactus family.

THE CORSICANS

Corsicans hold on to their traditional values and, while women are no longer the cause of vendettas, they maintain dominant family roles

The *paesanu*, his back bent double, tends his beans. Although he may be only a stone's throw away from the road, the passer-by will see little more than his straw hat, bobbing up and down. But peering out from under the rim, and without interrupting his work for even a moment, his keen eye has already made out who is behind the wheel. Local or stranger. The former will just be able to catch the greeting gesture of his hand, the latter probably won't even realise that their passing has also been registered.

Day in, day out, they're always watching: the shepherd on the hillside, the road worker resting under the shade of a tree, the old man on the bench in front of his house, his wife airing the sheets at the window, the boules player next to the war memorial. They hardly move their heads but they see everything. It is an involuntary action, this scrutinisation; a survival instinct moulded out of 2,000 years of dangers coming from across the sea, of foreign sails drawing ever closer. Today it is simply a question of recognising those who belong, "us", and those whose purpose on the island is unclear, "them". Are they just speeding through the countryside, or will they stop and maybe even venture to the bar and enquire about some thing to drink?

Corsican hospitality

That is something that the *paesanu* definitely hopes. Like so many islanders he needs several strings to his bow: he is shepherd, gardener and innkeeper rolled into one, and he likes uniting all these little jobs under the honourable title "farmer". He will serve his guest with a calm dignity that might seem almost cool; but then, even if the stranger has only stopped for a quick drink, he will always nod his farewell before getting down to another task. But maybe he wants a snack. In

LEFT: a time-honoured method of transport.
RIGHT: exchanging pleasantries while selling the catch of the day.

this case the *paesanu* will take the ham from its hook on the ceiling, carve some generous slices, then some sausage, and the crusty bread. He'll slice up a couple of tomatoes and produce a handful of olives, fill a large jug with water, and a smaller one with wine.

The stranger has become a guest, and as soon

as he has banished that initial hunger, the *paesanu* will strike up conversation. How does it taste? Well yes, the ham was smoked by a cousin, the bread baked by a friend in the next valley; he himself marinated the olives and he buys his wine next door.

Depending on the response, the *paesanu* will soon know if it's worth carrying on the conversation. If the guest is a tourist who has to get on, then it probably won't get beyond the small talk, about the weather and suchlike. But if it's an islander, even from the other side of the mountains where the *paesanu* hasn't been for ages, if ever, then the gossip will continue; after a lifetime of peeking from under the rim of his straw hat, of picking up snippets from countless conversations at the bar, he'll know all about where the stranger comes from. So he lives in X on the other coast. Isn't there a valley with five mills there? Doesn't family A own property in those parts? Didn't the eldest of three brothers die recently? Why, of course, there are relatives of that clan on this side of the island as well, just two valleys away.

Anybody from the mainland, whether French or total foreigner, will find it completely impossible to latch on to the system by which the Corsican navigates with such amazing certainty. Even someone from the mainland who

cool quickly become a friend. But Corsican hospitality will only ever be extended to the individual; it will never be applied to a group, let alone an anonymous group of tourists. And hospitality always has to be earned, through openness towards the locals, accepting their ways and respecting their pride and their highly sensitive sense of honour. Then it doesn't really matter where the stranger comes from.

Contradictions in character

A social psychologist doing research on the island asked the Corsicans what they considered to be their most important virtues. A clear

has lived here for decades will find it hard. Whether or not he will, eventually, become one of "us", whether he can ever consider himself to be *parmi nous*, will sometimes even be decided at that first *spuntinu*, the first glass of wine with bread and ham. In the meantime, every newcomer to this tightly knit community remains a potential intruder.

It wasn't so long ago, maybe two decades at most, that village children would repel the evil eye of a stranger by pointing their outstretched index and little fingers towards him, as he passed through. But just as the Greek *xenos* denotes a stranger as well as a guest, so on Corsica can someone whose initial reception was

first place was invariably occupied by hospitality, then came emotionalism, solidarity and honour. However, on the list of their self-admitted character deficiencies, inhospitality also occupied third place, after aggressiveness and unfriendliness, before power-mongering and vindictiveness.

This inconsistency in the local character has always determined the image of the Corsicans in works of history, literature and music. As Edward Lear wrote in 1868: "The people are unlike what I expected, having read of "revenge" etc; they have the intelligence of the Italians but not their vivacity: shrewd as Scotch, but slow and lazy and quiet generally. It must be added that a more thoroughly kindly and obliging set of people so far as I have gone, cannot easily be found…"

But there is also a constant factor which serves to explain the contradictions of the Corsican soul. That is the solidarity of the Corsicans among themselves, which has developed over hundreds of years and proven itself time and again. While on the one side "them" might be taken by the foreigner as some kind of threat, it is only a feeling of "us" that gives the Corsicans their real strength and security. Family, relatives, clan and people are the natural bonds that make the Corsican identity so strong.

can also provide the seed-bed of passionate conflicts. Altercations often begin over matters of honour or when the meticulously heeded system of *quid pro quo* is not correctly observed. When this is applied beyond an individual family to a whole clan, interpretations tend to be rather over-sensitive.

The power of the clans

The clans, whose origins are lost in the mists of time, and whose existence is often denied, especially by those at the head who pull the invisible strings, continue to play a prominent role in the life of a Corsican. Only when he leaves

The sense of belonging to an extended family provides the individual with a safety net of relative security that will accompany him from the cradle to the grave. From babysitter to teacher to employer, whether in Bastia or Paris, down to the pall bearers who have spontaneously leapt out of the crowd during someone's funeral, there is always a helping hand from some near or distant branch of the family; one doesn't expect to have to depend on anyone else. But these intimate elements of solidarity

LEFT AND ABOVE: boules is a popular pastime, often played in the village square. The benches lining the square also make a good venue for discussion.

the island can he escape traditional constraints. But even then, this requires a conscious act of emancipation, which will cease to be valid should he ever return.

If Colombani, the ministry official, returns on holiday from Paris, where he probably helps to cultivate the Corsican phobia of central government, then he can be sure that the people of his home village will be full of admiration for his social status. But at the *fucone*, his own hearth and home, his word counts for no more than that of the *zia*, the grandmother, or of his brother, who is "only" a shepherd – and often it counts for less. That he is a man of great influence in Paris, and that he may also have

Vendetta

Not so long ago, firearms could be seen hanging not only above bar counters and bistro fireplaces, but also behind bank counters and church pulpits. They may have been old, decorative carbines, but they were unmistakable symbols of a traditional readiness to take the law into one's own hands if need be. The principle of self-administered justice grew up in an atmosphere of uncertainty based on the partiality and venality of a well-established judiciary. The courts of justice established by the occupying forces which ruled

the island for over 600 years, the maritime republic of Genoa and the Bank of St George, showed a marked tendency to favour those from their own ranks who were on the winning side. Injustice on the part of these gentlemen was of as little concern to the courts as affairs of honour amongst the Corsicans themselves.

They were only prepared to take on such matters upon payment of hefty fees, but how many Corsicans were in a position to find the necessary cash? And so the native islanders, accustomed to self-defence since time immemorial, resorted to settling matters of personal vengeance by means of the bullet or stiletto, usually in the back. Sometimes generations of families were engaged in honouring the vendetta (Corsicans use the word "vindetta"). Peace, if it ever came, was brokered between families by the parish priest.

Vendetta corsa is still written on the penknives in the island's souvenir shops. If the murder of a Genoese enemy led to military retaliation, the killing of a fellow-Corsican would lead just as inevitably to a counter-assassination. Constant retaliation meant entire clans were extinguished. Between 1683 and 1715 there were almost 30,000 victims of arbitrary law. Pasquale Paoli was the first to end this self-destructive butchery by establishing a legal system which was beyond bribery and which guaranteed justice for everyone.

But when France annexed the island and tyranny reared its head once more, so too did the principle of "an eye for an eye". This time it was a true vendetta in highly personal affairs of vengeance where the local inhabitants were reluctant to allow a foreigner to pass judgment. Furthermore, the penal code introduced by the new rulers seemed too weak to the passionate Corsicans. The blood of the perpetrator was the only way of cleansing a besmirched family honour. Most of the time, the original offence which started the vendetta bore very little relation to the severity of the reprisal. Thirty six murders took place over a disagreement over a chestnut tree and the theft of a cock resulted in 14 deaths. A man marked by the curse of the vendetta took refuge in the *macchia* – but he knew that his death was only a matter of time. Into the undergrowth fled, too, the *bandits d'honneur* who had killed a gendarme, a customs officer or some rich oppressor. The silence of the populace was as impenetrable as the thorny vegetation.

Prosper Mérimée, the poet who created *Carmen*, based his novella *Colomba* on a tribal drama of this kind. Balzac, Dumas and Maupassant also carved for the Corsican vendetta a place in literature. The last of the vendettas is thought to have come to an end in the 1950s and there is no concrete evidence that the vendetta continues to exist in its original form today. Nowadays, vendetta manifests itself not so much in killing but in the destruction of property; for example the supermarket that gets burnt down the day before it's due to open because it provides unwanted competition in a seaside resort. But the perpetrators of such deeds can still be fairly sure of the silence of their fellow citizens. ❑

LEFT: Jeanne Fioravanti as Colomba in Ange Casta's film.

secured his nephew a nice little job over there, will cause some envy in the community at large, although not amongst his immediate family circle.

Whether or not such envy erupts into a dispute really depends on which larger community such families are attached to. If they belong to the same clan, the flames will probably be quenched by a respected elder. Between two different clans, however, an event that induces jealousy, however trivial, can easily decide the outcome of the election of the next mayor. The power of the clans reaches beyond party divisions, a fact that explains why a basically con-

the Corsican spirit. Neutrality in dealings both among and with Corsicans is just about impossible. The mainland French, however sympathetic they may be to the struggles of minorities elsewhere, often consider their Corsican compatriots irresponsible trouble-makers, their actions inexplicable.

Male honour, female honour

Another cliché with which the Corsicans are so often branded is that they are arrogant machos who oppress women. Visitors may feel there is some justification for this, as they watch the daily comings and goings from the chair of a

servative electorate can vote for a communist. Whatever his political orientation may be, the main thing is that he is their man, who can be relied upon to represent their interests.

Corsicans readily state their position, even if this defies all possible logic. It seldom has anything to do with party membership cards. The fact that they tend to get easily worked up over issues is the result of a history that has never let them get a word in edgeways. Planting bombs is a more extreme means of articulating what they feel. Indifference has never been part of

ABOVE: Corsicans are polite people who take their time with casual conversation.

street café. From sunrise till sunset, the vast majority of people you will see will be men; men strolling under the plane trees, drinking espresso or pastis at the bar, often involved in some lively conversation about world or local events. Their dazzling white shirts with impeccably ironed collars provide clear evidence of where the womenfolk spend most of their day.

A French women's magazine once described the sacrifices Corsican women have to make in a traditional, male world. But despite her disadvantages, the Corsican woman enjoys a high social status. From time immemorial she has played out her role as matriarch and may sometimes be happy to stand apart from the imperious men, the noisy hotheads and all the swaggering at the bar. While this involves her being tied to the home and doing all the housework, it is also a position from which she exerts a great deal of authority.

The first megalithic sculptures on the island were life-sized phallic symbols or depicted warriors. It is interesting to note, however, that when the Corsicans sought a leader in their first great liberation struggle against the Genoese, they were unable to find a man thought worthy of the role.

While history attaches a great deal of glamour to the swashbuckling deeds of male free-

dom-fighters of the likes of Sampiero Corso, the heroism of Corsican women in the revolts of the past and in the resistance of the last war was every bit as great as that of the men. But legend also ascribes an almost male toughness to Corsican women. After all, was it not the wife of General Gaffori who was prepared to sacrifice her own child for liberty? Didn't women pour molten pitch over the heads of French soldiers as they stormed the fortress? And wasn't it the woman who would dip a piece of a dead man's clothing into his own blood and pass it on to a younger member of the clan, the signal that it was now his turn to carry out the vendetta?

The woman's power no longer manifests itself in such extreme ways. Be that as it may, when it gets to eight o'clock the confident man in the bar will put his empty glass to one side, wipe his boule ball clean and put off the next little conspiracy until tomorrow in order to race back home for dinner. And woe betide he who comes too late. And although she may not sit down to eat with her husband, the *mà* usually directs proceedings from a standing position, apron and all; she listens and absorbs, and when it comes to making a decision she often has the last say.

Break with tradition

Over the past few years, precisely because until now Corsican women have kept to their traditionally accepted roles, they have brought some uneasiness into the seemingly secure realm of men. Now more and more women, particularly younger women, have acquired real skills and pursue careers in business, law and medicine, for example.

In the world of today, their training and abilities liberate them from the constraints of the man's world and the system of allocation of the political families or the clans, and enable them to be independent.

Even in local politics, their matriarchal awareness enables them to have a clear view of proceedings. Sitting on the district council for the first time, a woman is far less vulnerable than a man who has only obtained his title primarily as a pawn in the game of parish-pump politics. At the same time, one will rarely meet a Corsican woman who flaunts her emancipated position. She was always conscious of her traditional value and has no need to boast. She is also too clever for that. Now that she brings her metropolitan, almost provocative chic into play, she can treat the old power game between the sexes as a bit of a joke.

"*So Corsu, no se fieru*" – "I'm Corsican and proud of it": this profession is based on the knowledge that despite all the centuries of oppression and annexation, the essential Corsican identity has remained intact. ❑

LEFT: Corsican women have the same freedoms as women in France.
RIGHT: seafood features heavily in Corsica's cuisine, here a catch of crab is landed.

THE CORSICAN LANGUAGE

Spoken today mainly in rural areas, the revival of the Corsican language has been a hot political issue with nationalists since the 1970s

Although French is the official language of Corsica, you'll almost certainly hear people speaking the island's native tongue, Corsican – or *Corsu* – especially in more remote areas and by the older generations. A Romanesque language bearing traces of Latin, Arabic and Ligurian, it's more accurately described as a group of closely related dialects, influenced above all by Tuscan. With its expressive, accented rhythms and intonations, Corsican sounds nothing like French but a lot like Italian – indeed, Italians can be easily understood by most islanders, even those who've never crossed the Tyrrhenian Sea or studied the language of their former colonial overlords.

Having survived a seemingly terminal decline in the 20th century, following decades of social and economic upheaval, Corsican today is enjoying something of a renaissance. All schools on the island now teach it, several radio stations broadcast Corsica-medium programmes, and the profile of the written language in the printed media has never been higher.

Such advances have been driven largely by the island's nationalists, for whom the mother tongue represents a cornerstone of insular identity. Efforts to stem the saturation of Corsican by French in education and political life have become one of the prime fronts in the ongoing battle between Paris and Corsica's autonomists. Wrangles over issues such as which forms of place names should appear first on road signs may seem petty to outsiders, but they are frequently cited by paramilitary groups as justification for the continuing campaign of violence against the French state (hence the ubiquitous black graffiti sprayed over the French versions on signposts).

For its part, the French government – while happy to pour millions of euro of subsidies into

---

LEFT: the Corsican newspaper with the largest circulation is the local daily, *Corse-Matin*.
RIGHT: the island's language has become an area of deeply held opinions between the island and France.

the island each year – has been conspicuously reluctant to make any concessions when it comes to claims for a separate Corsican language. "Give the Corsicans the status they ask for their language" or so the argument goes "and the Bretons, Savoyards, Alsaciens and Basques will demand the same". The Corsican

language issue is, in short, seen by many on the mainland as the thin end of a wedge that could ultimately divide the nation itself.

Early linguistic history

The linguistic assimilation of Latin began with the Roman conquest of Corsica in 259BC and by the time of the empire's break up had given rise to a tongue the chroniclers of the second and third centuries AD described as a "*lingua corsa*".

This probably comprised three distinct dialect groups, corresponding to the traditional cultural fault lines that still prevail to this today (in the *départemental* divisions and rivalry between Ajaccio and Bastia): the north; the south; and Bonifacio (always regarded as something of a world apart from the rest of Corsica).

During the medieval period, Pisan rule saw Tuscan become the language of state. Corsican continued to be widely spoken in the villages and to a lesser extent as the medium of trade and commerce, but it did so without the anchor of a written form or any significant status. Over time the island's aristocracy adopted whichever brand of Italian was in ascendance, whether Ligurian or Tuscan or Genovese, travelling to Italy to study in Padua, Livorno, Pisa and Rome.

Toulon, bleeding its interior villages of their life blood, eroding the oral tradition and family ties which had preserved the Corsican language for thousands of years.

The first written language

Partly in response to this decline, the first attempts to fix a written version of Corsican were made at the end of the 19th century, when the island's first Corsican-language newspaper – *A Tramutana* – appeared. It was followed in 1920 by the magazine *A Muvra*, which became a mouthpiece for the nascent autonomy movement. Around this time, a pro-

This Italo-Corsican duality survived long after 1769, when the advent of French rule began the gradual gallicisation of the island and its language. However, French only really began to penetrate the more remote villages with the introduction of compulsory education during the Third Republic. In this period, from the early 19th century onwards, formal suppression of Corsican in schools hastened its rapid decline, as did massive emigration. More than any other region of France, Corsica provided administrative cadres for the expanding colonies in Africa, South America and Asia, and there was a mass exodus of unskilled rural labour to Marseille and

gramme of linguistic regeneration was also launched, with the promotion of plays, poetry competitons and translations of French and Italian novels into Corsican.

However, the continued impoverishment of the island's economy between the wars saw emigration rise and the use of Corsican dwindle still further. Some regarded a return to Italy and Italian culture as the only way to reverse the trend, and during the 1930s, a number of students and prominent intellectuals accepted Benito Mussolini's offer of generous grants to study on the mainland as part of a wider Fascists attempt to "re-Italianize" Corsica (along with other parts of France he regarded as spiritually part of Italy). In the end, however, Il Duce's military occupation of Corsica in 1942–43 dispelled what little pro-Italian sympathy there remained. The ensuing battle to liberate Corsica from its occupiers only served to reaffirm pro-French sentiments, and to this day many older Corsicans regard the occupation as an outrage and betrayal.

Linguistic nationalism

The nationalist resurgence of the 1970s saw the language issue come the forefront of political debate. If Corsican was to survive, it had to be

the spiny anthius fish (common in the waters around Corsica and known as *le barbier* in French) a *pesciu rossu* , whereas it's a *castagnola rossa* in Ajaccioor or a *trecua* in Bonifacio and *tracodi* in Porto-Vecchio.

Critics on both sides of the nationalist divide still complain that the "academisation" of Corsican, which to some extent still continues to this day, has favoured one form over another, stifled diversity and created false distinctions. But the process did pave the way for includsion under Deixonne, and hence the creation of a university at Corte, where the language is now taught to degree level.

taught in schools. But before it could fall within the terms of the Deixonne Act (according to which regional French languages were to be integrated into school curricula) it was necessary to standardise what had hitherto been merely a loose amalgam of dialects. Although mutually intelligable, the various spoken forms of Corsican differ greatly, with syntax, pronunciation and even vocabulary reflecting a person's origin. Capcorsins, for example, call

LEFT: the Corsican language became eroded with the mass migration of the 18th to 19th centuries.
ABOVE: in the 1980s it was thought the language would be dead within two generations.

In spite of such gains, extensive research carried out in the 1980s to study the use of Corsican in daily life concluded that unless something even more drastic was done to revive the native language it would be extinct within two generations.

Corsican in schools

The findings came as a wake-up call to the Regional Assembly, which voted soon after that Corsican should be made compulsory in schools. The decision was overruled by the national government, but since then the revival of Corsican through education has, more than any other single issue, dominated debate between the island's politicians and Paris. At primary level, schoolchildren study Corsican for 3 hours each week. In theory, attendance is optional, but in practise there exists considerable peer pressure from nationalist parents to support the teaching of the language, which receives preferential funding by the island's council. Nevertheless, while 76 percent of primary pupils follow Corsican classes, this figure drops off to 17 percent at secondary level.

Intense debate rages among the islanders themselves over how these figures can best be improved. Staunch nationalists fume about

Corsican being "relegated to the status of a foreign language in its own country", and advocate compulsory classes at all ages. "Any politician who declares himself against the obligatory teaching of Corsican in schools" railed the editorial of the Corsica Nazione weekly, *U Ribombu*, recently, "is an enemy of the Corsican people".

At the same time, many parents fear that promoting Corsican at the expense of French and Italian will disadvantage their children in the long run. One only has to look at the number of 18 year olds who include it as a Baccalaureate subject (typically 2 percent) to see what a low-status subject it has become.

The language of the future

The essence of the problem is that as long as French remains the language of education, government, law and the media, Corsican will continue to decline. Many doubt that even radical positive discrimination of the kind being demanded by nationalists will reverse this drift. The fact remains that the overwhelming majority of Corsican parents – even those who speak Corsican as a first-language – converse with their children in French, and that only a tiny proportion of youngsters speak to each other by choice in pure Corsican.

The few surveys that have been carried out into the subject point to a decline from 70 percent to 10 percent in the number of fluent Corsican-language speakers over the last two generations. That means only around 15,000 islanders nowadays have an active grasp of the native language, and most of those are elderly people and living in the villages of the remoter valleys.

There are, however, causes for mild optimism. Among young people, it is definitely cool to be Corsican these days. Few may be able to hold abstract conversations in the language, but interchanges in the street and schoolyard between teenagers are regularly punctuated with Corsican words and phrases (notably the ubiquitous "*Aiò!*", an expostulation that can hold a range of meanings, from "wow!" and "really!" to "hey, take it easy!" and "I don't believe you!", depending on how it's pronounced).

The upsurge in popularity of Corsican music among younger islanders also bodes well for the longer-term health of the language. Groups like I Muvrini, who enjoy mass appeal on the continent, are a great source of pride, and even traditional a cappella polyphony receives its fair share of youthful recruits.

All the same, it will doubtless take a lot more than a revival in the island's art and youth culture to make Corsican a truly living language once again. As the satirical weekly, *Le Canard Enchaînée*, recently quipped, "One day there won't be many people around speaking Corsican, but you'll have no trouble finding someone to sing it". ❑

LEFT: the teaching of the Corsican language in schools is a fiercely debated topic among parents and politicians.

Music

"It was like hearing a song from the depths of the earth, from the dawn of time". The English writer and Corsophile Dorothy Carrington, author of the acclaimed *Granite Island: A Portrait of Corsica*, was mesmerized when she first heard Corsican polyphonic singing in the late 1940s, and the island's unique choral tradition continues to exert strong appeal, both at home and abroad. After wine, U Cantu – a cappella song – is Corsica's most important export.

Bearing influences as diverse as Neolithic chant, Arabic liturgy and Genoan madrigal, it evokes perhaps better than any other art form the sense of mystery, grandeur and brooding melancholy that pervades both the Corsican landscape and troubled psyche of its inhabitants. Few who hear its swelling harmonies, passing dissonances and elaborate ornamentation, which sometimes sounds as if it could have drifted across the Mediterranean from North Africa, fail to be moved. It's no coincidence that polyphony has become as integral to the island's sense of self-identity as the Moor's Head flag.

Having lapsed into virtual extinction by the 1960s, the form was rescued during the nationalist cultural revival a decade or so later. Young militants who had learned the old ways of singing from their grandparents, but who'd perhaps sung only in church and at village festivals, suddenly discovered in the traditional music the power to stir patriotic sentiments at rallies. It was in such contexts that the most famous singers of the present day – such as Jean-Paul Poletti, Petro Guelfucci and the Bernadini brothers (of I Muvrini fame) – first forged their reputations.

Today, polyphony has evolved considerably since its folksy renaissance and found a much wider audience. Groups such as I Muvrini, who incorporate traditional singing into electric guitar, keyboard, bass and drum arrangements, are household names on the continent, filling stadiums in Paris and Marseille. Other ensembles, such as the wonderful A Filetta – led by the man widely acclaimed as being the greatest living voice of this generation, Ghjuvan-Claudiu Acquaviva – have delved into the music's roots and

developed a purer form, unencumbered by modern instruments, that has lent its force to several film scores. Women, too, have begun performing in public what had for generations been regarded as a strictly male preserve. Wives and sisters of men violently killed in vendetta would in traditional society sing a *voceru*, a dirge, to incite their relatives to vengeance, but this was a rare exception to the rule. Then, in the mid-1990s, came the ground-breaking group Donasulana, formed to mark the death of a close friend, who recorded one of the most magnificent polyphony albums to date, *Per Agata*. Among their number is the diva Jacky Michaelli, whose

searing solo renditions of traditional *voceri* vividly evoke the terror and grief of vendetta wakes.

Polyphony recitals take place regularly throughout the summer, at venues across the island. Posters advertising gigs appear in towns and on roadsides, and the Casa Musicale in Pigna hosts regular concerts of both singing and playing of traditional instruments (such as the Corsican cittern, which is still made in the village). Other chances to catch top-quality choirs occur at song festivals held annually in Calvi and Corte, while if you're anywhere near the Niolo Valley in September, you could make a detour to listen to the rare *chiami e rispondi* singing (a competitive form in which adversaries improvise musical insults). ❑

RIGHT: a man singing an imporvisational *chiami e rispondi*, a call and response that is similar to blues music.

THE "SANTA" FESTIVAL

The Santa di u Niolu is Corsica's most important religious festival, when

thousands of pilgrims gather to celebrate the Nativity of the Virgin

The broad, picturesque, upland plain of Calacuccia, the largest community in the Niolu, is surrounded by a chain of high mountains soaring up to altitudes of over 2,000 metres (6,500 feet). In former times the peasants and shepherds up here lived from the forests, largely comprised of chestnut trees, from modest cereal and fruit farming and from their large flocks of sheep and goats which grazed on the mountain pastures. In this remote fastness they had no need to fear attack by enemy invaders. And so they built their houses scattered at random across the mountain slopes. Here, in contrast to the coastal areas, you will find no fortified castles perched on the hilltops.

A shepherds' meeting

"In this region dwell the strongest men on Corsica, patriarchal shepherds who have faithfully maintained the tradition of their forebears", wrote Ferdinand Gregorovius in his history of Corsica in 1852, describing the rugged inhabitants of the Niolu.

Every year on 8 September, the Festival of the Nativity of the Virgin Mary, they still celebrate the largest and most important folk festival on the island, at which customs and traditions handed down across the centuries are brought back to life. The people gather together, not only to honour the Madonna, but also to commemorate the old traditions which united Corsicans for many hundreds of years. The festival, which takes place in the tiny hamlet of Casamaccioli to the south of the lake of Calacuccia, occurs during the season when the flocks are being driven back down into the valleys from the mountain pastures.

In former times the sheep and goats spent the entire summer grazing the mountainsides,

PRECEDING PAGES: a shrine to the Virgin Mary.
LEFT: priests taking part in the Santa festival.
RIGHT: the Santa Maria della Stella statue, venerated for its miracle-working powers, is carried in procession through the village.

watched over by the shepherds. In September, when the days become shorter and the arrival of autumn heralds the beginning of the cold season of the year, they would begin the withdrawal to the milder coastal regions. It was an occasion for rejoicing, and also a good opportunity for the shepherds and upland peasants to

exchange news and views before the flocks embarked upon the hazardous descent via the Scala di Santa Regina. There are many places away from the road where even today you can still see the staircase-like footpaths by which the mountain-dwellers and their flocks ascended and descended the slopes. Nowadays the vast herds of animals which once migrated up and down these ancient paths no longer exist.

Popular celebration

The Festival of *La Santa di u Niolu*, however, has remained the meeting point for shepherds and upland peasants, and also for many Corsicans who have left the island in search of better living conditions, and who return specially for the Festival of the Nativity of the Virgin. Casamaccioli attracts up to 10,000 visitors for the three-day event.

The traders erect their stalls on the spacious marketplace. Local handicrafts and Corsican ham and cheese specialities are offered alongside clothes, toys and household items. An essential part of the scene are the pious pictures and religious items in sugary hues spanning all the colours of the rainbow, and which at least serve as reminders of the reason for the market. Hidden away in the furthest corners of the square, roulette tables are set up,

an old crucifix in front of the altar. The congregation throngs into the square surrounding the church.

As soon as the Mass begins, a group of five men strike up a traditional chant. On holy days only the upland shepherds sing the folk Mass, known as the *paghiella*. It is regarded as the purest example of true Corsican folk music, which, despite the lack of written records, has been preserved in its simple, archaic form across the centuries.

It follows an ancient, polyphonic tonal system. The first voice – *a prima* – sets the rhythm and the pitch. It is underlined by the bass – *u*

for the Corsicans are passionate gamblers. The more money the relations have brought with them from the mainland, the higher the stakes. There also used to be a big cattle market here, but this has now disappeared.

Traditional folk Mass

The bustling activity between the stalls and displays does not begin until after the religious service, which is celebrated according to tradition on the spacious square in front of the parish church with its free-standing tower. The Santa Maria della Stella, a brightly painted wooden statue of the Virgin Mary is carried with great ceremony out of the church and placed next to

boldu – whilst the third voice – *a terza* – sings a high-pitched contrapuntal melody. The voices mostly sound rough and hard, occasionally becoming gentle or slightly nasal.

The origins of the music, which follows an octosyllabic verse rhythm, lie buried in obscurity. It may well have developed from the Italian madrigal, or from elements derived from oriental music.

At the end of the Mass, a group of men shoulders the pedestal upon which stands the statue of the Virgin Mary. They carry it round the village square to the rhythmic ringing of bells. Between the colourful stalls, the procession of white-robed penitents of the Fraternity of St Anthony forms the so-called *granitula*, a spiral procession common to many Corsican religious gatherings. The column coils up in the form of a sea-snail, unrolls and then coils up again in a visual allegory of life from its origins until death and the resurrection.

The story of the *Santa*

The local priest relates to listeners the story of the miracle-working statue in whose honour the festival takes place. On a stormy night back in the 15th century a ship had been blown off course near Galéria. Its situation seemed hopeless, but the captain prayed to the Virgin Mary for assistance. In his despair he vowed to donate the most beautiful statue of the Madonna he could find in Genoa. Immediately a strange light appeared above the Franciscan monastery at the foot of the forest of Tafonatu. The captain kept his promise, and the statue was duly erected in the monastery church.

During the 16th century, when the Turks destroyed the monastery, the statue of the Madonna was saved. It was carried by a mule high up into the mountains of the Niolu, where it remained in safety. When the beast reached the village of Casamaccioli, it suddenly threw its burden to the ground. The statue was placed in the Chapel of St Anthony, near the cemetery. The next day it miraculously reappeared in the middle of the village. After this had happened several times, the shepherds of the Niolu built a church dedicated to the Virgin. Ever since then, they have celebrated the festival of the Nativity of the Virgin. In recent years, the Santa Maria della Stella statue has become venerated for its miracle-working powers.

The singing contest

During the afternoon of the first day, on a square shaded by spreading chestnut trees, the mountain shepherds gather to compete with one another in poetic improvisation and oratory. With microphones belonging to the Corsican radio station in their hands, they stand ready to broadcast their singing talents in the language of the island. Musicians strike up a simple,

monotonous melody, to which the participants improvise their own lyrics. The *chiam' e rispondi* are above all sarcastic musical dialogues, in which the vocalists demonstrate their wit and repartee. Comments and responses fly thick and fast with the contestants introducing contemporary subjects which will arouse the emotions of the listeners.

The verses invented by the older men are full of poetry and wisdom; however, there are also a few younger bards who have mastered this traditional art of musical dialogue, which only comes to an end when no one can think of an answer. The singer who is best able to express

himself in a cutting, striking manner will be rewarded by the applause and laughter of the onlookers. This musical form, cultivated above all by the shepherds, is part of the island's folkloric tradition and has been handed down from generation to generation.

Women are excluded from the patriarchal contest (in days gone by their lyrical talents were put to use in the singing of lullabies, *voceru,* or *lamentu,* lamentations of the dead), and the circle of listeners is also predominantly male. The strange songs of the Corsican mountain-dwellers do not fade away until the sun has finally disappeared behind the ridges of the surrounding peaks. ❑

LEFT: spectators wait expectantly as the singing contest to get underway.
RIGHT: singing the *paghiella,* a distinctive Corsican polyphony and traditionally the preserve of shepherds.

THE OCCULT

*In an island so steeped in tradition, it is no surprise that its inhabitants
have some unusual ways of protecting themselves from evil*

Three drops of oil fall from the fingertip on to the plate filled with water. According to the laws of physics they ought to flow together on the surface of the water. But on the contrary! They disintegrate into a thousand minute globules which suddenly cannot be seen, as if they had never existed. Is there a

do not explain everything. Is there an explanation at all? Who could analyse and confirm procedures before which the human intellect capitulates?

And yet – the tears of the *Signadora*, the relief of the *occhju* victim, the repetition of the theatrical demonstration with the drops of

rational explanation for such a phenomenon? At such a moment words like "reason" and "rational" cease to have any meaning.

The laws in operation are those of the *Signadora*, who is engaged in the process of freeing someone from the Evil Eye, the *occhju*. The disintegration of the oil on the china plate tells the *Signadora* that the customer sitting opposite her is the victim of malevolent powers. And she sees it as her task to set him free.

This ritual, which cannot be explained by science, has its origins in the deepest recesses of the collective island memory. Religious references play a role in the proceedings; signs of the cross are used as part of the ritual, but they

oil, which this time flow instantly together – does this not show that something very mysterious has taken place here? That an unknown force, incomprehensible and yet effective for a few moments, has healed by its exorcism of evil, by its banishment to an indescribable place?

Although any observer can follow the apparent procedures making up the ritual and its trappings, it is pointless to try to understand the lip movements of the *Signadora*. When they start to utter what sounds like a prayer, the moment has arrived when the door to a magic universe is opened, only to close again immediately. Evil has admitted defeat, leaving room for a feeling of well-being. The tiredness and exhaustion, the entire malady, all the manifestations of the *occhju* are no more than a bad dream. But the *Signadora*, who has absorbed these harmful vibrations, must now rest in order to free herself from them once more. For a brief moment it is as if she has fulfilled the role of a sort of lightning conductor for some unseen power. As an initiate who is certain of her abilities she is not only able to drive out evil, but also – when necessary – to heal physical ills, to treat sunstroke or alleviate the pain of a burn.

The *Signadora* is not a witch. She is the guardian of an ancient tradition which can only be learned on Christmas night, when the evil spirits go into hiding. At any other time the handing down of the magic formulas would have no effect. Although it will only seldom be required, one must show the supernatural power that one is worthy.

For those who have never experienced the performance of the *occhju* ritual, a moment in which time stands still, in which centuries converge upon each other, there is one further method of protecting oneself against evil. Some Corsicans, both men and women, wear a carved branch of coral around their necks: a reddish "hand" which will ward off all evil. These talismans are a gift at birth and are preserved throughout one's life as magic symbols.

Magic? Is that not just a term to cover everything which one does not understand? In other words, things which cannot be explained with reason and logic. Should one see the *Signadora* as some sort of magician? And what is a *Mazzeru*? A man of whom it is said that his baptism took place in sinister circumstances without the blessing of the Church. And who, from a certain night during his life onwards, is able to see into the "Beyond". He is feared, the *Mazzeru*. The word is probably best translated as "Wizard". His shamanistic powers are demonstrated in dreams, when a mysterious power forces him against his will to go out in the middle of the night and to observe scenes which only he can see: the funeral of a villager who is as yet still unaware that he will die. The *Mazzeru* is a man to be avoided, for no one

wants prior warning of such events. "Villager" is a very important word. Outside the settlements in the interior, the *Mazzeru* no longer exists. And even in the hamlets strung out along the steep mountainsides he is no longer to be feared, because here, too, he is almost forgotten.

There are still a few of these unusual men – not many, for they are a dying race, following the inevitable fate of so much that has disappeared from the remote villages of the interior through the inexorable exodus of the inhabitants. In the very places where nothing seems to have changed very much, there has been a huge transformation which affects people, their tradi-

tions and their beliefs, and which means that the *Mazzeru* will also one day cease to exist.

Really? Are there not still shadows in the depths of the collective memory, which at night are roused to life once more? They populate the twilight for those who wish to hear and see them. What remains is the mysterious character of the island, its *macchia*, its mountains, its rocks, all of which acquire a soul as night falls. And what can one say about a region which appears alien even in bright sunshine, where there are no shadows and where man, surrounded by the *macchia*, can forget the world for a moment in order to sink back into the irrational? ❏

LEFT: those seeking to free themselves from the *occhju* (Evil Eye) visit the *Signadora*.
RIGHT: the ritual involves dropping three drops of oil onto a plate to see how it disintegrates.

LAGAULOISE®

BIERE   BIER

RICARD

MORT
SUBITE

GUEUZE • KRIEK
FRAMBOISE
CASSIS • PECHE

FOOD AND DRINK

Eating traditional Corsican food is a wholesome pleasure, while the
local beers and wines make an excellent accompaniment to a meal

The much-travelled writer Kasimir Edschmid was of the opinion that the imagination demonstrated by a nation's kitchens was closely linked to its deepest emotions. Corsica is a part of France, it is true, but it does not share the sophisticated cuisine of *La Grande Nation*. Corsican cooking is much simpler. It could be described as unrefined Mediterranean in style: home cooking, in fact. All superfluous trimmings are avoided. The food is mostly prepared and served in a natural way; the composition of the various dishes follows the pattern of the seasons. It is remarkable that, despite Spanish, French and Italian influences, the island has been able to preserve its own culinary individuality – thanks largely to its characteristic spices and seasonings.

Hearty soups

You are most likely to be able to sample traditional Corsican dishes in a small restaurant well away from the holiday centres on the coast. Sometimes there is no written menu and the waiter or waitress will recite a list of all the specialities the kitchen has to offer. A hearty soup is recommended as a first course. Usually a terrine is placed on the table, and as most Corsican soups are very filling you will hardly need anything else to follow.

One typical example is *aziminu*, a sort of bouillabaisse containing all varieties of local fish. Otherwise, the *suppa corsa* is usually a vegetable soup so thick that you can stand your spoon in it. The ingredients vary from region to region, from family to family and from season to season: potatoes, cabbage, onions, tomatoes, pasta and broad beans, combined according to the chef's imagination in accordance with what the garden can offer that day. It is not for vegetarians as it contains bacon. Another popular soup is *suppa di castagnia*, made with chestnuts, garlic, herbs and meat. A winter dish, it

LEFT: colourful adverts for beer featuring the local brew, Pietra.
RIGHT: variety of local olives for sale.

is served warm. Another very tasty starter, and a good choice for vegetarians, is *cannelloni al brocciu* made with local sheep's cheese and served with tomato sauce. Supreme among the island's typical cold *hors d'oeuvres* until recently was blackbird pie *(pâté de merle)* but the bird can no longer be captured so the soup

is off the menu. Instead, you may well find snails with anchovies *(escargots aux anchois)* or snails with mint sauce *(escargots à la menthe)*. Corsican ham has a unique flavour, for it is marinated in wine with rosemary, garlic and pepper before being smoked over a fire made of wood from the *macchia*.

Gourmet pigs

If your hunger is only moderate, you could decide to try a main course of Corsican sausages, the *figatelli*. These are small sausages which are eaten raw, fried or grilled. The main ingredient is finely chopped pig's meat, fat and liver, which is laid in a marinade of wine, fresh garlic and peppercorns. Afterwards the mixture is stuffed into sausage skins and smoked over a fire of aromatic wood from the *macchia*. A typical dish is *pulenta* made with *figatelli*, chestnut flour, *brocciu* cheese and meat dishes. The traditional black pudding *(sanguin, boudin)* of Corsica also includes its own particular ingredients. Apart from fresh pig's blood and small cubes of bacon, it also includes – according to region – raisins, chopped apple, onions, milk, nuts or brains, packed together into a skin and placed in boiling water.

The pork on Corsica has a highly individual and unusual taste, for the domesticated pigs are

the *mesgisca*, or fillet of goat. Certain rules must be observed in grilling the meat; it must be turned on myrtle branches above a fire which is made of juniper and mastic.

Fish and seafood

Fish and seafood *(fruits de mer)*, such as mussels *(moules)*, sea urchins *(oursins)*, crabs *(crabes)*, spiny lobsters *(langoustes)* and oysters *(huîtres)* should all be sampled on the coast, where the freshness is more or less guaranteed. A colourfully assorted plate of all the sea creatures with which the waters surrounding Corsica abound is not the cheapest of lux-

allowed to roam free across the island. They feed in the woods on chestnuts, acorns, roots and herbs. Most menus include a pork chop *(côte de porc)*. Prepared on the grill, and seasoned with the piquant spices of the *macchia*, the homely-sounding dish becomes a gourmet speciality. Amongst the typical stews is ragoût of pork with haricot beans *(tianu di fave)*. *Porc rotî aux aubergines* is roast pork flavoured with garlic and laurel and sautéed aubergines.

Lamb and goat's meat also feature prominently on the menu. There is, for example, a ragoût of lamb and peppers, known as *piverunata*, or *riffia*, a skewer upon which lamb's offal is roasted. A particular speciality is

uries, but probably one of the more rewarding ones. In small, relatively simple restaurants you can often make your own selection.

If you are really lucky, the chef will even join you at your table for a few minutes and describes the state of the day's catch. Particularly delicious are sole, gilthead *(daurade)*, mullet *(rouget)* and sea bass *(loup de mer)*. The method of preparation? As you like it. If you choose to have your fish grilled or deep-fried, you will discover that no one is prepared to economise on the garlic and herbs from the *macchia*. To be recommended, if you decide on fish while far from the coast, are the delicious trout *(truite)* from the local rivers and streams.

Classic dishes include *grondin aux olives* which is oven-cooked gurnard served in a sauce made of egg, oil and vinegar with tomato and olive. *Rouget au fenouil* is baked mullet served in a sauce of onion, fennel and olive oil.

Brocciu – deserts and cheese

Cheese is an excellent end to a meal; the sheep and goat cheese of Corsica are as famous as their aroma is notorious. The main ingredient of Roquefort, for example, is produced from Corsican ewe's milk. The uncrowned king of the island's cheeses is undoubtedly the *brocciu*, a soft cheese of sheep or occasionally goats'

order cheese after a meal in a restaurant, the owner will probably come to your table with a selection on an old wooden board, so that you can make your own choice.

As far as sweet desserts are concerned, you will certainly find plenty of suggestions on the menu. Most typical are the cakes and pastries made of chestnut flour; apart from the *brocciu* doughnuts mentioned above, *canistrelli* are another popular choice. They are prepared from a dough of chestnut flour, yeast, aniseed schnapps, oil, water and a pinch of salt, small spoonfuls of which are placed in boiling water. The cakes are cooked when the dough rises to

milk, which is seasoned with aromatic *macchia* herbs. Its uses – as you will gather from the study of many a menu – are almost limitless. *Brocciu* is used in the preparation of a number of sweet specialities, including *fritelles au brocciu* – little doughnuts made with chestnut flour and deep-fried in olive oil, or *fiadone*, a delicious cheesecake with rum, gin or brandy and lemon juice, served either cold, hot or flambéed.

The cheeseboard contains a wide range of mild and strong varieties of cheese. If you

the top; after being dried in a cloth, they are then deep-fried in hot oil for 10–15 minutes. If you are offered fresh *canistrelli*, your dessert choice has really already been made, although another popular speciality are the local *crêpes* or pancakes, which on Corsica are also often made with chestnut flour and coated with citron liqueur.

A good way to end to a meal is *torta castagnina*, made with chestnut flour mixed with vanilla sugar, milk, grappa, chopped almonds, hazelnuts and raisins or pine nuts.

Honey is another of the island's specialities. The many aromatic plants growing on Corsica – mint, lavender, orange trees, chestnut, rose-

LEFT: free-range pigs *(cochons coureurs)* are left to roam the countryside to improve their meat.
ABOVE: fish plays a large part in Corsican cuisine.

mary – produce a honey with an unforgettably spicy tang. The colours range from white to dark brown; the flavours are just as varied, from mild to very strong.

Vin de Corse

Corsica's wines are certainly worth trying, although this was not always the case. During the 1960s and 1970s they acquired a bad reputation as the result of a series of adulterated wine scandals. New standards for judging the wines were laid down and they are subjected to continuous stringent controls, and the co-operative cellars now produce excellent quality

wines. In 2000 there were 2,900 hectares (7,166 acres) of vines on Corsica. Most of the *vins du pays* are produced on the east coast – wine produced in Sarténe has won three gold medals at the Grand Concours de Paris.

Among the best grapes used on Corsica is the *Vermentinu*, which produces a dry, fresh wine, particularly on Cap Corse. It is light in colour with a nose of flowers, apples and almonds. Then there is the *Sciacarellu*, a grape grown especially in the region surrounding Ajaccio and Sartène and unique to Corsica. It produces light coloured reds with a peppery palate and aromas of red fruits, spices, coffee and flowers of the maquis. *Nielluciu*, a black

grape grown principally in Patrimonio and the Casinca, is often compared with a good Chianti and matures well. The grape makes deep red wines with a liquorice bouquet with hints of red fruits and a woody note. Also in the Patrimonio district the muscat grape is used to produce a delicious dessert wine. A vineyard in Calinzana (Domaine Orsini) produces a small quantity of sparkling muscat wines. Mild red wines with a fine bouquet are produced in Sartène, whilst the white wines from Porto Vecchio are particularly good accompaniments to fish dishes. *Nielluciu* grapes and *Vermentinu* grapes are also found on the east coast.

Vin de Corse is a label applicable only to wines whose origin and quality are tested annually – in other words, so-called AOC wines (*Appellation d'Origine Contrôlée*). They must have a natural alcohol content and a yield of no more than 50 hectolitres (1,100 gallons) per hectare (2.47 acres). Wine of excellent quality is awarded the description VDQS. The AOC zone of the wine will be on the label of the bottle, as will the name of the wine maker, preceded by the words *Clos* or *Domaine*, which guarantees the fact that the wine has been made in the winery or estate on the label. Labels to look out for red wines include AOC Patrimonio, Ajaccio, Coteaux du Cap Corse, Figari, Porto-Vecchio, and Sarténe. The best white wines will come from Patrimonio, Muscat du Cap Corse, Coteaux du Cap Corse and Vins de Corse. All are AOC. The best rosés are bottled in AOCs Porto-Vecchio, Patrimonio and Vins de Corse. Apart from the Patrimonio white muscat dessert wine mentioned above, a red aleatico is also produced. The Cap Corse produces a rare white dessert wine called Rappu, which can only be purchased from the wineries that produce it.

Other alcoholic specialities of the island include the apéritif *Cap Corse*, as well as citron and myrtle liqueurs. A schnapps is distilled from the fruits of the strawberry tree *(arbutus)*. Pastis, another apéritif, is an aniseed liqueur. Three brands of beer are made on Corsica. Amber-coloured La Pietra lists chestnuts as an ingredient, Colomba is a delicious strong beer flavoured with myrtle, while Serena is a pale, light beer with the Moor's head on the label. ❏

LEFT: traditional meal of mutton stew.
RIGHT: restaurant serving traditional Corsican food.

CORSICA IN LITERATURE

Corsica's beautiful landscape and traditional ways of life have inspired many writers and poets. A few of the best known are examined here

The earliest literary account in which Corsica is mentioned is Homer's *Odyssey*. The poet tells of the experiences of the Greeks in the land of the Laestrygons, a wild race of man-eating giants who consumed several of Odysseus' companions. In later descriptions from classical literature the island and its inhabitants are described in slightly more flattering terms, but its sinister, eerie and unruly character are always of prime importance. Seneca, who was exiled on Corsica for eight years in AD 41, describes the island as a "treeless corner of the earth, where virtually nothing grows on which its inhabitants can feed." In his *Epigrams* he curses it as a "terrible place, surrounded by rocks, where you will find nothing but barrenness". His antipathy was, of course, largely due to the fact that he lived here against his will and saw the island as a prison. And yet it seems likely that at least part of the Stoic philosophy which characterises his work can be traced back to the mark left on his mind by the solitude of Corsica.

A study of the history of Corsica and the customs of its inhabitants will explain why for centuries the island was ignored in the development of European literature. The Corsicans' traditional poems and songs – the *voceri, ballate* and *lamenti* – were passed on from generation to generation in an exclusively oral tradition, arising primarily in the mountain villages which were cut off from the outside world. The perpetual struggle against attacks and conquest from across the sea prevented the development of an independent literary tradition on the island.

Travellers' tales

During the 17th century there appeared the first travel journals written by soldiers stationed on the island, or by adventurous individuals who dared to visit the remote interior regions. It was not until 1729–1840, however, during the years between the beginning of the Corsican War of Independence and the year in which Napoleon's ashes were transported back to Paris, that the island appeared as a separate entity on the European – in this case primarily French – literary scene. Numerous writers visited Corsica.

They created a picture of the island as a paradox, both radiant and shadowy, idyllic and demonic. The strange habits and customs, strict moral code, love of freedom, tradition of banditry and above all the vendetta combined to produce an exotic portrait in which the boundaries between reality and myth became strangely blurred.

The authors of the 18th century preferred to people their novels with legendary or historical heroes. The unaccustomed traditions of the Corsicans were depicted in a more or less naturalistic manner: their blood feuds, devotion to honour and close family ties as well as their hospitality and loyalty.

LEFT: Honoré de Balzac thought that Corsica was the "back of beyond".
RIGHT: Prosper Mérimée also wrote about the island.

The years 1838–39 and 1840 marked the visits of three famous French writers to the island: Honoré de Balzac, Prosper Mérimée and Gustave Flaubert.

Honoré de Balzac

Corsica was just a stopover on the way to Sardinia for Balzac. Prevented by untoward conditions from continuing his journey, he spent two weeks in Ajaccio. He describes his impressions in various letters to Madame Hanska, later published in the form of a travel diary. For Balzac, Corsica is above all the birthplace of Napoleon: "Here I am in Napoleon's native

Prosper Mérimée

The writer responsible for creating for the island a permanent place in the annals of literature was Prosper Mérimée. He was the first to succeed in transposing the customs and laws of Corsica from a mist of exoticism by providing an explanation of their origins. In 1829, a decade before Mérimée arrived on the island as the Inspector General for Public Buildings, he was inspired by the novels and travel accounts of his predecessors to write the novel *Mateo Falcone.*

In the novel, a father kills his own son because the latter has broken the honourable

town!" In an outburst of lyricism he praises the island as "one of the loveliest countries on earth"; mostly, however, he sees it as the "back of beyond", mysterious and hostile, inhabited by wild, unknown men who suspiciously shut themselves off from the outside world and foreign influences.

The experience of loneliness and solitude, far from familiar civilization, impressed him as strongly as the uncompromising sense of fairness and traditional code of honour. Whilst none of Balzac's novels is set on Corsica, traces of the island's landscape and people do occur in the works set in Brittany as well as in *La Vendetta*, which is set in Italy.

tradition of hospitality towards a stranger hiding in the *macchia*. The bandit – alone, persecuted and betrayed, the victim of the child's misdemeanour – then becomes a hero. The boy, despite his youth, must die a traitor's death.

Mateo Falcone has only one son, whom he loves passionately, and in whom he has placed all his hopes. But the family honour requires that he be put to death. The novella, in which Mérimée develops a dramatic description of the merciless nature of Corsican laws, convinces by its restrained, detached narrative style, which makes the portrayal of the island all the more sinister.

Prosper Mérimée created a lasting monument for the island in his novel *Colomba (see also page 78)*, published in 1840. The theme of the story is an authentic family feud in Fozzano, a village in the Sartenais. The main protagonist is Colomba, a young Corsican girl, who tries to incite her brother, returned to the island after a number of years in France, to avenge their father's murder. Orso, conditioned by the laws and customs of France, refuses to comply, but is nonetheless aroused by the passion, mercilessness and cunning of his sister, progressively succumbing to the spell of the traditional values of his Corsican homeland. Columba is obsessed with thoughts of the vendetta, and he duly becomes her agent.

Her "serious, sad beauty" symbolises her native island. The central scene in the novel is the lamentation for the dead, led by Colomba at the deathbed of a deceased neighbour. A passionate *voceratrice*, she weaves into the lament her sadness and anger at the unavenged death of her father, awakening in Orso the long-forgotten "wild instincts".

An atmosphere of latent hostility pervades the novel. The author reveals with great precision the deep-seated roots of the hatred which moves Colomba, the "black dove". The prevailing sombre tone is enlivened by the humorous and ironic portrait of the bandits, the *seigneurs de la montagne*. They relate a number of stories elaborating upon the customs of the shepherds and outlaws and revealing the natural character of the island dwellers, whom neither Church nor aristocracy have been able to tame.

Mérimée regards vanity as one of the fundamental characteristics of the Corsicans; it is a trait which also dominated Napoleon's character. The writer sees it as one of the principal explanations for the vendetta. He sees revenge as a primitive form of duel and, at the same time, a result of the unjust rule of the Genoese, which made it necessary for so long that it eventually became custom.

Overwhelming beauty

Gustave Flaubert's experience of the island was quite different. He visited Corsica in 1840, when he was 19. Whilst his predecessors attempted to come to terms with Corsican customs, he was overwhelmed by the beauty of the countryside, the sea and the transparent Mediterranean air. His impressions are recorded in his letters to his sister, eventually being published for posterity in his *Mémoires d'un Fou*. Corsica aroused in the young traveller a remarkable talent for describing the natural world, a hallmark of his later work.

Apart from nature, what interested Flaubert most was the lawlessness hidden in the *macchia*. He elevates the bandit to the position of

an "honourable man", celebrating him as the "hero of the Land of the Sun". Flaubert, a young man seeking adventure and fleeing from the norms of civilization, turns his attention to the outsider whose lifestyle, far from society, personifies for him the longed-for life of freedom.

Flaubert's description of the island, full of natural scenes and anecdotes, in which women play only a subordinate, sketchily presented role, reflects the romantic dreams of a traveller of the time. He was the first poet to portray the island, its light, its scents and its unique beauty of mountain and sea with such sensitivity and poetic enthusiasm. ❑

LEFT: the drama of Corsica reflected in this engraving of Sarténe by Edward Lear (1868).
RIGHT: the island has been the inspirational to the arts.

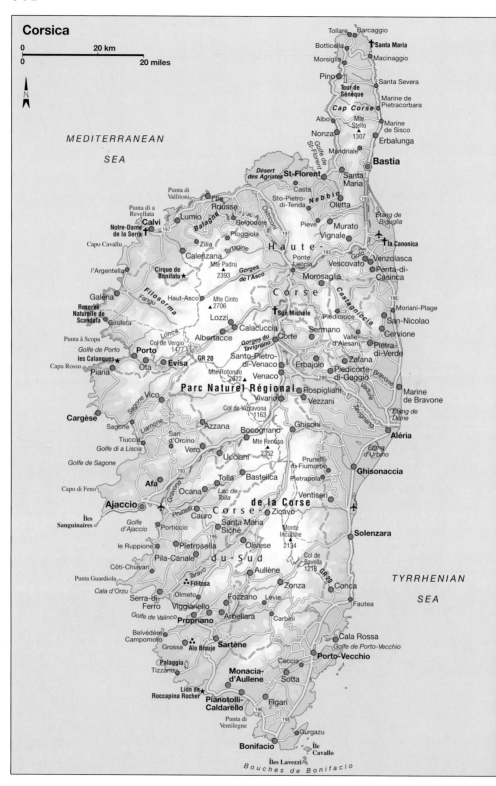

Corsica

0   20 km
0   20 miles

N

MEDITERRANEAN
SEA

Tollare Barcaggio
Botticella   † Santa Maria
Morsiglia   Macinaggio
Pino   Santa Severa
Tour de   Marine de
Sénèque   Pietracorbara
Cap Corse
Albo   Marine
Mte   de Sisco
Nonza   Stello   Erbalunga
        1307
Mandriale
Bastia

Punta di   Désert
Vallitoni   des Agriates   St-Florent   Santa
Punta di a   l'Île   Casta   Maria
Revellata   Rousse   Sto-Pietro-   Nebbio   193
Calvi Lumio Balagne   di-Tenda Oletta
Notre-Dame   Belgodère   Ploggiola   Pieve   Murato   Etang de
de la Serra   197   Zilia   197   Vignale Biguglia
Capo Cavallu   Calenzana   Tartagine   Ponte   193   la Canonica
l'Argentella   Cirque de   Mte Padru Gorges Leccia Goto Venzolasca
             Bonifatu ★ 2393 de l'Asco   Vescovato Penta-di-
Galéria   Haut-Asco   Corse   Morosaglia   Casinca
Réserve   Fangu   Mte Cinto   San-Nicolao   198
Naturelle de   2706   Lozzi   San Michele Piedicroce   Moriani-Plage
Scandola Girolata   Calacuccia   Sermano   San-Nicolao
Punta à Scopa   Lonca   Albertacce   Gorges du   Valle   Cervione
Golfe de Porto Col de Vergio Tavignano   Corte d'Alesani Pietra-
les Calanques ★ 1477   GR 20 Santo-Pietro-   Zalana   di-Verde
Capu Rossu   Porto   Évisa   di-Venaco   Erbajolo   Piedicorte-
Piana   Ota   Mte Rotondo Venaco   di-Gaggio
            2622   Parc Naturel Régional Marine
Cargèse Vico   Vivario   Rospigliani   de Bravone
      Azzana   Col de Vizzavona Vezzani   Etang de
Sagone   1163   Diane
Tiuccia   Sari   Bocognano Ghisoni   Aléria
Golfe di a Liscia d'Orcino Mte Renoso   Etang
         Vero   2352   d'Urbino
Golfe de Sagone   Ucciani   Prunelli-
Capo di Feno   Tolla di-Fiumorbo   Ghisonaccia
Ajaccio Afa   Ocana Bastelica Pietrapola
Îles   Prunelli Lac de Ventiseri
Sanguinaires Cauro Tolla Corse   Solenzara
Golfe   Porticcio Santa Maria Zicavo
d'Ajaccio   Siché Monte
le Ruppione Pietrosella 196 Incudine
Côti-Chiavari Pila-Canale Olivese 2134
Punta Guardiola   du-Sud Col de
Cala d'Orzu Filosa 193 Aullène Bavella Conca
Serra-di- Olmeto Fozzano Levie 1218 TYRRHENIAN
Ferro Viggianello   Fautea SEA
Golfe de Valinco Arbellara Zonza
Propriano Carbini
Belvédère- Cala Rossa
Campomoro Grossa Alo Bisuje Sartène Golfe de Porto-Vecchio
Palaggiu   Ceccia Porto-Vecchio
Tizzano   Monacia- Sotta
Lion de   d'Aullène
Roccapina Rocher ★ Pianotolli- Figari
Caldarello 196
Punta di 198
Ventilegne Gurgazu
Bonifacio Île
Cavallo
Îles Lavezzi
Bouches de Bonifacio

PLACES

*A detailed guide to the entire island, with principal sites
clearly cross-referenced by number to the maps*

Because of its extremely diverse landscapes, Corsica might easily give the impression of being much larger than it actually is. But wherever you happen to land on the island, nothing is very far away. Having scarcely even arrived at a place like Ajaccio and done the tour of the museums and monuments to Napoleon, you can be off, doing whatever your heart desires; seeking out some lonely beach on the west coast, negotiating the hairpin bends of some mountain road, or even beating your way through the *macchia* in search of the remnants of past civilizations.

The following pages allow you to take your pick from the island's wealth of sights and sites. Leaving Ajaccio, the tour starts by heading to the Alta Rocca, and then goes south via the monuments to the island's megalithic past in the Ornano, through the rugged Sartenais and on to Bonifacio, precariously perched on its clifftop above the waves. Then it's up the rugged west coast, past such wonders of nature as the Calanche cliffs of Piana, and on to Calvi, dominated not only by its Genoese citadel, but also by the impressive hills of the Balagne rising in the backgound and studded with picturesque villages and their bold, Pisan churches.

Before the tour of lonely Cap Corse, the next port of call is the pretty port of St-Florent and its equally enchanting hinterland, the Nebbio, where the very best of Corsica's wines can be savoured. Bastia is a convenient launching pad for a drive down the east coast, with many an opportunity for a fascinating detour into the interior, including the Castagniccia, the land of chestnuts. Then it's up to Corte, Corsica's "secret capital", once the stronghold of Pasquale Paoli, and today the centre for explorations of the island's high mountains and valleys like the Niolo and Asco. The next chapter then details the country south of Corte. Impressive country this, as anyone with stamina enough to tackle some of the hiking trails is bound to testify ❑

PRECEDING PAGES: the mountain village of Ste-Lucie-de Tallano; an impressive mountain backdrop to the Golfe de Calvi; group of mountain bikers and the Aiguilles de Bavella.

Map
on page
116

AJACCIO

*Napoleon's birthplace is a chic, Riviera-style town of palm-lined squares,
with an ochre-washed old quarter containing an art gallery holding the
country's largest collection of Renaissance art outside Paris*

The best way to appreciate Ajaccio's (Aiacciu) setting in its broad, magnificent gulf is to view it as one arrives by ferry. The ship enters the semi-circle of the harbour, which is protected by the citadel and the harbour mole; behind it the houses extend up the slopes, and the town towers above the yachts and fishing boats below. Palm trees along the quayside, street cafés, fishermen mending their nets: a first walk along the mole (Jetée de la Citadelle) is an intensely Mediterranean experience. From here you can get the very best impression of the town as a whole, and of its "two-storey" appearance: the colourful façades of the Old Town below, and the rather less picturesque modern, concrete housing blocks further up.

A brief history

The town's name could have come from a Roman camp that was once situated here, if one takes the word *adjacium* (resting-place) as its root. But the Corsican word for sheep-herding, *agghjacciu*, also comes very close. Whatever the derivation, the town as we know it today was founded as late as 1492 by the Genoese, who ceded administration of the island to the private Bank of St George. Many members of the Genoese nobility and around 100 families from Liguria settled here.

Corsicans were not allowed to live here at first, and stayed outside the town for security reasons. But in 1553 Sampiero Corso captured the town, marking France's first ever intervention in Corsica, and the French started building the citadel. In 1559 Ajaccio was once again in the hands of the Genoese, who extended the fortress still further. Today, the citadel is still being used for military purposes by the French army, and is closed to visitors. In 1769, just a few months after France had annexed the island, Napoleon Bonaparte

was born in Ajaccio. Even though the town's most famous son did very little that was beneficial either to Ajaccio or Corsica in general, his birthplace still revels in his fame to this day, proudly styling itself the Cité Impériale, a title more than emphasised by all the monuments and museums here. However, the crown in the city's coat-of-arms (above a pillar supported by two lions) dates back to Genoese times. In 1811, Napoleon honoured Ajaccio by making it capital of the whole island – or rather of the French Département Corse. The harbour thus gained rapidly in importance. Since 1975, however, the island has been made up of two *départements* once again, and Ajaccio is now the capital of Corse du Sud.

Seen in terms of its population figure of 59,000, Ajaccio is really little more than a provincial town. But you very soon notice just how lively this former resting place can get when one drives off the ferry and plunges headlong into the tumult of the town's traffic, which only slackens off briefly at lunchtime.

Visitors intending to take in all of Ajaccio's galleries and museums are advised to invest in a Passmusée, which covers the six main sights for only €10. They are available from the museums themselves and from the tourist office on Square Campinchi.

Foch and around

The ideal place to savour Ajaccio's Mediterranean atmosphere is the **place du Maréchal Foch** Ⓐ, just above the harbourfront, where townsfolk come for their evening *passeghjata*, or leisurely stroll. Open to the gulf on one side, the palm and plane-lined square inclines slightly uphill to a towering marble

statue of Napoleon dressed as the First Consul in a Roman toga, around its base, four lions spout water.

Another essential stop on the Bonaparte trail is the **Hôtel de Ville** (Town Hall), on the east side of the square, built in 1826. Inside its lobby, a statue of Napoleon's brother Jérôme Bonaparte, King of Westphalia, greets the visitor with outstretched arm. Up on the first floor there is the **Musée Napoléonien** Ⓑ, (open 9am–noon, 2–6pm, closed Mon am and Sun pm; entrance fee) containing several mementos of the town's most famous son, including a copy of his baptism certificate and the death mask taken at St Helena, contained in a sumptuous chamber.

On the red velvet walls of the Grand Salon there are portraits of various members of the family, and hanging from the ceiling is a highly ornate chandelier made of Bohemian crystal – presented by the Czech Republic on the 200th anniversary of Napoleon's birth. Other highlights of the Musée Napoléonien

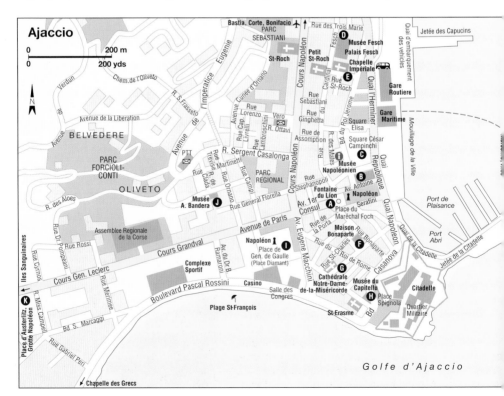

Map on page 116

include the Hall of Medals, housing a collection of medals and coins, the latter commemorating outstanding events from 1797–1876.

Directly behind the Hôtel de Ville, **square César Campinchi C** holds a colourful fresh produce market (open Tues–Sun, 6am–2pm). The stalls here offer not only delicious fruit and vegetables, but also such Corsican specialities as *maquis* honey, chestnut cake and Corsican wine. The *charcuterie* and the fresh, white *brocciu* cheese are garnished appetisingly with green ferns or leafy twigs, possibly a reminder of the fact that pigs, goats and sheep enjoy a great deal of freedom in the woods and meadows of the island's interior – something that lends their meat and their milk a particularly fine flavour. Fish of every size and colour is sold at the **fish market**, at the southwest corner of the square, along with oysters, mussels, crabs and lobsters. At weekends, the "non-food section" of the market becomes the focus of attention. Textiles, belts and all sorts of appliances are laid out on the ground for sale, mostly by North African traders.

From the Napoleon statue on place du Foch, follow the pedestrianised rue du Cardinal Fesch north into the *borgu* (old harbour quarter). The tall houses here, with their partly crumbling, partly restored façades, contain tiny handicraft shops, boutiques and cafés. Narrow, dark alleys and stone staircases branch off this street until – somewhat surprisingly – a broad square opens out on to the generously proportioned **Palais Fesch**. The black bronze statue of Cardinal Fesch, Napoleon's uncle, stands out in stark contrast against the yellow façade of this edifice, which was built by Napoleon III. It has undergone extensive renovation work. Joseph Fesch was a half-brother of Letizia Bonaparte, the Madame Mère. His nephew Napoleon I, who was six years younger, not only helped him reach his high rank in the Church but also lent his support to Fesch's secular passion for collecting Italian paintings from the 15th to the 18th centuries, many of which were spoils of war. The **Musée Fesch D** (open daily 9.15am–

noon, 2–5pm, closed Mon am, and Fri/Sat pm in July/Aug; entrance fee) contains those works in the collection not later sold off by Napoleon's brother, Joseph, including canvases by Botticelli and Titian. Ajaccio itself is only represented in one rather modestly-proportioned painting by Peraldi, hanging next to a corridor window facing the sea: it shows a view of the town around 1882.

In the north wing of the Palais Fesch is the **library**, founded by Lucien Bonaparte in 1801, which numbers several valuable antique books among its treasures. The south wing of the building is taken up by the **Chapelle Impériale E** (open same hours; entrance fee), the Bonapartes' funeral chapel, where Fesch lies buried in the crypt alongside Napoleon's parents and various other members of the family.

Much less tranquil than the rue du Fesch is the **cours Napoléon**, the town's main traffic artery, which runs above it. Even here, though, cafés have placed

GHT: fishing nets and tackle the harbour.

their wicker chairs out on the pavement, the terraces growing grander and more expensive the closer to the posher south side of the street you get.

The old town

Napoleon's birthplace is the main point of interest in the old town. It is most easily reached from the statue on place Foch via the rue Bonaparte, at the corner of which a little niche set into the wall contains a 17th century figurine of La Madonuccia or "little Madonna", as the town's patron saint is named.

The **Musée National de la Maison Bonaparte**  (open 9am–noon, 2–6pm, closed Mon am, Sun pm; entrance fee) is not situated in the rue Bonaparte, however, but on the small place de Letizia in a side-street, the rue St-Charles. Opposite is a small, tree-lined square containing a bust of Napoleon's son, the Roi de Rome. The façade of the house is decorated with the family's coat-of-arms, and a memorial plaque situated above the entrance announces Napoleon's birth here on 15 August 1769. The vestibule contains the sedan-chair in which his mother, Letizia, feeling the pains of oncoming childbirth, was swiftly carried home from a service in the cathedral. The furnishings are, however, no longer the same as they were during Napoleon's childhood. The Casa Buonaparte was destroyed in 1793 when the family were forced to flee from the Paolists and leave Ajaccio because of their French sympathies.

Go up the stairs and enter the first hall on the first floor, and you will find a highly elaborate family tree of the Bonaparte family, with entries made as recently as 1959. These upstairs rooms, with their memorabilia in glass cases and family portraits on the walls, are furnished more as museums than living quarters. Then we see the rooms designed by Letizia when she returned from her years in the countryside: her living-room furnished in the Paris chic of the time, her sleeping-chamber and also the room in which she is said to have given birth to Napoleon – assuming, of course, that it hadn't already happened in the sedan chair on the way back from church.

We now enter the 12-metre (40-ft) long salon, in which Napoleon is said to have eaten a meal with friends on his last ever visit to the house in which he was born, and then "taken French leave". He left his hat on the table as a decoy manoeuvre and disappeared down to the floor below through a trapdoor, in order to reach his ship unobserved and travel off to further adventures on the mainland. This secret escape route ends up in a vaulted cellar, where a Corsican oil-mill can still be admired today.

If you follow the rue St-Charles you will reach the **Cathédrale Notre-Dame de la Miséricorde** , an unpretentious-looking Renaissance edifice consecrated to the town's patron saint. La Madonuccia is meant to have protected Ajaccio from a plague epidemic in 1656.

Above the altar of the first chapel to the left is a valuable Vierge du Sacré Coeur by Delacroix. The chapel is decorated with stuccos thought to be the work of

LEFT: statue of Napoleon Bonaparte in the courtyard of place du Maréchal Foch

Map
on page
116

Tintoretto. In the second chapel we see a marble statue of the Madonuccia. Her feast, 18 March, is celebrated each year by the citizens of Ajaccio. Napoleon was baptised in this cathedral on 21 July 1771, in the marble font to the right of the main entrance. He also requested to be buried here if Paris were to "exile his corpse" – as stated on a plaque to the left of the entrance to the cathedral; this never did become Napoleon's final resting place, however, since Paris, as is well-known, did not wish to do without its dead emperor.

A private collection belonging to an old established Ajaccien family (furniture, paintings, sculptures, tableware) can be seen at the **Musée du Capitellu** ❸ (open Mon–Wed 10am–noon, 2–6pm; entrance fee) near the Citadel. There are also some remarkable watercolours and portraits by Aglaé Meuron, an artist born in Ajaccio in 1836.

In the glass display cases is a rare edition of the first history of Corsica, written by Agostino Giustiniani, and the *Code*

ELOW: place
ı Maréchal
ɔch, the heart
˙ Ajaccio.

Corse, a set of laws for Corsica written by Louis XV in 1796. The final room contains a painting which is thought to be be work of Turner's nephew, entitled *Sunrise over Bavella*.

Along the cours Grandaval

Two more striking statues of Napoleon lie along the town's main east–west thoroughfare, the cours Grandval. At its eastern end, in the **place de Général de Gaulle** ❶ (known locally as the Place Diamant) the emperor is depicted on horseback, dressed as the Emperor of Rome, wearing golden laurels, and surrounded by his four brothers dressed in togas. This broad square – a skateboarders' paradise, but a bleak expanse of broiling concrete in the summer – affords a fine view of the sea. It also doubles as the roof of a car park.

Anyone interested in learning more about the history of the town and the island should make the short detour north of the cours Grandval to the **Musée A.**

Bandera  (open Mon–Sat 10am–noon, 3–7pm; entrance fee) in the rue Général Levie. Of particular note here are the photographs of bandits, and later documents relating to World War II (Ajaccio being the first town in Metropolitan France to have been liberated by Allied forces in 1943). There is also material and displays relating to prehistoric times and the Moorish raids on the island. From the place Diamant, the broad cours Grandval leads in a straight line to the **place d'Austerlitz** , another large square at the end of which Ajaccio's most imposing Napoleon memorial was erected in 1938.

Rising from the top of a high white pyramid, the emperor is shown in a familiar pose: wearing his frock coat and bicorne hat, the fingers of his left hand thrust inside his jacket. Between the steps on the way up, his famous military victories are engraved in stone. He used to enjoy playing hide-and-seek here as a child – in a grotto behind the monument. The **Jardins de Casone** around it are the

venue for the Fête Napolienne in mid-August (around Napoleon's birthday), featuring processions in period costumes and a firework and sound-and-light display.

Maps:
City 116
Area 124

Route des Sanguinaires

The town doesn't just revel in the past glory of its most famous son, though – and certainly not in the summertime, when life here primarily revolves around the sea and the beaches. Anyone who is not just passing through should at least take an excursion out to the Iles Sanguinaires, either by boat or on the Petit Train des Iles, a small open-top train with a warning bell. Both begin at the harbour.

The **route des Sanguinaires** runs along the north coast of the Golfe d'Ajaccio, and passes the **Chapelle des Grecs** , founded in 1632, where the Greek Orthodox community used to come to worship. The Greeks first settled in Ajaccio after their expulsion by the Turks in 1731, before finding a permanent home in Cargèse. Some lines from Joseph Bonaparte's memoirs are engraved above the entrance.

Just beyond the chapel is the impressive **cemetery**, with its many family vaults and tombstones spread over the steep hillside facing the sea. Among them is the final resting place of local crooner Tino Rossi – known as the "Corsican Nightingale" – who became a household name in France in the 1950s and 1960s. The route then passes several more beaches and ends at the **Pointe de la Parata** , crowned by a Genoese watchtower built as a defence against the Moorish raiders, with the **Iles Sanguinaires** in the middle distance. Sanguinaire means bloodstone, and the name turns out to be very apt at sunset, when the rocks turn a reddish-ochre colour – an experience that really should not be missed.

The lighthouse on the largest of the islets, Mezzo Mare (Grande Sanguinaire), is renowned for having accommodated Alphonse Daudet in 1862 – a windy sojourn that inspired one of his much loved *Lettres de Mon Moulin*. You may want to take one of the daily boat rides around Mezzo Mare from Ajaccio. ❏

LEFT: fishing off the rocks a the edge of town.

The Napoleon Cult

There is hardly a street or square in Ajaccio which does not in one way or another recall Napoleon and his clan. At the foot of the monuments, the eternal gratitude of his native island is proclaimed – but what reason does the Corsican people have to be grateful to the Emperor of France? Because he "carried out our vendetta on all those who caused our downfall", as Paoli asserted? Or because today he can be marketed so successfully – as a sight, a motif on T-shirts, postcards and mugs, as the inspiration for the names of cafés and bars? Napoleon himself is hardly likely to turn in his grave, for as he once remarked, "Providence created in me a Corsican rock, from which all strokes of Fate simply run off like water."

But what was Napoleon's relationship to Corsica really like? "I was born as my fatherland lay dying." The words of the young man express an ambivalent attitude to his native island which was mirrored in the career of his real father. Carlo Buonaparte was a descendant of a Tuscan family who became involved in the Corsican struggle for independence. He became the confidant of Paoli; whilst pregnant with Napoleon, his wife Letizia Ramolino accompanied him to the Wars of Independence. On the day of the defeat at Ponte Nuovo she felt the child struggling "as if it wanted to fight before it was even born".

Napoleon was born in 1769 on the Day of the Assumption; he was the second son in the family. The fight for Corsica was over for the moment; his father, Carlo Buonaparte, did not follow Paoli into exile, but chose to stay in Ajaccio and to adapt to French rule. Napoleon's childhood on the island was a happy one. Of all Letizia's children – she bore thirteen – "Nabulione" was the most boisterous. A ruffian and a precociously cheeky child, he soon acquired the nickname "Rabullione". When he was nine, he went to the military academy at Brienne. He always remained somewhat aloof from his fellow-pupils, wrapped up in his dreams of Corsican independence and imagining himself as the saviour of the island. He adapted his name to the French much later, when he was a general in the French army.

He took advantage of the revolutionary turmoil in France to enjoy an extended period of home leave in Corsica, meeting up with Paoli, who had been his idol during his youth, and who had returned from exile. The bubble burst when Napoleon's brother Lucien spread the rumour in the Jacobin Club in Toulon that Paoli wanted to hand Corsica over to the English. The warrant for Paoli's arrest gave rise to a vendetta on behalf of the Paoli clan against the Bonapartes, who were forced to flee from Ajaccio. Napoleon's comet-like career began in Paris; as commander-in-chief and later as emperor he finally forged the links between Corsica and France. His compatriots were forced to adapt to his plans to make France a major power. But Napoleon remained a Corsican in his concern for his clan: irrespective of their abilities, he elevated his relatives to the thrones of Europe. At the end of his life, during his exile on the island of St Helena, he often felt homesick for his homeland. He was certain that even with his eyes closed, just by the smell alone, he would recognise his native island. ❏

Map
on page
124

AJACCIO TO PROPRIANO

*This varied route covers two of the scenic highlights of Corsica's southwest
coast – the gulfs of Ajaccio and Propriano – taking in the world-famous
prehistoric site of Filitosa and a string of picturesque granite hill villages*

"Almost colourless, its outlines uncertain, it swam in the early morning mist, a creation half-materialised, an ectoplasm of the sea in trance", wrote Dorothy Carrington of her first glimpse of the Golfe d'Ajaccio in 1947. Framed by the distant snow-flecked crags of Monte d'Oro, the bay remains an extraordinary spectacle, especially when viewed from one of the high ridges surrounding it.

Having skirted the flat delta formed by the rivers Prunelli and Gravona, the main route from the capital to the south of the island – N196 – passes **Campo dell'Oro airport** (so named for the golden grain fields that were formerly here). It was on the edge of this plain, at the huge **Tour de Capitello**, that Napoleon and 50 of his most loyal French sailors were besieged in 1753 by Paolist rebels. He managed to escape with his life, but slipped secretly back to the same spot later that year to rescue his mother, uncle and sister. The tower still stands, in spite of Napoleon's vengeful attempt to blow it up after he became emperor.

The Rive Sud

The Tour de Capitello flags the start of the gulf's southern shore, or **Rive Sud**. A string of modern resorts have sprung up behind the beautiful beaches that punctuate this turquoise coastline, with terracotta-roofed villas stacked up the hillsides of eucalyptus and *maquis* inland.

Directly opposite the capital, and linked to it by a daily ferry service, is the largest of these, **Porticcio ❹**, a smart little resort frequented by well-heeled Ajacciens. The campus of supermarkets, shops and banks at its centre form the area's hub, but possesses little charm. Exclusive villas, some with their own boat jetties and helipads, flank the D55 as it winds southwest past a succession of crumbling Genoese watchtowers. At **Le Ruppione ❺**, a striking

sweep of golden sand opens up, washed by transluscent water that's shallow enough to provide safe bathing for small children. Beyond here development gradually peters out and the *maquis* begins to encroach on the roadside verges. Its edges bounded by clumps of red rocks and pines, the last of the Rive Sud's noteworthy beaches is **Plage de Verghia**, 13 km (8 miles) southwest of Porticcio, where there's a large car park, campsite and café, but little else.

Verghia ❻ is marked on some maps as **Port de Chiavari** – in times past, before the road was surfaced, it served as the harbour for the well populated village of **Côti-Chiavari ❼**, high up in the hills behind. The tortuous D55 winds up there

LEFT: calm
anchorage at
Porto Pollo.
RIGHT:
eroded rock
formations,
Golfe d'Ajaccio.

today through a protected forest of holm oak. Increasingly spectacular glimpses of the gulf are yielded by gaps in the tree cover, and from the village square you can look over the tiled rooftops of Côti-Chiavari's pretty stone houses and church to a magnificent spread of hills and sea.

For this area's ultimate panorama, however, press on a kilometre or so further along the main road to Le Belvédère hotel *(see Travel Tips page 269)*. Its terrace is perfectly placed to make the most of an amazing natural viewpoint above the gulf, encompassing most of the island's northern watershed.

Having negotiated a series of dramatic switchbacks, the road re-joins the main D155 at the hamlet of **Acqua Viva**. Shortly beyond here signboards point the way to a hidden cove that's a perfect place to pull over for a secluded swim. Reached by a rough dirt track, **Cala d'Orzu** ❽, huddled in the lee of the headland dividing the gulfs of Ajaccio

and Propriano, may be remote, but it made international headlines in 1999, after one of the shack-restaurants on it was blown up. This was not an exceptional event in Corsica, but on this occasion undercover police, acting under the direct orders of the island's governor, were found to be responsible. The ensuing political furore cost Préfet Bonnet a couple of years in prison and nearly brought Lionel Jospin's government down.

Porto Pollo

Once across the spur above Cala d'Orzu, a deserted hillside of fire-scorched *maquis* falls away to the awesome **Golfe d'Ajaccio**, the most southerly of the fjord-like inlets cleaving Corsica's west coast. In the 14th and 15th centuries, piracy made life miserable for the inhabitants of **Porto Pollo** ❾, but these days this fishing village at the gulf's far western rim is enjoying a renaissance as a low-key resort, with a handful of smart little hotels, restaurants and dive schools strung along its single

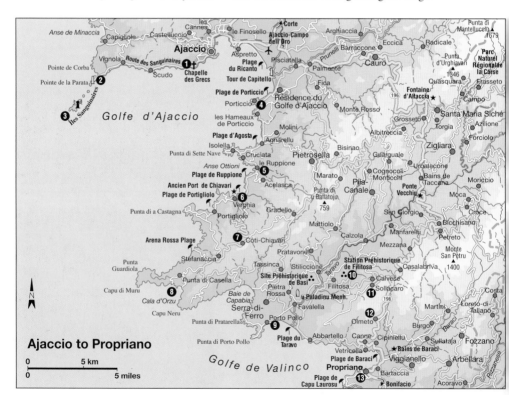

Ajaccio to Propriano

0   5 km

0   5 miles

Map
on page
124

street. At the end of the road, a small marina overlooked by a café makes a perfect spot to enjoy the views across the water to Campomorro. Porto Pollo presides over the mouth of the beautiful Taravo Valley, visited in large numbers thanks to its prehistoric site, Filitosa, only a 15-minute drive inland.

Filitosa

Many old shepherd legends revolve around Corsica's menhirs, which date from the megalithic period. In 1946 Charles-Antoine Cesari discovered several of them on his land in the hamlet of Filitosa. The **Station Préhistorique de Filitosa ❿** (open summer daily 9am–sunset; entrance fee), the Cesari family's well-preserved prehistoric site, which has been the subject of archaeological research by Roger Grosjean since 1954, is the best place to study the development of the island's megalithic culture and its replacement by the "Torréen" civilization – so named by Grosjean because of the

BELOW: Station Préhistorique de Filitosa.

tower-like fortresses they built *(see page 22)*. You can buy Grosjean's excellent book *Filitosa, Haut Lieu de la Corse Préhistorique* in the Cesari family's bar and restaurant. More up-to-date and richly illustrated is *Lumières de Granite* by the archeologist Lucien Aquaviva and Filitosa owner Jean Dominique Cesari. Stone-Age monolith carving reached its high point around 1400 BC, when statues began to take on increasingly human form. Between 1300 BC and 800 BC, however, the megalithic culture gradually declined.

The small **museum** at the entrance is best visited after a stroll around the whole area. To make it easier to distinguish between them, the menhirs, all of which represent men, have been quite simply numbered, and an avenue of pine trees leads us first to Filitosa V: a massive, 3-metre (10-ft) high rock statue with a head divided into two halves, upon which the chiselled outlines of a long sword and a dagger in its sheath are clearly recognisable. On the back of the statue there

are faint indications of a shoulder blade and also of the spinal column.

The "Torréens", Grosjean believed, streamed into southern Corsica between 1600 and 1400 BC, and were far superior to the megalithic population. If the armed granite statues were supposed to represent the invaders and help defeat them via some kind of magic spell, then this turned out to be a rather futile defensive strategy. The "Torréens", according to this theory, invaded Filitosa, once populated by shepherds, and smashed their menhirs or used them in the construction of their own places of worship.

The **east monument** resembles a walled-in burial mound. The ramp leading up to this tumulus is remarkable, as is the 15-ton block of stone forming part of the wall. No one is really certain what took place here. Taffoni rocks were used as hiding places by the megalithic people, while the Torréens later built dwellings from them. Foundations can be seen to the left. Under the shade of olive trees we now reach the **central monument**, a round "Torréen" building used for religious purposes. Fragments of simple menhirs and menhir statues – face down – were incorporated into the walls, but have since been retrieved, and are now either upright once more or leaning against the monument. The statues are unarmed and may have represented the megalithic dead, or simply served as tomb guardians. The midday sun is weathering them more and more, and those with oval faces are the easiest to make out.

The grim but clearly defined features of Filitosa IX (to the right of the entrance) are very arresting. On the other side of the "Torréen" building are the three fragments of the menhir-statue Filitosa VI, a sword-bearer with a very realistic, almost clown-like expression.

The most important "Torréen" complex is the **west monument**, a labyrinthine structure composed of three chambers, two rock caves and a spring. The main chamber, the Cella, is divided into two

BELOW: Filitosa contains a significant alignment of anthropomorphic menhirs.

Map on page 124

sections. Connecting passages lead to underground cavities, which may have been used for storing food, weapons or cult objects. The remains of a fireplace may point to it having been used as a temple of fire.

Below, in the valley of the Barcalojo stream, the five menhir statues first discovered here stand in a semicircle in front of an olive tree. Their facial features are scarcely recognisable, but daggers and swords can be clearly seen. The statue Tappa I (named after the place it was found, roughly 400 metres/440 yards away), with its strange head, is particularly striking. A faceless "mummy" or a phallic symbol erected by farmers for fertility purposes?

The **Centre de Documentation Archéologique** contains more menhir-statues that have been restored: Scalsa-Murta holds a sword, his back is protected by armour and a helmet containing two holes can be made out; they may once have contained Viking-style horns. Fili-

tosa XII was discovered – split into two lengthwise – in a shepherd's hut, where it was being used as a door lintel. Particularly distinctive here are the positions of the arms and hands.

Finally, Tappa II is impressive for the manner in which its facial features are only hinted at, in a similar way to some modern sculpture. Alongside the mysterious statues there are glass showcases displaying pottery fragments, millstones and other finds documenting daily life in Filitosa from the Early Neolithic period to medieval times.

Sollacaro and Olmeto

Continuing up the side of the Taravo Valley from Filitosa, the D57 winds eastwards to one of the most attractive and historic hill villages in this area, **Sollacaro** ⓫ (Sudacaru).

It was here in October 1765 that the first meeting took place between the Scottish dilettante, Dr Johnson's biographer James Boswell, and the hero of Corsican

BELOW: the countryside surrounding the Golfe d'Ajaccio.

Independence, Pasquale Paoli. They had been introduced to each other by Rousseau, and Boswell's subsequent *Journal of a Tour to Corsica* (1768) had immediate success and was consequently translated into several languages.

Sollacaro also used to be a seat of the d'Istria family, whose most famous member was Vincentello d'Istria, a 15th-century viceroy of the King of Aragon. If a medieval legend is to be believed, a nasty drama of revenge took place in their nearby seat. It is the tale of the beautiful Savilia, who is said to have enticed a count of the d'Istria family to her castle by promising to marry him. On visiting her, however, he did not end up in the marital bed as expected but in the castle dungeon instead.

Every morning the beautiful mistress of the castle would parade naked in front of his prison in order to mock him for his ugliness: how could he even have dared hope to possess such a wonderful body as hers? The humiliated count managed to

escape at some point, though, thus clearing the way for his revenge. He returned with his men, destroyed his tormentress's castle and put Savilia in a hut at a cross-roads on a pass – so that all the men who passed by could have their way with her. Word of this must have spread very quickly among the local male population: the unfortunate Savilia is said to have survived the onslaught for just three days.

The ridgetops high above Sollacaro can be reached by following the D57, which joins the main highway, N196, at the **Col de la Celaccia**. Fine views of the Golfe d'Ajaccio are revealed from here as the road bends downhill to **Olmeto** ⑫, situated at the head of a steep-sided valley.

One of the castles belonging to the powerful della Rocca family stood on a bluff overlooking the village in former times; today only ruins remain. Much olive cultivation goes on in the area surrounding the town. An inscription on a simple house on the right-hand side of the road announces the fact that Colomba Carabelli used to live there: she was a heroine of the vendetta, and Prosper Mérimée met her in 1840. The events upon which his tale *Colomba* were based took place in a small village north of Sartène called Fozzano *(see page 143)*.

Town of work and play

Propriano ⑬ (Prupiá) is a tourist town first and foremost (receiving 23,000 visitors during the summer), but an attractive one all the same. The town centre, with its church up on the hill, gives every sign of having developed quite naturally, and many people from the surrounding countryside come here to do their shopping. The bars often play host to sailors, because the harbour – which was developed as a centre of the export trade for the south of the island – is now busy once more, ever since French Algerians began cultivating cereal, fruit and wine in the vicinity.

Two hour long boat sightseeing excursions in the Golfe de Valinco can be organised via the tourist office. Ferries to mainland France and Sardinia also leave from the port. ❑

Map on page 124

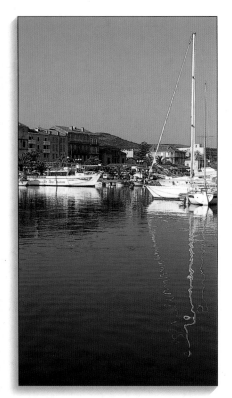

LEFT: yachts moored in Propriano's harbour.
RIGHT: clouds gather above the Golfe de Valinco.

Map
on page
134

THE SARTENAIS

*Sartène – "the most Corsican of Corsican towns" as Prosper Mérimée
described this region's sombre capital – provides a base for forays into a
hinterland strewn with enigmatic standing stone sites and lonely beaches*

Inland from the tourist resorts lining the Golfe de Propriano, the landscapes of Corsica's sparsely populated southwest – a region known as the Sartenais after its principal town, Sartène (Sarté) – is dominated by the prominent peak of Uomo di Cagna. Its summit boulders eroded into a weirdly human formation, the mountain surveys an expanse of rolling *maquis* that at first may seem featureless and unwelcoming, but on closer inspection reveals a wealth of prehistoric sites, snug fishing villages and hidden beaches.

Once beyond Sartène, worth a stop for the brooding atmosphere of its old town and some superb vistas over the Rizzanese Valley, few roads peel off the main highway to penetrate this remote area. The Sartenais is definitely a corner where stout footwear and a sense of adventure will pay dividends, especially for flora enthusiasts, with meadows and verges carpeted in Mediterranean flowers during the spring and early summer. Wine lovers should also note the existence, hidden away in the roadless side valleys spreading inland, of some of Corsica's most renowned vineyards – sources of spicy, *maquis*-scented wines and a rare red muscat to rival the more famous dessert whites of Cap Corse and Patrimonio.

Sartène

The hilly landscape here is so cheerful and inviting that the first sight of **Sartène ❶** up on its mountain can often come as quite a shock. Could this really be Mérimée's "*la plus corse des villes corses*"? It not only looks grim and forbidding, it's actually quite ugly, too, at first glance. The high blocks of houses seem to be clustered together very haphazardly. First impressions are deceptive, though: as one rounds the final few bends before entering the town it already looks very different, with its parks and gardens full of palm trees, orange trees and bright flowers, and by the time you reach the square it becomes clear that the town is far more in harmony with the landscape than initially seemed to be the case.

It may turn its back to it in one sense, but in another Sartène shows it its heart. For this central square, the focal point of town life with its plane trees and palm trees, is only built up on three sides. The fourth, open, side faces the valley. This open centre is typical of mountain towns in Corsica, and it can sometimes even be found in small villages as well.

The finest house in the square, apart from the town hall, is the palace that once belonged to the Genoese governor, and today the building houses the headquar-

ters of Sartenais wine. The dark, cool vaults here are a good place for some *dégustation*, wine purchasing and information-gathering before you travel off to the vineyard of your choice out in the surrounding countryside.

Also in the square is the town's main church, the **Eglise Ste-Marie**, an austere structure built of grey granite. The wooden cross and iron chain in the doorway, often the subject of curiosity among visitors, are used for a very serious procession: the Catenacciu, or Grand Penitent, dressed in a red robe and hood through which only his eyes can be seen, drags the cross and the chain through the town barefoot on the evening of Good Friday each year.

A gateway below the town hall leads through to the lower town, the medieval Old Town – or rather, one of the two Old Towns, for the upper town is equally old. Power and wealth, influence and political importance were distributed between the two parts of the town at different times, and the question of whether living down in Ste-Anne is nobler than living up in Borgo is probably still a bone of contention even today – though no longer the excuse for wholesale slaughter it was in former days. Sartène's notoriety as capital of the vendetta stems from its divided Old Town.

Feudalism was still rife here as late as the 19th century. The town was run by just a few families, some of them genuinely noble, others self-styled nobles because of the sheer amount of land they owned. Each family had its own supporters and dependants among the simple townsfolk, and so the various rivalries, combined with the vendetta tradition, cut through every social rank, and for tactical and practical reasons, straight through the entire town as well.

The two quarters became fortresses, and people were still barricading themselves into the houses here as late as the 19th century. It was only in 1834 that the French finally succeeded in getting the two rival sections of the town to sign a

LEFT: war memorial in the old town.

Map
on page
134

peace treaty. A solemn announcement to this effect was made in the church, and an oath was sworn.

The lower part of the Old Town gives every indication of having had a shady past, too: any sunlight that does manage to penetrate the high walls of grey granite very soon vanishes in the narrow streets and winding passageways. The Old Town is very much alive, however. Children play on stairways, and women carrying shopping bags go in and out of the houses.

The old people are the only real locals left, however. Many of the young families come from the Maghreb states, and work on farms owned by *Pieds Noirs*. As is the case in many small towns in Western Europe, the immigrant workers have been left with the shoddier housing. The odd craftsman here and there attempts to make some money from tourism, and cheese and honey are also on sale.

In the Borgo quarter it is not so much the old streets but the newer palazzi that

strike one at first. When the barred windows are flung open here to let fresh air into the salons, and the family arrives in a state carriage drawn by majestic horses to play its role in the town for several days, one can sense that the power structures haven't really altered very much.

Above the Borgo, the **Musée de Préhistoire Corse** (open Mon–Sat 10am– noon, 2–6pm; entrance fee) was at the time of writing being moved to new premises high on the hill above the town. Its remarkable collection, covering nearly 7,000 years of history with finds drawn from across the island, includes jewellery, weapons and human remains, as well as displays showcasing the latest archaeological research findings.

Sartenais' prehistoric sites

The itinerary continues southwestwards from Sartène, following the N196 as far as the Bocca Albitrina, where a right fork followed by another right turn soon after, and finally a left turn at the third junction

BELOW: discussing events on Sartène's main square.

encountered (on to the D21 signposted for Grossa), leads to the prehistoric site of **Alo Bisuje ❷**. Piled up on the roadside, a mound encircled by a double wall of broken boulders is all that remains of a neolithic settlement dating from 1700 bc, which was later colonised and rebuilt by the Torréens.

Not one of the larger structures, it nevertheless exhibits all the typical features of *castelli*, especially the combination of roughly-assembled sections of rock and carefully-built wall. Four passageways with bends in them fan out, swastika-like, from an unwalled, almost circular central area.

To reach the region's other prehistoric vestiges, return to the D48 and follow the signs for Tizzano. A green metal gate 1,500 metres (1,640 yds) on the right after the Domaine la Mosconi vineyard marks the start of the track to the **Alignements de Palaggiu ❸**.

The site was first excavated by Roger Grosjean, the first archaeologist to undertake a serious study of Corsica's megalithic culture, who unearthed many of the menhirs here and had them placed upright once more.

And there they are: an army of 258 stone men, standing firm in a lonely stretch of landscape. Some of them are wearing daggers and swords. Their weapons are only vaguely hinted at with scratch marks, possibly to enhance their effectiveness, at least if we are to believe Roger Grosjean's theory that they may have been some kind of magic deterrent. The stone men are arranged in groups and face in various directions, some towards the rising sun, and others towards the Uomo di Cagna, the most striking peak in the chain of mountains to the south.

A little further to the north, the road branches off towards **Cauria ❹**. Here, you should leave the car at the end of the road and continue on along one of the scenic footpaths signposted to various prehistoric sites. They include dolmens,

BELOW: Alignements de Palaggiu.

Map on page 134

alignments, groups of menhirs, all of them possibly forming part of a central place of worship and once again pointing towards certain salient features of the landscape: the Uomo di Cagna, the Lion of Roccapina. The summer solstice, of course, also plays an important role in many prehistoric sites. One dolmen is placed in such a way that it catches the first rays of the sun after the winter solstice.

This **Dolmen de Fontanaccia** is the largest on the whole island. Granite blocks as high as a man support a crossways slab 3.4 metres (11 ft) long and 2.6 metres (8.5 ft) wide. Cauria is the name of this mountain area, across which these monuments are distributed. A path leads through a grove of chestnut oak, along the edge of which 36 smaller standing stones can be seen, the Menhirs of Rinaggiu.

On the way back to the parking place – or starting from there to Rinaggiu – you will meet impressive rows of unarmed Stantari ("petrified ones") and Paladini, menhir-statues with swords and daggers. At the foot of one of the menhir statues a vessel was found which had apparently served as a painting bowl more than 3,500 years ago.

Two statues still bore traces of red paint. The stone warriors were not only painted, however, they also had horns, judging by the impressions in their helmets. Indeed, some of the stones are so well carved that it is even possible to tell what kind of weapon the megalithic masons wanted to depict.

Grosjean came up with the theory that the megalithic people wanted to represent their enemies with these statues – the "Torréens" who had invaded their island. And it was also the stone statues of Cauria that suddenly reminded him of similarities in an Egyptian temple relief of Medinet-Habu, leading him to suppose that the Torréens may have been identical with the Shardana.

The **Uomo di Cagna**, a mountain peak in the Cagna range which seems to have played an important role geometrically in the layout of these extensive megalithic cult sites, is remarkable in its own right: it is a huge spherical rock that has been

eroded so much by wind and weather that it now balances on top of a very slender base. Apparently it used to serve as a landmark for ships arriving from the south; it is certainly the most noticeable feature of the landscape for miles around.

The Sartenais coast

The rugged Sartenais tumbles to an appropriately wave-lashed shoreline, backed by miles of unbroken *maquis* where wild boar herds still roam free in large numbers. Road access to this wonderfully pristine stretch of coast is limited to only three points, but the intervening portions can be reached on foot: a cleared and intermittently way-marked path winds across the granite outcrops and flotsam-covered coves between Campomoro, Tizzano and Roccapina (anyone attempting to follow this route for more than a couple of hours should take along adequate water as there are no dependable springs on the way) and an IGN map as the route

**Map
on page
134**

regularly plunges into dense, thick undergrowth. Spread behind a graceful arc of soft sand, its opalescent bay overlooked by a massive Genoan watchtower, **Campomoro ❺** presents an arresting spectacle as you descend on it via the D121 from Propriano (an alternative route takes you from the Bocca Albitrina and Alo Bisuje, described earlier, via the hamlet of Grossa.

Although almost overrun by campers in high summer, for the rest of the year this tiny village remains a sleepy, unfeasibly picturesque backwater. Walkers and hikers will find plenty of inspiration in the recently inaugurated coastal path stretching south across the island's wildest shoreline, dotted with giant outcrops of weirdly eroded granite. The trail starts just below the watchtower (open 9am–7pm) and can be followed (by adequately equipped hikers) all the way to Tizzano and Roccapina.

The deep waters of the gulf are rich in marine life, and a couple of sub-aqua schools have also sprung up to provide access to some of the dive sites just beyond the harbour. From Campomoro, a high, sinuous backroad wriggles inland via the villages of Belvédère and Grossa, passing the prehistoric site at Alo Bisuje en route, to join the D48, connecting Sartène with the region's most remote coastal village, **Tizzano ❻**. Little more than a scattering of holiday homes grouped on a hillside above a small boat jetty, the settlement lies all but deserted in the winter, but throughout the summer months it sees a steady stream of visitors, largely due to its proximity to the impressive **Cala di l'Avena** beach around the corner to the north. The village is the only permanently inhabited settlement on the Sartenais coast.

Opposite the harbour, the remains of a crumbling Genoese fort crown a low hillock. Soon after it the driveable track degenerates into a footpath which can be followed northwards to the lonely **Tour de Senetosa** and its working lighthouse, and thence to Campomoro in five or six hours of rough walking.

While the majority of the Sartenais beaches can only be reached on foot, arguably the most beautiful of them, **Roccapina**, is skirted by the main N196. Heading south from Sartène, look out for the Auberge Coralli, from where a rutted *piste* runs downhill to the beach, a gleaming white strip of shell sand hemmed in by a pair of steep headlands.

Roccapina is famous above all for the eerily lifelike figure of a lion, the **Lion de Roccapina ❼**, worn into the rocks overlooking the bay, which rises next to the inevitable ruined watchtower. The hollows in the surrounding boulders are said to have served as a hideout for the bandit, Barrittonu, and his gang, whom local rumour insists salvaged a trunk of treasure lost when the ship transporting it ran aground on some rocks off Roccapina. The precious cargo, a present from the princely states of India in 1887, was bound for Queen Victoria to mark her jubilee, but was never officially recovered. The haul includes a purse of valuable Indian diamonds. ❏

LEFT: sailing boat moored near the shore at Tizzano.

The Catenacciu

The *Catenacciu* procession in Sartène isn't the only Easter-week custom the visitor can experience on Corsica, but it is certainly the most spectacular. *Catenacciu* means "The Chained One". The event takes its name from the 14 kg (30 lb) iron chains which for the rest of the year can be viewed in the church. Even the weight of the cross is common knowledge: 32 kg (70 lbs). It requires little to imagine what it must be like to drag such a burden through the Old Town of Sartène. Only one man enjoys the honour and the torture of completing this penitential circuit on Good Friday each year. The supplicant is enveloped in a red hooded robe from his head to his naked feet. He drags the chain attached to his ankle. Nobody knows who he is apart from the parish priest and the monks in the monastery perched up above the town. The priest selects the man in question – supposedly from a long waiting list which stretches out well beyond the next five years. Having been chosen, the winner spends a day and a night in prayer in St Damian's monastery preparing himself for the procession. From the late afternoon the town centre is closed to traffic and crowds of spectators begin to assemble at the best vantage points. At 9pm the lights are all extinguished. Everyone falls silent. There is a sudden flickering as candles are lit. Twinkling lights can be seen at windows and in doorways. Then comes a surge of movement, whisperings. And finally he appears, the *Catenacciu*, the Grand Penitent in the red robe. Bent double under the weight of the cross, he sways, stumbles and finally falls to the ground. That is part of the ritual – and may even be genuine. As he collapses, only one man comes forward to help him: the Little Penitent. Dressed in a white, hooded robe, he represents Simon of Cyrene. The red- and white-robed figures are followed by eight men in black, the *Penitents Noirs*, bearing a wooden effigy of the dead Christ wrapped in a shroud. Behind follows the procession of those whose participation is based on piety rather than curiosity: men, women and children, bearing candles and quietly chanting the invocation *Perdono mio Dio,*

perdono mio... The priest, by contrast, is far from quiet as he takes up the microphone as the procession approaches the half-way point, the square in front of the church. Question, answer, incantations – the strange ritual of the Stations of the Cross. Then they move off into the darkness once more, their voices echoing in the narrow alleyways, the candles flickering under archways. The two historic town centres, the lower and the upper, are linked by the route of the *Catenacciu* – no wonder, after the feuds between the different districts during the past. The journey of the *Penitent Rouge* ends where it began, beside the parish church of St Mary. The entire procession lasts three hours. In the meantime, the onlookers have dispersed: the pious have taken their places in the church, while the less pious have gone for dinner. The next day, the photo of the *Catenacciu* in his red robe will adorn the front page of the local newspaper. Not even the reporter knows his identity, so there will be no startling revelations. Respectfully – and wisely – he too will stick to the rules. ❏

RIGHT: the Catenacciu (Grand Penitent) bears the cross.

Map
on page
144

ALTA ROCCA

*The prehistoric settlement of Cucuruzzu and picturesque villages perchés,
overlooking miles of forest to the peaks of the island's spine, provide
ample incentive to explore this quintesentially Corsican region*

Immediately inland from the gulfs of Valinco and Sartenais, a tract of thickly wooded valleys sweeps north towards a horizon dominated by the grey bulk of Monte Incudine (southern Corsica's highest peak) and the distinctive needles of the Bavella massif. The compact stone villages nestled on the ridges of this region, known since ancient times as the Alta Rocca, formed the heartland of the della Rocca warlords until their subjugation by the Genoese in the early 16th century. Little impact on its notoriously rebellious inhabitants was made by nearly 500 years of colonial occupation that ensued, and the now depopulated settlements remain distanced from the mainstream of island life, with a staunch tradition of independence and its own rich folklore.

The route stringing the largest Alta Rocca villages together ranks among the most picturesque in Corsica, yielding impressive views of the interior hills and passing a number of important historic sites. Foremost among them is Cucuruzzu, near the village of Levie (Livia) which, although far less famous than Filitosa, possesses an eerie of its own.

The Rizzanese Valley

The principal gateway to the Alta Rocca is the lush Rizzanese Valley, south and east of Propriano. Just as the *route nationale*, N196, begins its looping climb up to Sartène, a side road (the D69) peels eastwards to hug the Rizzanese River, from whose banks radiate the vineyards of the renowned **Domaine de Fiumicicoli** (open Mon–Sat 9am–noon, 2–6pm, Sat only in winter). The *domaine*'s label sports the distinctive profile of the **Spin' a Cavallu ❶**, an immaculately preserved 13th-century Genoese bridge spanning the river nearby. The name means "horse's back", but the nag that gave it its name must have been pretty gaunt-looking. The

road leading to this bridge goes up steeply, makes a bend at the top and then dips straight down again just as steeply to the other bank. The road is very narrow and really only suitable for carts, horse-riders and mule trains. Many such bridges were built on Corsica during Genoese rule, and this one, the best-preserved of all, still serves its original function.

A couple of kilometres beyond Spin' a Cavallu, a more modern bridge carries the road across the Rizzanese. Bear left on the far side and you'll find yourself contouring uphill on the D19 to Arbellara and, a couple of kilometres beyond there, **Fozzano ❷**, the typically austere stone village famed as the setting for Prosper Mérimée's best selling vendetta novel,

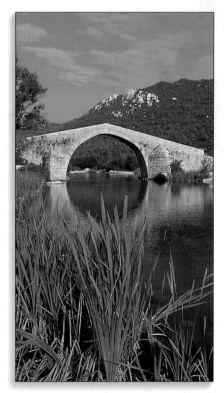

Colomba. Written in the mid-19th century, the book was based on a real life feud that took place between the village's two clans, the Carabellis and Bartolis over the preceeding decades. Its success gained a certain notoriety for the story's heroine, the raven-haired, cold-hearted Colomba Bartoli, who came to epitomize the pivotal role played by women in Corsican vendettas. By the time of her death she had become a tourist attraction in her own right – even Flaubert called by on his teenage tour in 1840. Her house, one of several gaunt granite buildings dating from the Genoese era, still stands on the edge of the village, while her tomb – alongside that of her son, slain in the vendetta – is housed inside the church.

To reach the next village of note, backtrack to the river and follow the D268 up the opposite flank of the valley to **Ste-Lucie-de-Tallano** ❸ (Santa Lucia di Tallo), whose distinctive roofscape is one of the defining images of the Alta Rocca. Ste Lucie was the seat of the rebel Corsi-can clan leader, Sinuccio della Rocca, who resisted the Genoese occupation in the late 15th century. Between battles, the warlord also amassed an impressive collection of Renaissance art, the remnants of which may be seen in the **Eglise Paroissiale**, facing the square, which harbours a beautiful bas relief of the Virgin and Child. Further up the hill at the **Couvent St-François**, consecrated by Rinuccio, hang several paintings by the Spanish artist Castel Sardo. The village's other novelty is a curious, and very rare, kind of rock bearing black and white rings called diorite orbiculaire. The Bar Ortoli in the main square has a few sample pieces on display.

The Fiumicicoli Valley

From its conjunction with the Rizzanese just upstream from Spin' a Cavallu bridge, the smaller Fiumicicoli Valley funnels northeast, its sides carpeted in dense *maquis* and, as it narrows towards the river's headwaters, pristine oak and chest-

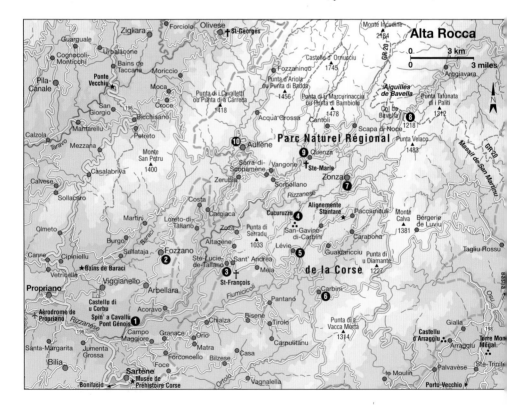

Map on page 144

nut forest. A perfect place from which to gain a sense both of the region's dramatic landscape and its ancient heritage is the prehistoric site of **Cucuruzzu** ❹, also known as the **U Pianu de Levie** (open daily 9.30am–7pm; entrance fee), signposted off the D268, 5 km (3 miles) east of Ste-Lucie-de-Tallano, from where a narrow backroad strikes a further 4 km (2½ miles) to the parking field and main entrance. A series of numbered posts guide visitors along the trail, hemmed in by moss-covered oak forest, to the site of the monuments.

Like other, similar fortified settlements, Cucuruzzu, which dates from the 14th century BC, utilises a rocky hilltop to incorporate the natural rock into the structure of the town. The walls are made of huge granite blocks, some of which weigh several tons. Entrance is via a roughly-formed stairway between a huge split rock. It leads past subterranean chambers, casemates, billets, and niches for storing provisions. A walkway leads round to the east side of the fortress to a terrace, which is bounded on one side by the Cyclopean walls of the central monument, surrounded by the cult area.

The chamber is entered through two successive openings framed by huge lintels set on massive vertical rocks that serve as pillars. The interior vaulting is quite ingenious, particularly when one considers that the stones are held in place without any kind of mortar.

Outside, the summit of the monument can be reached by a kind of staircase. From up here the visitor can really appreciate the strategic location of the site. On the eastern extremity of the rocky spur it is possible to make out the basic foundations of the houses of the former village, and also the remains of the fortifications that once surrounded it. In every direction the view stretches far across the *maquis* and forests, valleys and mountains.

A further Cyclopean structure, the **Castellu de Capula**, can be reached either directly from Cucuruzzu (20 minutes) or from the car park. Unlike Cucuruzzu, the site was continuously occupied from the Bronze Age right up to medieval times, when the castle was finally destroyed after a long period of clan warfare in 1259. Archaeological finds from this area can be viewed at the museum in **Lévie** ❺ (Livia), administrative capital of the Alta Rocca, 3 km (2 miles) beyond then turning off the D268 for Cucuruzzu.

Occupying a recently revamped building in the Quartier Pratu, downhill from the main street, the **Musée Départementale** (open Mon–Sat 10am–noon, 2–4.30pm; entrance fee) holds a skeleton of a woman in her mid-30s carbon-dated to 6,570BC; fractures on her legs indicate she must have been disabled and thus cared for, which makes this some of the oldest evidence of social support ever discovered in Europe. The museum's other prize exhibit is an ivory statue of Christ donated by Pope Sixtus V to his home village in the late-16th century.

From Lévie, the D59 plunges steeply downhill through a forest of decaying chestnut trees to the floor of the Fiumicicoli Valley, and then scales the other side

to reach one of the Alta Rocca's remotest settlements, **Carbini** . The Romanesque **San Giovanni Battitista**, on the edge of the village, attests to its religious importance during the Pisan era. Prosper Mérimée oversaw extensive restoration to the chapel in the 19th century, and you can still make out much of the original geometric carving and mythical sculpture lining the walls.

Next to it, a three-storey bell tower with unusual pierced arcades is all that remains of the later **Eglise St-Quilico**, thought to have been the birthplace of the Giovannalani sect who were alleged to have held mass orgies in front of the main altar of the church. In fact the accusations were merely drummed up by the Vatican as an excuse to wipe out the heretics, whose members were hunted down and burned by papal troops on the hillock overlooking Carbini (now surmounted by a commemorative crucifix). Those who escaped were tracked to Ghisoni, where they endured a similar fate *(see page 245)*.

The high Alta Rocca

Overshadowed by the bare, grey granite bones of the watershed, the high Alta Rocca forms a transition zone between the forested river valleys that comprise the region's heart and the mountain wall bounding it to the north. Once free of the tree canopy, the views open up, the air grows clearer and the road verges sprout snow poles.

The most convenient hub for exploring this area is **Zonza** , whose typical stone houses and red terracotta roofs are framed by the awesome backdrop of the Aiguilles ("Needles") de Bavella. The surrounding woodland is criss-crossed by a network of well-marked trails on which visitors can work up an appetite for the village's excellent Corsican cooking.

Still more dramatic hiking is offered 13 km (8 miles) further northeast along the D268, which climbs from Zonza to the spectacular **Col de Bavella** . Presided over by the white-painted statue of Our Lady of the Snows, the pass and its dis-

BELOW: family of hikers, Aiguilles de Bavella.

Map on page 144

tinctive landscape of soaring cliffs and twisted Corsican pines has fascinated travellers since Edward Lear painted it to such dramatic effect at the end of the 19th century. Most people who venture up here these days do so to walk one of the superb trails that penetrate the watershed from the pass; these include the infamous GR20, one of whose most memorable stages threads through the needles. The route – known as the "Variant Alpin" and marked with red and white paint flashes – begins behind the statue of Our Lady.

Five minutes later double yellow lines branch off to the right. If you follow these markers for about two hours you will reach Spire III, which is easy to climb and gives you a good view back across the other two Bavella spires. If you continue to follow the GR20 markers at this stage you will reach the Réfuge d'Asinao, the starting point for climbers with their eye on **Monte Incudine** (2,134 metres/7,006 ft). From here it takes approximately two hours to reach the summit.

Less adventurous travellers not wishing to stray too far from their vehicles may get a taste of the rugged granite landscape of the high watershed by pressing on beyond the Col de Bavella and the tiny summer village of tin-roofed cabins clustered below it. From here, the remaining portion of the D268 begins its spectacular descent to Solenzara – a route often dubbed the most scenic in southern Corsica.

To continue the Alta Rocca tour, however, you should return to Zonza and take the D420, winding westwards around the headwaters of the Rizzanese to pretty **Quenza** ❾, set on a natural balcony overlooking a great expanse of forest.

On its main square, next to a babbling fountain, the **Eglise de St-Georges** harbours an unusual pulpit carved with twisting serpents and a Moor's head – an image thought to symbolise the defeat of the Saracen pirates who raided deep into the region in the late medieval era. The key to the church is kept in the village bar opposite. Erected long before the village is thought to have grown up, possibly to avoid the attentions of the pirates, the

Romanesque chapel of Ste-Marie stands 300 metres (328 yds) southwest on the edge of Quenza. Built around AD 1,000, the building retains its original stone roof tiles and features beautiful 15th-century frescoes inside.

The last, and highest, sizeable settlement in the Alta Rocca is **Aullène** (**Auddé**) ❿, 13 km (8 miles) west of Quenza. Straddling the crossroads of the interior's four main routes, it is well frequented in summer by tourists, most of whom stop to eat at the Hotel de la Poste, housed in a 19th-century coaching inn just off the square.

A short way further up the road, the village church has a chestnut-wood pulpit similar to the one in Quenza, supported by four very finely-carved sea-monsters and a Moor's head. Another interesting feature of this pulpit is the sculpture of a hand holding the Cross, projecting from its right-hand side. The key to the church is held at the Maire – ask at the hotel outside office hours.   ❑

RIGHT: mountain biker cycles past the Aiguilles de Bavella.

Map
on page
152

BONIFACIO

Nowhere in Corsica has been more photographed than this extraordinary clifftop town, whose medieval walls, rising seamlessly from vertical white escarpments, stare across the straits to Sardinia

The only people to start their tour of Corsica at its southernmost tip will be those who arrive by boat, from Sardinia. On the journey over, their eyes will have already grown accustomed to the stunning view of Bonifacio, and they may therefore not be quite so overwhelmed on arrival as visitors who approach by land. But however you get here, you'll feel bound to concur with the sentiments of the French poet Paul Valéry: "as far as sheer beauty is concerned, Bonifacio is the unrivalled capital of Corsica".

The builders of Bonifacio converted this wonderful natural setting into a magnificent theatre stage. The Old Town consists of a small cluster of houses, built on the topmost overhanging ledge of white chalk cliffs, a dizzying 65 metres (200 ft) above the sea. Whether viewed from offshore or from the clifftop promenade, their location on this perch looks decidedly precarious; it seems that almost at any minute they might just drop off the edge. The sea pounds against the cliffs from two sides. In the course of millions of years the waves have eroded the soft chalk. But the town has endured; like a crown, man has triumphantly set it here upon the cliffs as if his sole aim were to stubbornly defy the forces of nature.

But nature didn't only produce the cliff face; behind, it moulded a protected harbour in the form of a 1,600-metre (1-mile) long inlet, where the water remains calm even if there is a storm raging out on the open sea. It is thought that this is the harbour referred to in the *Odyssey* when Odysseus tells of arriving at the fortress called Lamos, which was held by the Laestrygons, and entering a good harbour protected by an unbroken wall of rock with two headlands guarding a narrow entrance. The Greeks were forced to retreat by the Laestrygons; their king was a cannibal and he wanted to have them for his supper.

The Old Town

The **Old Town** can be reached by car by following the winding Avenue Charles de Gaulle. But a more impressive, though less relaxing way, is on foot, via the steps of the **Montée Rastello** Ⓐ that lead up from the harbour. The mighty ramparts above were built by the Genoese in 1195 to thwart any attempts at resistance by the "uncolonisable" locals whom they had banished from the town and replaced with Ligurian families (the little church on the right of the steps is that of the fishermen barred from the town).

Having crossed the avenue Charles de Gaulle, you arrive at the **Col St-Roch** Ⓑ and the natural belvedere which looks over the harbour on one side and out to

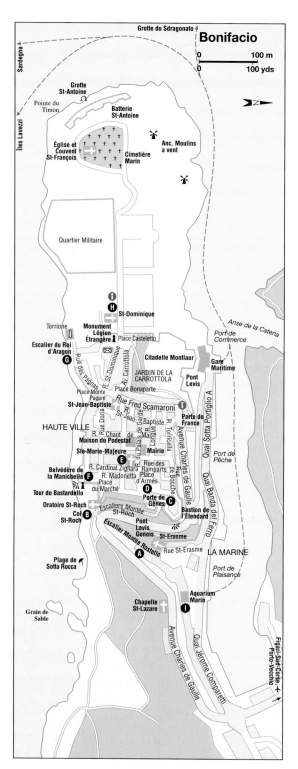

Bonifacio

sea on the other. Towards the south, the green coast of Sardinia can be made out across the narrow Straits of Bonifacio. Italy is only 12 km (7 miles) away. The colour of the sea changes from turquoise blue to emerald green, from cobalt blue to pale aquamarine, then loses itself somewhere in the sandy coloured current.

The view from up here can leave nobody in any doubt about the fact that this channel was created by the sea itself; it simply washed over, broke over and finally tore away the narrow isthmus that once connected Corsica with Sardinia. Islands and islets were created but they too eventually succumbed to the power of the sea. One of the tiny islands remaining is aptly called "Perduto", the lost one. From the Col St Roch, the visitor can continue to savour the view of the sea by following the cliff path towards the Pertusato Lighthouse, a 45 minute walk.

The Old Town itself is entered through the **Porte de Gênes** ⓒ, which until the 19th century was the only gate; the 16th century drawbridge and gates can still be seen. The Ligurian settlers constructed their tall, narrow houses packed next to each other to create a defensive shield. On the **place d'Armes** ⓓ to the right of the gate are the plinths of the four grain silos that provisioned the inhabitants during times of siege. The town's most testing time came in 1553 when it was besieged from the sea by the French and Turks under the command of the notorious corsair Dragut, with the Corsican freedom fighter Sampiero Corso mounting a rearguard action from the landward side. The Bonifacciens held out, but the siege was a waste of time because the whole island was handed back to the Genoese in 1559. This all occurred at the time when Henri II of France was waging war with Charles V of the Holy Roman Empire. The emperor himself had actually once stayed in Bonifacio: on returning from his campaign in Algeria in 1541, he was driven to these shores by a storm. Count Filippo of Bonifacio, who was known locally as Il Alto Bello, offered the emperor his

Map
on page
152

house as lodgings, and presented him with his favourite horse to ride. The story goes that when the emperor departed, the count had the unfortunate animal killed because nobody else should mount his steed once the emperor had sat on it.

Napoleon's sojourn in Bonifacio is recalled by a plaque on the house in which he stayed. At that time he was the commander of the second batallion of Corsican Volunteers, and laid siege to the tiny Italian islands off Sardinia, which he intended to capture for France. It was here that Napoleon sampled his first bitter taste of defeat.

Generations of builders added their own touches to the town. Beautiful patrician houses with balustrades, and arcades with splendid portals and loggias testify to the wealth of their former owners. The magic of the old streets is compounded by the arches which span the alleys from one house to another. Many of the houses in the Old Town bear the patina of age; some have fallen into complete decay.

However, since central government in Paris declared Bonifacio a "national monument" and offered cheap grants to the house owners, a great deal of restoration has taken place; some of the old palazzi have been returned to their former splendour. The attraction of the town as an international tourist destination has also encouraged the locals to do the place up a bit. But Bonifacio's essential character is still there; a certain amount of dull-pink, morbid decadence remains to remind one of the fact that we are still in Corsica, in Europe's beautiful, if somewhat sleepy south.

Sights in the Old Town include the **Eglise Ste-Marie-Majeure** Ⓔ in the rue du Corps de Garde which was begun by the Pisans in the 12th century and subsequently refashioned in Gothic style by the Genoese. Meetings of local notables used to be held in the large loggia in front, which was also where proclamations were made and justice dispensed. The palace of the ruling magistrate was situated directly

ᴇʟᴏᴡ:
ᴠiew over the
ᴘoftops to
ᴛᴇe tower of
ᴛ-Dominique.

Necropolises

The cemetery at Bonifacio lies next to the Church of St Francis, perched high above the sea at the far end of the limestone plateau. As you enter, you will feel transported to a miniature city outside the main town. The tombs stand cheek by jowl, their roofs surmounted by gables topped by a cross. A place of rest, deaf to the roaring of the surf at the foot of the cliffs – and also a mirror-image of life on this side of the grave. The tombstones tell of how the deceased must once have lived. If they were rich, stone edifices of hewn granite or white stuccoed walls soar heavenwards. Sometimes a mausoleum has been built in the shape of an elegant villa or perhaps to resemble a sacred monument, almost a cathedral in miniature. If it is open you can peer in at free-standing sarcophagi adorned with wreaths of pearls. On the graves of the less well-to-do, a massive stone slab, sometimes carved, declares who has been laid to rest below. If the dead

man was poor, his burial place will be marked by a simple wooden cross, sometimes decorated and simply pushed into the ground, or one of iron, its arms rusted by the salty sea breeze which wafts across the memories, along the frequently abandoned footpaths, caressing the pine trees, its wailings echoing like an eternal prayer. For Corsicans, as for other Romance peoples, death was never a tragic moment in which a loved one passed over into what they hoped would be a better life beyond. Death was a constant companion on this island where tragedies were a daily occurrence. Death is a familiar figure. He is feared because the ancient spell of Corsica has always waged war against the *imbuscata*, the evil with which the dead can curse the living. And yet, death is also honoured. Death is never far away, recalled in monuments both simple and grand. Apart from the many isolated tombs on the island, standing in solitude by the wayside or even in the middle of the macchia, each community has its own *campu santu*, its *cimteriu*: a place of respect, a place where the living recall the dead. It is a meeting place where Corsicans indulge their memories. But the dead are not only present here. Islanders believe they exert an invisible influence on the living. Until recently, death was to be heard in the *lamenti*, the moving dirges; it also formed the main theme of traditional folk poetry, and it gave rise to superstitions. The cemeteries along the Mediterranean, formerly avoided because of its perils and the infertile soils of the coastal margin, are more recent than those in the interior. The Corsicans seldom turned towards the sea. Apart from the residents of Cap Corse, the islanders preferred the mountain valleys, where they found protection and safety. Only in the vicinity of the towns built by the Genoese or near the settlements built during the 19th century will you find necropolises beside the sea, facing out across the water. In the past, towns like Bastia, Ajaccio, Calvi and Bonifacio, whose Genoese pedigree explains their fortifications, buried their dead in such a way that there was no contact between the two worlds on either side of the grave. But by ensuring that the cemetery lay not too far from the town they still gave their heirs the chance of honouring the dead with their presence. ❑

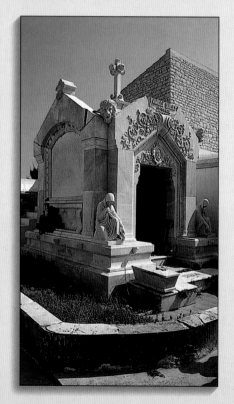

LEFT: Corsican people believe in the *imbuscata* – the evil with which the dead can curse the living.

Map on page 152

opposite. The church contains a Roman sarcophagus from the 3rd century and, above it, a beautifully sculpted Genoese tabernacle representing the torso of Christ.

An ivory and ebony casket said to have contained the relics of St Boniface is kept in the sacristy, together with the relic of the True Cross which used to be carried up to the **Belvédère de la Manichella** ⑥, 65 metres (213 ft) above the waves. Here the waves were blessed in the hope of bringing calm. And here on this very same terrace once stood a certain first-lieutenant Bonaparte; he had just been defeated by his enemies, but was madly in love.

From the belvedere, backtrack to rue Doria and keep left at the fork to reach the head of the **Escalier du Roi d'Aragon** ⑥ (open daily 11am–5.30pm; entrance fee), a staircase of 187 steps leading from the cliff edge to the waterside. The *escalier* is often erroneously said to have been the work of the King of Aragon, who is supposed to have cut it from the chalk during a siege in 1420, but in fact it's

considerably older and was probably used centuries before that by townsfolk to reach a well.

Until 1963, the **Citadel** at the western end of the promontory was the main garrison of the Foreign Legion, and so could not be visited. Although there is still a military presence, it is now possible to walk right to the end and to visit the two old windmills as well as the ruins of the **Franciscan Monastery** and the Church of St-François.

The **Church of St-Dominique** ⑥ on the south side of the Citadelle was begun in 1270 by the Knights Templar and completed by the Dominicans in 1343. The pillars of the nave are decorated with delicate paintings of the *Fifteen Mysteries of the Rosary* and there is also a particularly fine *Resurrection* and a wonderful *Descent from the Cross*. The 800-kg (1,763-lb) wooden sculpture *Martyre de St-Barthélémy* is carried in the Good Friday procession. Tradition has it that St Bartholomew was flayed alive while

BELOW: sundowners at the harbourside.

working as a missionary in Armenia, and the sculpture depicts the infidels fulfilling their gruesome task.

The harbour

The centre of the action in Bonifacio is undoubtedly the **harbour**. There are bistros and restaurants, souvenir shops and smart boutiques, a number of bars and the odd hotel, as well as the **Aquarium Marin ❶** (open 10am–8.30pm; entrance fee) stocked with local fish (which are all released at the end of each season). Boats to neighbouring Sardinia leave the harbour just about every hour.

Providing many of the inhabitants with a secure income, tourism has become the mainstay of the local economy. In recent years, fisheries, wine cultivation and the cork industry have suffered a noticeable decline. Many of the fishermen now work on pleasure launches during the summer season and the local fishing boats have now become crowded out by luxury yachts. The nicest time of day to

stroll along the quayside is the evening, just before dusk, when the last of the boats have berthed and the area is a hive of activity.

A couple of decades ago, things were much quieter here, although the place was always popular. You sat on hard benches at wooden tables and enjoyed crayfish, bouillabaisse and all kinds of seafood, the specialities of the few bistros down on the waterfront. Much has now changed; for want of space, restaurants have leeched into the old town. But crayfish remains the very special delicacy of Bonifacio. They live – as long as they are allowed to live – in the underwater caves beneath the cliffs and are served freshly caught. But as demand now outstrips supply, extra live crayfish also have to be flown in from further afield.

With its rugged chalk coast, Bonifacio has very little to offer in terms of paradise beaches. The best beach lies 10 km (7 miles) to the north, along Corsica's flat east coast. The Golfe de Porto-Vecchio has some of the best beaches on the island (*see page 160*) and has become a prime holiday destination.

During the daytime, a flotilla of **excursion boats** depart from the harbour on sightseeing trips. These vary from short 45-minute jaunts to nearby *calanaches* (inlets) and *grottes marines* (sea caves), famed for the play of light on their walls, to longer crossings to the **Iles Lavezzi**.

Chief among the landmarks of this deserted archipelago, nowadays protected as a nature reserve, is the **Cimetière de l'Achiariono** on the main island of Lavezzi itself, where victims of the 1855 sinking of the *Sémillante* are buried. All 773 crew and passengers on board the ship, which was carrying troops to the Crimean War, perished after the vessel ran aground in a fierce storm – the worst ever disaster in the maritime history of the Mediterranean. Most were placed in unmarked graves, their bodies having been so badly disfigured by the battering of the sea. A stone pyramid on the tip of the island stands as a memorial. The island is home to many rare species of wild flower. ❑

LEFT: Bonifacio's harbour. **RIGHT:** the Bastion de l'Etendard towering over the Marina.

Map on page 152

Map on page 160

BONIFACIO TO PORTO-VECCHIO

Transluscent turquoise water and perfect white sand are the hallmarks of Corsica's far southeast, whose coastline is backed by low maquis dotted with well preserved Torréen ruins

Except in summer when its coastline is deluged by holidaymakers, the far southeast corner of Corsica, between Bonifacio and Porto-Vecchio, is among Corsica's least-populated regions. The strong, salt-laden winds that blow in off the Straits of Bonifacio scour the coastal lowlands, where the scrub is dense and cultivable ground a rarity. Inland, the Massif de l'Ospédale marks the southernmost extension of the central range, its rocky slopes scarred by patches of charred forest – this is a prime area for bushfires, and Canadair sea planes swooping down to dump loads of water on to plumes of smoke is an all too common sight in hot, dry weather.

Regional history

Human settlement of this remote, exposed region dates back more than 6,000 years, and a crop of particularly prominent Torréen *castelli* dating from the 2nd millennium BC have led to speculation that the warlike agriculturalists responsible for some of the Mediterranean's most impressive prehistoric monuments first colonised these southeast plains before pressing northwest.

In later centuries, malaria rendered the lowlands virtually uninhabitable: transhumant shepherds would descend here in winter when the mosquitos had died off, but follow the receding snowline north in the spring. Some of the first farmers who braved the spectre of annual fevers to dwell here permanently did so in order to escape a bloody vendetta in the mountains – their descendents still account for the bulk of the population of the villages scattered around the skirts of the mountains hereabouts.

The arrival of the Genoans in the 13th century saw the emergence of both Bonifacio and Porto-Vecchio as important mercantile centres, with a thriving trade in cork and wine. Malaria, however, eventually got the better of them too, and the region struggled economically until the US army's DDT programme in 1947 rendered the sunny shoreline safe for tourist development.

Thanks to the mighty chalk cliffs fringing the far south, the beaches around Bonifacio are on the whole disappointing. The same, however, could not be said of the coastline further north, which boasts some of the finest, whitest sand and bluest water in the whole Mediterranean.

As a result, development has made a greater impact here than elsewhere, with numerous holiday villages, large-scale campsites and villa complexes to accommodate the annual invasion of affluent Italians. To experience the seashore between Bonifacio and Porto-Vecchio at

its best, therefore, it best to arrange a visit which does not coincide with the Italian tradition of the *grandes vacances*.

The beaches

Scything northeast across a swath of wind-stunted *maquis* scattered with dry-stone farmhouses and boulder outcrops, RN198 is the far southeast's main artery. Around 14 km (9 miles) north of Bonifacio, a roadside hoarding flags the turning for **Plage de Rondinara** ❶, an extraordinary shell-shaped cove lined with gleaming silver sand. Aerial photos of the bay adorn postcard racks across the island, but it lies sufficiently far from the main road to escape severe overcrowding, even at peak season. Behind the bay, a well equipped campsite provides the area's only ammenities.

The next beach north, **Plage de Santa Giulia** ❷, would be Corsica's most beautiful were it not for the existence of a large holiday campus overlooking it, which ensures that the exquisite white sand is jammed with people all summer long. All the same, it's well worth a visit just to experience the unbelievably turquoise water, which wouldn't look out of place in the Seychelles.

Keep heading north for 3 km (2 miles), and you'll come to the turning for another exceptionally picturesque strand, **Plage de Palombaggia** ❸. Ranks of umbrella pines fringe the dunes here, and the translucent water is studded with distinctive red rocks, but the beach, lying within easy reach of Porto-Vecchio, is far from a secret. To sidestep the crowds, stroll south to the quieter **Asciaghju beach**, where there's a simple campsite but little else.

Ceccia and Tappa

For those who prefer not to spend their time in the water or on the beach, a pair of Torréen *castellu* sites provide a worthwhile detour away from the *route nationale*: opposite the turning for Palombaggia, look for a lane cutting inland. This will bring you out after around 3 km (2 miles) at the tiny hamlet of **Ceccia** ❹, 5 km (3 miles) southwest of Porto-Vecchio

on the D859, where a single tower was erected between 1500 and 1350 BC on a conspicuous spur. You have to clamber up a steep path from the village to reach the crest, from where the views over the scrubland and hills inland are appropriately atmospheric.

One kilometre (½ mile) further southwest down the D859, the larger *castellu* complex at **Tappa** ❺ (open all year; free) rises from a low hillock, ten minutes' walk from the main road on private farmland . A ramp gives access to the largest structure here, in which several chambers yielded pottery, grindstones and tools when excavated in the 1970s, suggesting that the building was used for milling as well as storage. This area southwest of the Golfe de Porto-Vecchio is thought to have been the one first colonised by the enigmatic Torréens *(see page 22)*.

Porto-Vecchio

The Golfe de Porto-Vecchio possesses some of the best beaches on the island and

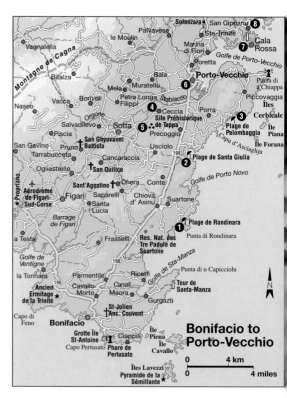

Bonifacio to Porto-Vecchio

Map
on page
160

for this reason the area has been a prime holiday destination for decades. There is something for everyone here: campsites and nude bathing, marinas, club villages, holiday villages, hotels, small pensions, as well as private accommodation; and all looking out over a deep blue sea that is seldom too rough.

It's hard to believe that once upon a time this stretch of coast was swampland. When Genoa developed the natural harbour and built its first fortress on top of a mighty cliff of porphyritic rock, the entire garrison was wiped out by disease within ten years. That was in the year 1539. Before the Genoese, Greek seafarers had settled here, and even earlier the Torréens. But they all succumbed to the anopheles mosquito, whose breeding grounds were also the breeding grounds of malaria.

The only people who knew how to survive in these parts were the Corsicans themselves, accustomed as they were to the prevailing conditions. In summer they left the coast and lived in the hills above the gulf, not returning until the autumn. It was only after World War II that malaria was finally irradicated. After that the door was open to all.

In the summer the narrow streets of **Porto-Vecchio** ❻ (population 8,000) are teeming with visitors. Founded in 1539 and set on a hill, the town was set up as a Genoese stronghold. A third of Corsica's wine is exported from here, but the town's top priority is shopping and tourism. The only historical attraction worth seeing is the fragments of well-preserved walls encircling the medieval centre, whose narrow streets are still lined with their original Genoan tenements. Apart from that, the town is dominated by the creations of the booming tourist industry – supermarkets, petrol stations and holiday apartments – although the modern marina is lined with pleasant cafés serving good food.

North of Porto-Vecchio

North and east of Porto-Vecchio, the gulf shelters a string of secluded upscale developments, frequently opening on to their own private coves of orange sand. The villa belt culminates at **Cala Rossa** ❼, a picture-postcard pretty spot where one of Corsica's smartest hotels overlooks a gorgeous reddish sand beach sheltered by mature pine trees.

A less exclusive atmosphere prevails further north on the D468 at **San Ciprianu** ❽, a large crescent of white sand backed by a *village de vacance*. The pick of the beaches in this area, however, has to be the **Plage de Pinarellu**, another 7 km (4 miles) north. From the foot of a stately old Genoan watchtower, a bay of vivid white sand and turquoise sea arcs to a wooded headland. Due to its easy accessibility from the *route nationale*, overcrowding can be a problem here during the summer, in which case, head south through the pine forest backing the beach towards the fancy three-star site *Camping Le California*, which flanks a scenic but much less fequented cove that's popular mainly with nudists from the neighbouring *centre nudiste*. ❑

BELOW:
fishing boats
moored outside
Porto-Vecchio.

Map
on page
166

THE WEST COAST:
AJACCIO TO CALVI

*Surging straight out of a cobalt-blue sea, the red porphyry cliffs and
mountains of the west coast form one of the island's defining landscapes,
at their most dramatic amid the contorted rocks of the Calanche de Piana*

Corsica's west coast is one of the finest pieces of natural landscape in the entire Mediterranean. Popular subjects for photographers along the coast road from Ajaccio to Calvi include: the strange-looking red rocks known as Les Calanques (the Calanche), at Piana; the deep rocky bay at Porto, with its old watchtower; the fishing village of Girolata, which can still only be reached either by water or on foot even today; and last but not least, the view of the town of Calvi from the heights above.

The coastline is markedly jagged, with rocky outcrops enclosing broad bays where good swimming beaches can almost always be found. Best equipped with holiday amenities is the huge Golfe de Sagone, while the narrow Golfe de Porto is also a popular destination for excursions. The high mountains nearby are always part of the dramatic landscape; their white peaks stand out against the sky until well into May each year, and their vast tracts of forest are easily and quickly accessible from the coast.

Sagone and Vico

The road from Ajaccio starts off by going inland, and it isn't until the top of the **Col de San Bastiano** that there is the first really good view of the sea. The road then leads down from the pass into the broad **Golfe de Sagone**, where three small rivers meet the coast. Between them, the ranges of hills extend down towards the coast, finishing as promontories surmounted by watchtowers, and dividing the gulf into several small bays.

The landscape here consists of *maquis* up on the hills, farmland in the fertile river-valley plains, vineyards and olive plantations here and there on the valley slopes. The villages, though, can only be

seen in the distance, situated high up, away from the coast. The coastal strip is an area that was freed from the danger of malaria only relatively recently, and its fine sandy beaches, rather than its fertile flood plains, are the real reason for any housing development taking place here now.

Hotels, shops, bars and apartments are a distinctive feature of **Sagone ❶**, and the smaller town of **Tiuccia** nearby seems to have similar aspirations. From the southernmost of the bays, with its beach, a detour leads upwards along the River Liscia into the **Cinarca**, once ruled by the mighty counts of the same name, whose castle overlooked their domain from a

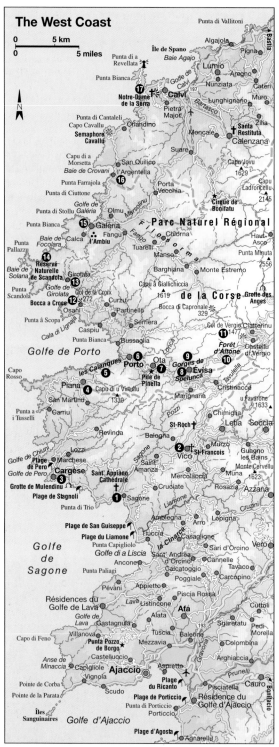

The West Coast

0   5 km
0   5 miles

hill top. The farmers also settled high up in the valley here, and laid out terraced fields below their villages.

If winding roads don't bother you, try doing a round trip inside the Liscia basin along the smaller back roads, from **Sari d'Orcino** to **Ambiegna**, then on to **Casaglione**, past the ruins of the Castello Capraia – seat of the counts of Cinarca – and then back down to the coast again.

Another worthwhile detour leads to **Vico ❷**, historically the most important town in the area. The road curves out of the Sagone Valley and up through *maquis*-covered hills and forests to the Col de St-Antoine, a former junction of traffic routes. Behind it lies the old town of Vico, overlooking the valley and surrounded by forest. The bishopric was moved here from Sagone for a while, when the coast fell victim first to the Saracens and then to malaria. The town still looks serious and dignified today, with its tall, grey houses.

A short distance from here is the former Franciscan monastery, now inhabited once again by monks, who will gladly show you round the church. Today, on the site of historic Sagone, the former bishopric, only the ruins of its cathedral remain. A menhir statue was used in the foundation wall.

Cargèse to Porto

The most interesting place along the Golfe de Sagone is where a tiny, narrow valley faces out towards the sea, with two churches up on the ridges on each side of it, facing each other. Together they form the centre of the small town of **Cargèse ❸**, which stretches away behind them on a small plateau above the steep cliffs. The "gulf" separating the two churches is symbolic, too: one of them is Roman Catholic and the other Greek Orthodox.

Cargèse was founded in the 18th century by Greek refugees from Turkish rule. These days, its protective power is no longer Genoa but France, and the oath of loyalty it once swore to Genoa is now merely symbolic, in the shape of

Map
on page
166

the flag kept in the church and used during processions. An arrangement was swiftly made between the Greeks and the Catholics in Cargèse, and anyone who visits Corsica in springtime can witness a very colourful combined Easter Monday celebration, in which both confessions take part. The **Greek church** is definitely worth a visit. The interior is incredibly impressive, and some of the icons are masterpieces – the refugees brought them from their homeland. Cargèse, by the way, with its hotels, restaurants and shops is also a very pleasant place to stay. Delicious seafood is served at the restaurants down in the small harbour. Swimming and beach life takes place in the bays some distance away from the town; those who prefer seclusion can find it out along the rocky headlands.

For many people, the Golfe de Porto is the main reason for Corsica's reputation as the "isle of beauty". It's true that some of the views here sometimes make people forget that they are driving – which is particularly dangerous considering the number of bends along this stretch of road. The reddish colour of the rocks here is at its most vivid and striking, standing out starkly against the deep blue of the sea, and there are many fascinating variants of it, ranging from the bizarre formations of the Calanche to the red houses, built from the local rock.

The coast road goes past the outskirts of **Piana** ❹, and most tourists, with only the Calanche and Porto on their minds, tend to drive straight past – much to the advantage of this village, which has thus succeeded in remaining unspoiled. Men wearing peaked caps sit chatting in front of the cafés in the little village square.

Piana is built on a rocky spur 400 metres (1,300 ft) up, overlooking the sea. A small road winds down to a small beach, but it's actually a better idea to enjoy the view of the sea and the rocky coastline from above. Some of the houses here could have come straight from a picture postcard. The late 18th-century church here is the venue for an Easter Granitola procession.

Les Calanques ❺ (the Calanche, *see page 171*) , are unusual wind-eroded porphyry of vivid red and orange colours. It is best to view the rock formations on foot, but part of it can be seen from the D81. In the morning sun the Calanche have yellow-orange tones, which turn to red by the time the sun begins to set, and then fade to violet as the sun sinks below the horizon.

A narrow valley, almost a ravine, in the red rock; the mouth of a small river; a pebble beach; and a natural harbour. They all contribute to the picturesque beauty of **Porto** ❻. Before the tourists arrived this is all Porto was: a small harbour, where the village of Ota, a bit further upstream, kept its boats. The people of Ota, prosperous and keen on tradition, have not simply left tourism to its own devices here, but have successfully kept one eye on the architectural planning. Even if the odd modern hotel here may look just a little too box-like, at least its colour suits the general appearance of the place.

If you want to avoid the crowds here it

BELOW: view of the town of Porto and the beach.

is a good idea to visit outside the tourist season when it becomes a serious problem. A rocky promontory with a Genoese tower on top divides the bay into two sections. To the south there is the pebble beach, the mouth of the river, and a eucalyptus grove which until recently was a three-star camping area.

On the other side of the outcrop is the business centre of this tourist resort. The connecting road between the coastal route and the town centre is lined with even more shops and hotels: a good place for a stroll. At the base of the restored Genoese Tower, the new **aquarium** (open June–Aug daily 10am–10pm; entrance fee) displays various fish of the gulf.

Inland from Porto

Ota ❼, 6 km (3½ miles) further inland, is a world away from the busy holiday atmosphere on the coast. The people who come here tend to arrive with rucksacks and walking boots, and find their kindred spirits either at the hiking hostels *(gîtes d'étape)* or in the bar-restaurants, which serve definitive local mountain cuisine. Ota marks the end of one of the most popular hiking routes on the island.

It begins in the mountain village of **Évisa** ❽ and leads through **Les Gorges de Spelunca** ❾, in which several streams join together to form the Porto River. The walk isn't difficult at all as long as you wear sturdy shoes and have some water. Bring your swimming gear, too, because there are some very inviting places to bathe en route. The path, which leads down through the *maquis* for nearly 700 metres (2,300 ft), should be taken in fine weather: in the rain it quickly becomes slippery. Evisa is situated exactly between the sea and the mountains, and is no more than a stone's throw from either, making it a popular base for tourists keen on combining a swimming with a hiking holiday.

The road, lined with hotels and unpretentious restaurants, carries on up through the **Forêt d'Aïtone** ❿ to the **Col de Vergio** ⓫ (1,477 metres/4,800 ft) mountain.

BELOW: view from the coast road to Porto.

Map
on page
166

This beautiful forest is made up of tall Laricio pines with walking trails between the trees, and you will spot different varieties of local wildlife including eagles and sparrowhawks. Sightings of the wild ghjattu volpe (cat-fox), a large cat which lives high in the mountains, is very rare.

There are several fine views to be had from Evisa out across the valley containing the Gorges de Spelunca, with Ota, huddled on its steep slope, and the sea in the far distance. The way down into the Spelunca gorges begins at the cemetery in Evisa and ends at an old Genoese stone bridge. There are some fine places to swim and many visitors spend the day here.

The far northwest

There are more fine opportunities to photograph Porto and its bay as the drive continues along the coast road. The next feature of interest is the **Bocca a Croce ⓬**, a rocky spur overgrown with *maquis* dropping steeply down to the sea. From here one can also catch a glimpse of part

of the magnificently isolated coastal village of **Girolata ⓭**. It really is: no roads lead to it at all, apart from a hot and dusty mule track. But in the mornings in the summer season, one excursion boat after the other moors there, and its two fishermen's bars have now become wood-lined restaurants with terraces. Situated on a promontory and dominated by the coastal hills and its very own Genoese watchtower, this small coastal village still retains its own special charm. The boat trips along this stretch of coast from Porto, Calvi and Cargése provide glimpses of several other completely inaccessible bays, all of them forming part of the 700-sq.-km (270-sq.-mile) **Réserve Naturelle de Scandola ⓮**.

Created in 1975, the sanctuary protects a rich array of rare wildlife and plantlife, including 450 types of seaweed, which thrive here because of the water's exceptional clarity, and the much prized red gorgonian coral, these days harvested according to strict quotas for the local

BELOW: the village of Girolata.

jewellery trade. Dolphins and seals are also to be found. Bobbing around the base of the massive red cliffs, you might also sight an osprey nesting on an inaccessible pinnacle, peregrine falcons and their favourite prey, blue rock thrushes.

The coast road only skirts the edge of the Scandola reserve. It is a lonely stretch, punctuated by numerous bends. The next place on the coast is **Galéria** , a village that has opened up to tourism only recently. The centre of the village is still very much intact, and the street leading up to the church, lined with shops and houses several storeys high, projects an astonishingly prosperous image for such a remote place. Galéria is traditionally connected with the pastures high up in the Niolu. The sheep used to graze throughout the winter in the green countryside inland from the gulf; in summer they would then move up to the high mountains.

Long journeys like these belong to the past, however, for far fewer sheep are now reared on Corsica, and transferring animals to new pastures in trucks is safer and simpler. Demand for Corsican ewe's cheese has risen a lot over the past few years because of tourism, and since the selection is limited the prices tend to be pretty high. It's still well worth taking some home, though.

The fishing village down by the beach is also part of Galéria, and the seafood restaurant right next to the beach is popular among those in the know. A stretch of the old transhumance track that used to lead up into the Fango Valley has been converted into a section of the **Tra Mare e Monti** hiking route *(see page 252)*, which winds up the northwest coast from Cargèse to Calvi. The little river is framed by low-lying red cliffs, and here and there they form attractive bathing pools; the evergreen shrubs here are not the thorny variety, either. A good, old-fashioned *gîte d'étape* lies right on the route at **Tuarelli**, with its own *piscine naturelle*.

From Galéria the route now leads northwards again right above the coast before entering human habitation again at **L'Argentella** . This is a very odd place: half beach resort, half ghost town. It was named after a silver mine that closed years ago, and this adds a touch of adventure as far as campers are concerned: they can go off silver prospecting on the campsite.

The last section of the coastal route leads through the "Balagne Déserte", so named to distinguish it from its more fertile counterpart further to the east, the "Balagne" proper. It is indeed a desolate landscape, devoid of all human habitation, part *maquis*, part bare rock. Driving conditions are easier on the newly surfaced road inland, which is joined by turning right just after the bridge over the Fango River.

Doing this, though, does involve missing a highlight which the coast road has been keeping as a kind of farewell present: a small road leads off in the direction of **Notre-Dame de la Serra** . This tiny chapel is situated on top of a rocky knoll, and affords a very impressive panoramic view for miles around, with the citadel in Calvi right in the middle. ❏

BELOW: cycling through the Gorges de Spelunca.

Map on page 166

The Calanche

Recent research suggests that the islands of Corsica and Sardinia are not, as was once supposed, the remains of a separate Tyrrhenian block, but a part of the granite massive of Southern France that drifted away from the main mass and came to rest in its present position during the Tertiary period. And indeed, the type of red granite which so impressively dominates the landscape of the Estérel hills to the west of Cannes on the Côte d'Azur can also be seen along some stretches of the Corsican coast.

In other areas, however, it appears that the granite block of Corsica has undergone its own special geomorphological development. The most spectacular and best known example is the **Calanche of Piana**. Here the forces of nature have moulded the granite and porphyry just like a sculptor. Smooth columns and pillars alternate with hideously gnarled forms, grotesque faces, animal-like features and sharp profiles. The kind of erosion that has taken place here can hardly be found anywhere else the world, and can be explained by the special crystal structure of the rock created by particularly rapid cooling. As far as the variety of forms are concerned, these are further highlighted by the light that penetrates the cliffs. What might resemble a face in the morning can easily have turned into an animal form by the time evening comes around. The colours also change with the time of day. The morning sun produces yellow-orange tones, which turn to red by the time the sun begins to set, and then fade to violet and as it sinks beneath the horizon.

Trail maps can be obtained in Piana, although the routes are so clearly marked that there is little danger of ever slipping or falling. The approaches to the cliffs are marked by the Tête du Chien (Dog's Head) in the north and the bridge Pont de Mezanu in the south. Each is served by a car park. The third starting point is the Roches Bleues in between, which, although poor for parking, does offer a magnificent view from the bar. The most popular trail leads from the Tête du Chien to the Chateau Fort, a cliff formation above the coast. While it offers good views of the cliffs and the sea, it doesn't really penetrate the chaotic labyrinth of the Calanche itself. But it is still a walk worth taking, particularly in the springtime when all the fresh vegetation compounds the colour spectacle. Indeed, on all routes it would be a shame to allow the splendour of the rock scenery to totally detract from the surrounding flora: in addition to the variety of orchids, there is the rare alpine violet, a kind of clove; the heaths of fragrant rosemary will also delight the senses.

The second of the short routes leads along the top between the Tête du Chien and the Roches Bleues, although you'll actually get better views if you start at the Roches Bleues. Opposite the bar begins a route with a number of possible variants: the northern one is the easiest while the southern one provides the most dramatic scenery.

Here it is also possible to join the long route which runs all the way to the east as far as the summit of the Capu d'Orto – a memorable walk affording one of the island's finest panoramas. ❑

Map on page 174

CALVI AND THE BALAGNE

*Against a backdrop of snow-topped peaks, the fortress town of Calvi
provides an exotic base for trips into the northwest corner of the island,
where stone villages tumble from the feet of massive grey escarpments*

On Corsica's northwestern coastline, nature has created several areas resembling huge natural theatres, with broad dress circles, narrow stalls, bold balconies and a stage opening out onto the broad expanse of the Mediterranean and mainland Europe beyond. And to cap all these geographical set pieces, whenever there is a change in the weather the snowy peaks of the Alps come into view at the very rear of the picture. The white and yellow ferries only have 180 km (112 miles) of water to cross between Nice and the protected harbours of the Balagne's two main towns, Calvi and l'Ile Rousse – a far shorter distance than the one that brought Columbus immortality, but local legend has it that the Genoese explorer was born in the citadel in Calvi.

A cosmopolitan resort

Calvi ❶, which was already promoting itself as a cosmopolitan beach resort when St-Tropez, on the opposite shore, was still a sleepy little fishing village, is the heart of the Balagne. During wintertime, which actually resembles nothing more than one long, drawn-out March, the pace of life here is leisurely.

The many sunny moments of these quiet months combine just about everything that is attractive about the island and its rather old-fashioned charm: the glittering sea, the curving beach, devoid of people once more, the pine-groves behind it and then the foothills gradually sloping upwards, with their oaks and olives, their barren-looking, aromatic *maquis*, their distant villages halfway up the mountainside and above them a chain of 2,000-metre (6,500-ft) mountain peaks, whose snowy summits change colour as the day goes by, progressing from freezing blue to pristine white, then yellow, and then finally a red shimmer in the setting sun. A sense of cosy tranquillity then descends

over the imposing fortress, a contrefort further inland and the **Chapelle de la Madonna di a Serra**, situated just on the bend of the town's main street, which stays busy late into the evening.

Calvi's nearby airport brings a lot more visitors to the town than its rather impractical harbour ferry. Even when tourists are already occupying every other chair outside the cafés along the quays during the off-peak season, and a jazz festival at the beginning of June is already providing a foretaste of the crush to come, there are still a huge number of spare seats outside the cafés of l'Ile Rousse, Algajola and Galeria. The terraces outside the bars and bistros, situated next to a narrow one-way street and extending as far as the fisher-

LEFT: fishing boat in the marina at Calvi.
RIGHT: Calvi's old town.

men's nets right by the water's edge, are set up on a recently re-made traditional pavement and sheltered by sunshades.

During the peak summer months, this tiny coastal resort is filled with the kind of frantic activity favoured by the hordes of tourists that descend on it from France and Italy. Nowhere is free of it, not even the bungalows and campsites right out on the edge of the town.

Calvi's hinterland

The Balagne Déserte, situated only a few minutes' drive to the south of Calvi, could not be more of a contrast. It begins just beyond the promontory called the **Punta di a Revellata**, which extends far into the gulf. Prince Pierre Bonaparte, a nephew of Napoleon, sought isolation here once, a little further inland. After his cousin Charles Louis had become Prince-Président and then the Emperor Napoleon III, thus destroying any political ambition he may once have possessed, Prince Pierre had the castle of **La Torre Mozza** built in the

middle of the *maquis* for himself and his mistress. Women carried the building materials on their heads – including, for the record, a bathtub from Marseilles – from a jetty up into the hills. Today, even the ruins of this erstwhile dream of a life lived close to nature still have a rather royal atmosphere about them.

In the rear stalls of the huge natural theatre in which Calvi itself occupies the royal box, and the landing strip of **Ste-Catherine** airport forms the centre aisle, the dress circle area rises steeply. Behind it is another, smaller but still dramatic arena: the **Cirque de Bonifatu ❷**, a spectacular opening into the heart of the watershed range which can be reached by car via the D251.

With sheer cliffs soaring on both sides, the road winds up a steepening valley to its end at **Bonifatu**, where a welcoming *auberge-gîte d'étape* provides hearty Corsican specialities on a sunny terrace for the crowds of hikers who pass through. A network of well cleared and marked trails

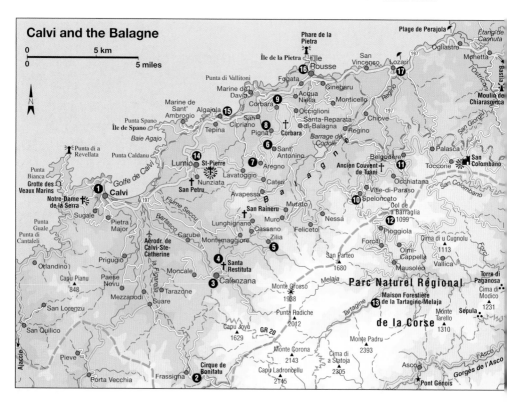

Calvi and the Balagne

Map on page 174

criss-crosses the pristine holm oak and pine forests lining the valley to the high ridges above, offering several inspiring day walks.

The trailhead for Corsica's most famous long-distance treks, the GR20 and Tra Mare e Monti, lies due north of Bonifatu in **Calenzana** ❸, stretched out at the foot of Monte Grosso. The dead straight D151 cuts across the coastal plain from Calvi to this, the largest village in the Balagne, whose small hotels, *gîte d'étape* and restaurants are kept busy from May until mid-October.

Once the daily exodus of walkers has clumped into the sunrise, a peaceful place to watch village life go by is the café on the main square, whose terrace is set opposite the impressive **Eglise St-Blaise**. An inscription on the belltower relates to the famous battle fought here in 1732 when German mercenaries, hired by the Genoese to help put down the Corsican revolt, were slaughtered by the locals. Some say that they did it with pitchforks

and spades alone; others that they opened their beehives and stung the enemy before finishing them off with knives.

Strung along the base of Monte Grosso at an altitude of roughly 300 metres (984 ft), a necklace of villages presides over the belt of olive groves beyond Calenzana, joined together by the D151. First stop on this scenic route should be the **Chapelle de Santa Restituta** ❹, just under a couple of kilometres (3 miles) out of the village. Although rebuilt several times since its original construction in the Pisan era, the chapel retains an 11th-century nave and, in its crypt, a 4th-century marble sarcophagus holding the remains of the martyr St Restitude, who was beheaded in AD 303 in Calvi. The medieval frescoes that formerly adorned the casket are also displayed. If the church is locked, ask for the key as the little *tabac* just below the square in Calenzana.

Zilia ❺, the next village along the road, is an olive-growing centre that has been enjoying a new lease of life as the source

ELOW: typical ive grove in e Balagne.

of one of the island's premier brands of mineral water, tapped at a factory on its outskirts. This area is also connected with the real-life Don Juan, Miguel de Leca y Colonna y Manara y Vincentello: his father came from Calvi and his mother from **Montemaggiore**, a few more winding kilometres along the road, from whose church square a spectacular view extends over Calvi and its gulf.

Inland Balagne

From Montemaggiore, the D151 climbs around a mountain spur to the **Col de Salvi** (509 metres/1,670 ft), and drops down the other side to **Cateri**, a typically compact Balagne village straddling the area's four main routes.

Heading north, still on the D151, you soon arrive at the turning for the region's oldest settlement, **Sant'Antonio** ❻, whose crow's nest of ancient stone houses, sloping walls and convoluted passageways cluster on the summit of a conical hill top. Remarkable views are to be

had from its snug café-restaurants and the terrace of its 16th-century baroque church, Sant'Annunsiata, adjacent to the car park below the village proper.

To continue the tour of inland Balagne, return to the main road and follow it north for a kilometre (⅔ mile) or so as far as **Aregno** ❼, with its simple but stunning Pisan Romanesque church of **La Trinità**, constructed of chequered green, ochre and white granite. Prominent among the primitive sculptures of beasts, geometric patterns and human figures adorning its exterior walls is a crouched man holding his foot, thought to be an allegory for Man paralysed by Sin.

Pigna ❽, the next village along the road, is a postcard pretty cluster of houses sporting blue shutters and new red-tiled roofs. Government grants have enabled local artisans and craftspeople to spruce Pigna up and reinvent it as a cultural centre. Its immaculately restored cobbled lanes harbour a dozen or more artisan workshops turning out produce from

LEFT: alley-ways of Sant' Antonio hilltop village. **BELOW:** traditional village street in Pigna.

Map on page 174

flutes to musical boxes, ceramic tiles and organic jam. Traditional music, both sung and instrumental, has also been revived here at the Casa Musicale, which hosts regular evening recitals in its classy little hotel-restaurant.

After a few more bends in the road, the monastery village of **Corbara** ❾ hoves into view, its cubic houses stacked steeply up the sides of a rocky bluff. The main attraction here is the ostentatiously baroque **Church of the Annunciation**, built in 1685. Inside, relics of an older church that stood on the same site include painted panels and carved wood furniture. A grand *palacio* two doors down, known locally as the Casa di Turchi, belonged to Davia Franchesini, a Corsican woman born in Tunis (after her Corbaran parents had been abducted by pirates) who married the Sultan of Morocco.

On the hillside above the village, the **Couvent de Corbara** is a working Dominican monastery with buildings dating back to its foundation in 1430.

When services are not being held, casual visitors may enter the whitewashed church and inner cloisters, while accommodation is available for those seeking spiritual retreat.

At this point, travellers either opt to break the inland itinerary by dropping down to nearby l'Ile Rousse, only 5 km (3 miles) from Corbara, or else turn around and head back uphill to Cateri, from where the D71 arcs in a broad semi-circle through the remainder of Balagne's major villages. Arguably the most photogenic of these is **Speloncato** ❿, whose shady square is lined by several picturesque houses, one of the village's two churches and also the private palace of a Corsican cardinal that has now been turned into a hotel. Very much the focus of the village still, it's an ideal place to observe typical Corsican daily life over a chilled *pastis* on the café terrace. The rocks on either side of the Speloncato are riddled with numerous grottos *(spelunca)*. Twice a year, on 8 April and 8 September,

BELOW: photogenic Speloncato.

assuming there are no clouds, the locals and their guests wait for the setting sun to reappear through the famous Pietra Tafonata (pierced stone), bathing the village in its light for several extra minutes.

In **Belgodère ⓫** (Belgudé), where Maurice Utrillo and his painter-mother Suzanne Valadon eked out a meagre existence shortly before World War I selling paintings of the surrounding villages and churches, the 16th-century church of **San Tumasgiu** harbours a serene painted panel of the Virgin and Child. Around the corner in the Oratoire de la Madonuccia, 500 metres (550 yds) or so from the central square, holds an even older art treasure in the form of a carved Madonna statue installed here in 1387.

The corniche begins its descend towards the beach at Lozari at this point, but the Balagne has three more attractive, though less well known valleys to offer.

To pick up the road to the **Giunssani**, northern Corsica's remotest micro-region, you'll have to double back to Speloncato.

Curving around in several ever-widening loops, the D63 scales the side of the mountain as far as the 1,099-metre (3,600-ft) high **Col de a Barraglia ⓬**. If you get out of your car at this point and take a few steps back towards the valley you will suddenly feel you are flying above the Balagne. The bird's-eye view from up here takes in the whole stretch of coast between the Balagne Déserte and the Désert des Agriates to the northeast. And if you turn round you will find yourself standing opposite the 2,393-metre (7,800-ft) high Monte Padru.

The valley basin in front of it contains the villages of Pioggiola, Olmi Cappella, Forcili and Mausolé, all surrounded by intense green foliage. Laricio pine covers the slopes of Monte Padru above, and the mountain torrents of Melaja and Tartagine are cool and refreshing even on the hottest days of the year.

Walkers should follow the road as far as its end at the **Maison Forestière de la Tartagine-Melaja ⓭**, from where a

BELOW: the village of Belgodère.

Map on page 174

network of superb trails fans out across the surrounding forest and mountainsides. Local tourist offices can supply leaflets outlining itineraries for the area, which range from leisurely streamside ambles to strenuous ascents of Monte Corona (2,143 metres/ 7,034 ft), the most northerly of the big peaks punctuating the Coriscan watershed.

Along the coast

First port of call on any tour of the Balagne's sun-drenched northern coast is the village of **Lumio** , known to the Romans as Ortis Culis ("Where the Sun Rises"). On its southern outskirts, just above the main highway, the beautifully preserved 11th-century **San Pietro e San Paolo** is a text-book Pisan church, with geometric window surrounds and a pair of monumental lions gazing mutely across the bay towards Calvi. While you're in the area, call in at Christian Moretti's **Centre d'Ethnographie et de Recherche Métallurgique** (open Mon–Sat 2.30–6.30pm), where knives are forged according to traditional methods using hand-mined ore from Cap Corse. The road forks at Lumio, with one direction leading eastwards into the Balagne and back to the beach at Lozari, and the other sticking close to the coast as far as the Désert des Agriates. Along the coast there are around half a dozen beach resorts, the first of which, called the **Marine de Sant'Ambrogio**, surrounding a fishermen's chapel, was conceived on a drawing board. There is a Club Mediterranée here.

Passing through this area, the road then leads through *maquis* and several bizarre rock formations as far as **Punta di Spano**, which has a small golf course set into a unique landscape.

Along the coast, below the broad and gently curving road, the Trinighellu, the island's little railway – in its summer guise as Tramway de la Balagne – can be seen rattling and whistling its way at regular intervals between one holiday village bay and the next.

BELOW: traditional Corsican cemetery, the Balagne.

Algajola ⑮ is a typical stop: a tiny resort on a long, yellow, sandy beach which actually belongs to the mountain village of Aregno. Algajola's small citadel, now privately-owned, was once an outpost of the Genoese fortress at Calvi. It also kept Pasquale Paoli at bay; the latter eventually thought he had found a chink in the armour of the hated oppressors when he founded a Corsican port to rival the Genoese Calvi at the red cliffs of the Isola Rossa, today's l'Ile Rousse ⑯. His plans failed to materialise, however, but the tower that once protected his harbour is now right at the centre of the second most popular tourist destination in the Balagne.

Guarded by a column of tall palm trees, a white marble statue of Paoli dominates l'Ile Rousse's plane-tree-lined square, situated right next to a fine promenade and also a sandy beach, divided up by beach cafés and rocky outcrops.

From the new harbour the view across the town encompasses a large area of hillside with two basin-like depressions – one of them beyond Algajola and extending up to Aregno and Cateri, the other concealed behind the Regino Valley. Both are natural catchment areas for the town, which has now spread far beyond its original borders.

Just as in the Calvi basin, all the people from further inland stream into the shops and supermarkets of this resort, and many for whom the sea is only a distant shimmer from their villages can usually earn a modest income here, though only during the peak season. L'Ile Rousse, which the Romans called Rubica Rocega, is hopelessly overcrowded in July and August, its beaches completely covered with sun-hungry bodies. A sewage treatment plant originally built to cater for the local population sometimes cannot cope with up to ten times its working capacity. So it is best to come here out of season for a holiday, even though some of the establishments are closed then.

East of l'Ile Rousse, two outstanding beaches are visible from the main highway as it hugs the coast en route to Bastia. Backed by a large holiday complex, Lozari Plage ⑰ is the most easily accessible, a broad sweep of steeply shelving, gold-grey shingle. For anyone with children in tow, however, a better option is Plage de Perajola, 5 km (3 miles) further east. Wide, sandy and shallow, the vivid blue bay is sheltered by the scrub-covered hills of the Désert des Agriates on its northern side; the catch is that reaching it involves a stream crossing. Drive along the remains of the old corniche road and park where you see a footpath dropping to the right.

A new road to Bastia via Ponte Leccia, the so-called "Balanina", has cut travel time drastically from one coast to the other. It leads through the formerly remote Valley of Ostriconi and has brought tourism and traffic a step closer to a string of villages whose 19th-century prosperity came to an abrupt end when the bottom fell out of Corsica's olive oil trade. The route which peels off the Balanina through the Désert des Agriates – the D81 – has also been upgraded, transforming what was until 1997 an adventure journey over unsurfaced roads.

Map on page 174

LEFT: high season on the beach at l'Ile Rousse

The Wind Rose

Windmills were once an essential part of the landscape of Corsica. The fact that they are now ruins is not because the wind has ceased to blow. It is due to the decline in trade with Genoa during the 19th century, which led to a decrease in the quantities of wheat and olives grown until ultimately there was no more work for the mills. The winds are as strong as ever. The massive erosion of the rocks, creating grotesque formations which evoke in the mind's eye an Indian's head or a dinosaur, is due in no small part to the "tossing breezes". They blow and roar from all points of the compass – although not at the same time, of course. On Corsica, each of these winds has a name. The *Scirocco*, which blows from the southeast, from the Sahara, brings with it desert sands – an unpopular souvenir amongst Corsicans. In Bonifacio the *Scirocco* only blows an average of four days a year, because Sardinia acts as a protective shield. Along the east coast, however, it is much more common: in Bastia it occurs, albeit in a mild form, on over 100 days each year. The opposite of the *Scirocco* is the wind which blows from the northwest, the *Maestrale* (French: "*Mistral*"), which blows southwards from the Massif Central and the Rhône Valley. It is a rough companion, whose gusts whip up the waves and create a hazard for winter sportsmen. "Beware of the *Mistral*!" in the weather forecast: should not be ignored. By the time it reaches Corsica the *Maestrale* has usually lost some of its strength, but it can still be unpleasant. It is experienced most frequently in Ajaccio – on 36 days a year. The *Mistral*'s easterly neighbour is called the *Tramontana*. It blows from the North, from the cold, wintry plains of the Po. As its name indicates, it comes from "across the mountains" and makes the islanders shiver, particularly the inhabitants of Bastia, who have to face it for two months each year. Continuing round the wind rose in clockwise direction, the next wind is the *Grecale*, which during the winter brings rain from the Apennines across on the mainland. If the wind blows directly from the east it is named *Levante*, after the sunrise. The opposite, the west wind, is known as the *Ponente*. Having set off from Gibraltar, the southwesterly *Libeccio* has crossed the entire western Mediterranean by the time it reaches Corsica. It brings rainfall in winter, which mostly falls on the west coast. Although that completes the list of the seven winds, there are still two missing. On Corsica, the *Mezzogiorno* is not a southerly, for the wind virtually never blows from that direction. Instead, following the original meaning of the word, it is applied to a wind which blows at noon. The breeze gets up at about nine o'clock, after the land mass has heated up faster than the sea, causing the air to rise and creating a current of air to fill the resulting vacuum. So the *Mezzogiorno* blows from the sea onto the land, reaching its greatest intensity at about midday. In the past, sailing ships returned to port at this time. During the afternoon, when the temperatures have equalised, the *Mezzogiorno* dies down. After sunset the drama is played in reverse, and the land breeze, *Terrana*, starts to blow, reaching its climax at midnight – the signal for ships to put out to sea. ❏

THE NEBBIO

Forming a huge amphitheatre of maquis *and chalk-speckled vineyards, the Nebbio encompasses all of Corsica's landscapes – from the beaches of the Agriates desert to the mountains of the coastal range*

Map on page 186

Pasquale Paoli was reputedly the first person to refer to the Nebbio as a "golden shell". And the region does indeed resemble a sea-shell as it rises up from the Golfe de St-Florent. The hills pile up, higher and higher, into the schist mountains whose peaks form the crest along the top. During Paoli's lifetime, the Nebbio was the bread-basket of Corsica. The Genoese, who pursued a strict agrarian policy on the island, ordered cereal to be grown here alongside its fruit and vegetables. Olives grow further up. The hills are a mixture of woodland and meadow, especially in the island's centre, where a narrow range of mountains halts the build-up of clouds to the west. To the north is the Patrimonio wine country, and to the west the vast, lonely expanse known as the Désert des Agriates.

St-Florent

St-Florent ❶ lies on the gulf of the same name. The town dates back to Roman times, when it was situated higher up, and further inland. It was here that the Pisan bishopric also grew up, thus providing continuity from antiquity via the early Christian period right through to the High Middle Ages, which was when Genoa placed its citadel on a rocky projection right next to the coast, and the town, forced to stay close to it, had to extend its housing to the surrounding marshland. St-Florent then became a strategically important harbour, and during the various wars that followed it was owned by Genoa, Corsica and France alternately, though its real conqueror was malaria. It was only when the nearby swamps were drained that its harbour was able to function properly once more.

Today's St-Florent is very French and very Mediterranean. Its cafés (bastions of the male population) still have a fishing-village atmosphere about them. Here you can live in style, the food is good, the holiday crowds never become a crush, and the central square is still predominantly a meeting-place for the locals, for *pétanque*, *pastis* and *politique*.

The key to the **Santa Maria Assunta** (Cathedral of the Nebbio) ❷ can be obtained from the Tourist Office (you'll have to leave a piece of ID as security). Although it is a Pisan cathedral, anyone with visions of the cathedral in Pisa will be disappointed.

It stands on farmland outside today's town, and is a simple building of pale limestone. Blind arcades adorn the façade and the tops of the graceful pilasters are decorated with a frieze. The cathedral is actually by no means as plain as it appears

PRECEDING PAGES: the waterfront in St-Florent.
LEFT: local men playing *pétanque (boules)* in St-Florent's town square.
RIGHT: harbourside stalls in St-Florent.

at first glance. More and more details catch the eye: the fabulous animals on the capitals, and the symbols, geometrical patterns and marks on the frieze.

Inside the building, in a glass case, the mummified remains of St Flor can be seen. The patron saint of the town, he was a Roman soldier who was martyred here in the 3rd century.

The Désert des Agriates

Les Agriates – also referred to as the **Désert des Agriates** – is the name given to the strip of land to the west of the Golfe de Saint-Florent. This area, which measures roughly 200 sq. km (77 sq. miles), was once fertile land but is now a barren wilderness – for several reasons. The farmers who grew their wheat here used to live beyond the gulf, on the steep slopes of the Cap Corse, where the sunny slopes were more suited to wine and figs than corn. For sowing and harvesting purposes they thus travelled across to the coast. The farmers shared the Agriates

region with shepherds, who brought their flocks here to winter pasture. The fact that the shepherds began to burn tracts of forest to give their flocks more room to graze probably did not concern the farmers unduly at first – until the resulting erosion starting affecting the water balance. Increased karstification also limited grazing possibilities. The farmers abandoned the region, and the valleys degenerated into steppe. Recently, however, the Agriates region has become more interesting again – thanks to tourism.

Excursion boats from St-Florent depart several times daily throughout the summer (the last boat returns at 4pm) to ferry visitors across the gulf to the exquisite **Plage du Loto ❸**, as perfect a beach as you'll fine anywhere in the Mediterranean, with fabulous blue water and pearl-white sand.

En route you get great views of the **Punta Mortella ❹**, whose watchtower was destroyed by no less than a youthful Horatio Nelson after a siege. The British

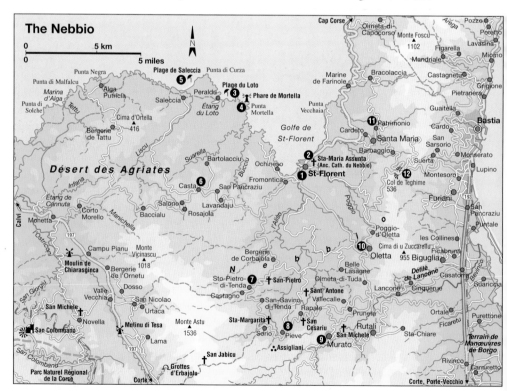

The Nebbio

Map
on page
186

navy was so impressed with the tower's ability to hold out against a superior force that it commissioned a whole string of them across the empire, known as Martello towers after this one.

From Loto, a gentle coast path meanders along a wild stretch of shore to the still more spectacular **Plage de Saleccia** ❺, reached after around 45 minutes on foot. A huge spread of soft white sand, it is the most unspoilt beach of its size on the island, although in summer season a steady stream of pleasure boats from St-Florent ensures peace and quiet is in short supply.

Skirting the desert between St-Florent and l'Ile Rousse, the main D81 may not approach the coast, but it does afford some spectacular views of the distant shore and hills of Cap Corse, and there is no shortage of small establishments selling Corsican cheese, honey and wine along the way. The only food and accommodation in the area is in **Casta** ❻, where you can join a horse ride or rent moun-

tain bikes for the rough trip to Saleccia; the tracks that lead from this road through the Agriates and over to the sea are unsuitable for normal cars. Hikers should take sufficient drinking water with them.

Inland Nebbio

It is possible to take a circular tour of the hills of the Nebbio from St-Florent. Take the D81 towards l'Ile Rousse for about 4 km (2½ miles), along the southern edge of the Désert des Agriates, before turning off to the left along the narrow and winding D62. To the west, the route is dominated by a 1,536-metre (5,039-ft) high mountain range, the highest peak of which is the impressive Monte Astu.

There are a number of tiny villages along the way. After 10 km (6 miles) is **Santo-Pietro-di-Tenda** ❼, whose houses are ranged along the Tenda ridge above the Aliso valley. In the centre of the village, which is surrounded by olive and chestnut trees, are two separate baroque

BELOW: the landscape of San Michele.

churches joined in a single façade by a square campanile. The route gets more rugged and mountainous as it continues to **Pieve** ❽, 7 km (4 miles) further on. Next to the church are the very weathered remains of two menhirs. Unlike their granite cousins in the south of the island, these ones are made of slate. Now and then one comes across very strangely constructed shepherds' huts: the ground plan is square, but the roof is round. The walls and roof, made up of layers of flat stones, blend into each other.

The biggest attraction of the journey is without doubt the famous church of **San Michele de Murato**, situated at a T-junction about 1 km (⅔ mile) from the village of **Murato** ❾. Considered to be one of Corsica's finest churches, it stands on a grassy spur, elevated in splendid isolation above the surrounding countryside. The 12th-century church is built of two kinds of stone: pinkish-yellow limestone and dark-green serpentine marble, running in relatively uniform stripes around the top of the building before becoming more and more untidy and irregular at the base. The whole structure looks weird and highly exotic.

Even more remarkable are the numerous motifs chosen by the stonemasons. According to local legend a mosque once stood on this site, and several people have interpreted the reliefs as representing the victory of Christianity over Islam. Severed hands are depicted, for instance, possibly signifying that the church once housed a court of law. Men, animals and fabulous creatures are all gathered here.

Another relief depicts the wine harvest: two men with an enormous grape that they have just hacked down with warlike curved knives. A further scene depicts Eve being tempted by the serpent and covering her naked body with a huge hand – naive Romanesque "expressionism".

To the east of Murato, the D62 connecting St-Florent with Bastia plunges into a deep ravine, the **Défilé de Lancone**, and then descends to the eastern coastal

BELOW: the church of San Michele de Murato.

Map on page 186

plain. Recently a broader, less winding road (D82) on the south bank has been constructed to lead down to the plain as well. The traveller can return to St-Florent by taking the D82 to the north, past the village of **Oletta** , whose church of **St-André** harbours a miraculous triptych that once called out to warn a mother than her baby's cot was about to catch fire. Dating from 1534, it shows the Virgin and Child flanked by Saints Reparata and John the Baptists. The square in the village witnessed a grizzly scene during the Paolist insurrection when local rebels were mutilated, quartered and crushed on cartwheels by the local French army commdander.

Patrimonio and hinterland

The wine country of **Patrimonio** , in the north of the Nebbio, is a complete contrast to the barren wilderness of the Désert des Agriates. Wine has been produced in Corsica since antiquity; it played a role while the island was under Pisan domination, and Genoa turned the Cap Corse peninsula and its surrounding area, as far as the corn land in the Nebbio, into a wine-producing region. In 19th-century French Corsica, more Corsicans were employed in wine production than in any other trade. But then, in 1874, the phylloxera (vine louse) arrived and destroyed as much as 85 percent of the crop. Most of the island's vintners gave up. Many emigrated. The few who stayed were faced with unexpectedly tough competition after World War II.

But it wasn't long before people who knew how to apply modern cultivation methods arrived: the *pieds noirs*, French emigrants returning from newly independent Algeria. They also introduced new grape varieties, and gave winemaking on Corsica a huge boost – but in many cases the island's wine was now being massproduced. Several local vintners called in the bulldozers, cut away large areas of *maquis* and planted the cheap varieties.

Now even France has remembered that Corsica used to have a tradition of quality

BELOW: the church at Patrimonio.

Map on page 186

wine-production, and honour has finally been restored to the island once more: Corsican wine now has a legal claim to the AOC (*Appellation d'Origine Contrôlée*) title. Patrimonio received its AOC in 1968. Most of Corsica's AOC wines are made from the island's original grape varieties, and several of them can only be obtained on the island itself.

The wine region of Patrimonio today comprises not only the central area around the village and its church, but also the surrounding slopes. Some vines here grow on shale, but limestone tends to predominate. The soil is a favourite with Nielluccio, a variety that probably came here from Tuscany centuries ago, and which today gives Patrimonio red wine its distinctive character. Wine from this region is definitely worth buying – especially red wine. The Muscat is also popular. But the real classic alongside the Nielluccio is the Vermentinu, also known as Malvasiu, which may even have been brought to the island by the Greeks. Here in Northern Corsica it

produces a white wine of distinction that is also strongly acidic. As far as taking wine home is concerned, it is best to stick with those vineyards that have experience in the wine export business, and to ask which wines are suited to long-distance travel and which are not.

Patrimonio is probably the only village on the island to have maintained and retained its prosperity for any length of time. Lots of small, dignified-looking vintners' houses, separated by ancient trees and encircled by vineyards, dot the slopes surrounding the village and its elegant parish church. There are a few craft shops, and also several restaurants providing Corsican cuisine. And it's also a good place for those interested in Corsican prehistory: a few years ago, a **menhir statue** was found in one of the vineyards here. It has now been erected just below the church.

A human head with shoulders can be made out on the top of a column – one of the "stone warriors" that are so numerous in the southern part of the island. This one, hewn out of pale-coloured limestone, is "only" 3,000 years old, and is now protected by a roof. When it was created the island's sculptors had already been producing menhirs for 2,000 years. Possibly forced to leave their settlements in the south of the island, the megalithic peoples brought this expression of their culture along with them and guarded it closely, while all around them a new epoch – the Bronze Age – had already been ushered in. The menhir of Patrimonio is thus the last reminder we have of a very advanced Stone-Age civilization.

Having left Patrimonio, the main road to Bastia continues to climb high above the village, yielding superb views over the gulf and Cap Corse coastline. The pass where it crests the ridge, the **Col de Teghime** ⑫, is marked by a memorial to the soldiers (of mostly North African origin) who died here fighting the Germans in 1943. The Free French forces' capture of this vantage point high above the town allowed them to fire on Kesselring's 9th Panzer division as it retreated to safety across the Ligurian Sea.

LEFT: typical roadside vegetation. **RIGHT:** goats grazing in the Gorges de Spelunca.

BASTIA

*Extravagant baroque churches, a pastel-washed citadelle and an old port
hemmed in by run-down Genoese tenements give Bastia
a more lived-in, authentic feel than its rival Ajaccio*

Map
on page
196

Bastia is an honest town, not a spruced-up, shiny tourist haven. There are fewer luxury yachts in the harbour here, and there's not a sandy beach for miles around. It is a busy port with real Tuscan flair, economically the most important town in Corsica, although with a population of only 50,000, it can hardly be called a major metropolis. On weekdays the town is one massive traffic jam – although since the construction of the road tunnel under the old citadel and port, this problem is nowhere near as bad as it used to be.

Bastia is the first contact many visitors will have with the island. This is where most of the ferries from the mainland arrive, while Bastia-Poretta airport handles more traffic than Ajaccio's Campo dell' Oro. In the past few years, nearly 2 million passengers each year have used the town as a gateway, making it the busiest French port after Calais.

Anyone arriving by car who gets sucked down into the **Voie Rapide** (expressway) will have missed the best view of the town, which is the old, semi-circular harbour with the church of St-Jean Baptiste. This church, visible from miles away across the water, has greeted homecoming seafarers for centuries. The streets of the Old Town, with their tall, narrow houses, rise up behind it like a huge amphitheatre, and high above them, in stark contrast, are the modern, white apartment buildings. But it is the old, dilapidated buildings that make Bastia so picturesque.

The history of the town

Bastia was founded by the Genoese. Their governor, Leonello Lomellini, occupied what was then a rocky crag above the fishing village of Cardo, and had a bastion erected at this strategic location. The Italian word for "bastion", bastiglia, gave

the town its name. The watchtower soon developed into a mighty fortress with high walls and battlements. In the 17th century the Genoese moved the seat of their Corsican governors from Biguglia to Bastia, and Pope Clement VII then awarded the settlement civic rights. Even after Corsica had fallen to the French in 1769, Bastia still remained the chief town of the island. Following the division of Corsica into two *départements* in 1797, Bastia remained capital of the northern one. Then, much to its displeasure, the town had to content itself with being a *sous-préfecture* when Napoleon I selected his native town of Ajaccio as Corsica's new capital.

It was only in 1974, when Corsica was divided anew into two separate regions,

**PRECEDING
PAGES:** Vieux
Port and
church of St
Jean Baptiste.
LEFT: fishing
boats in
Bastia's
Vieux Port.
RIGHT: street in
Bastia's
old town.

that Bastia once again became the administrative centre of the northern part of the island, or Département d'Haute-Corse. There is considerably less jealousy and resentment between Ajaccio and Bastia now that each administers one of the two *départements* on the island, but the two towns are very different: Ajaccio in architecture and atmosphere is very French while Bastia is far more Italian.

Industrialisation

The town's **Nouveau Port** (new port), was constructed between 1850 and 1870, and it very soon became the most important marine traffic and trading centre in Corsica. Over half of all the goods exported or imported by Corsica pass through Bastia. The economic boom, and Bastia's reputation for being Corsica's leading trading port, have both left their mark on the town's demographic structure. In contrast to other towns and even regions on the island, Bastia still provides enough jobs, and is thus succeeding in staunching the flow of young emigrants to the French mainland.

Bastia could be termed a workers' city, for working people do make up the largest section of the population here, at 39 percent (roughly 30 percent in Ajaccio). A cliché attitude on the island considers Corte to be the cultural centre of Corsica and Bastia the industrial capital, where it is said that "feet are on the ground and hands at work".

Two-thirds of Bastia's working population are employed in companies within the region, most of them small craft businesses and industrial firms. However, the town also offers its visitors a whole host of sights, and its colourful markets, quays and squares are full of bustling life. A day in Bastia (the average amount of time most tourists spend here) is certainly not a day wasted.

In 1983, the new road tunnel was built in order to cope with the town's appalling traffic, which used to be quite unbearable whenever the big ferries docked, or during rush hour. It runs directly from the docks under the old harbour and the citadel. Not everyone in Bastia was happy about this development, since it meant that many tourists bypassed the town centre entirely. Restaurant, café and boutique owners manned the barricades, but in the end the arguments in favour of the tunnel outweighed the complaints.

Further civic controversy was sparked off after a stand at the local football team's **Furiani stadium** collapsed in May 1992, killing 17 people and injuring 1,300. More than a decade later, compensation and liability claims are still being debated in the courts, while those responsible for the disaster have yet to be brought to book.

The other occasion Bastia made headlines in recent years was in 1996, when a car exploded in broad daylight in the Vieux Port. Planted by militant paramilitaries, its intended target was Corsican nationalist politician Charles Pieri, who was gravely injured but survived the attack; a colleague also caught in the blast, later died. The bombing unleashed a bloody series of reprisals and counter-

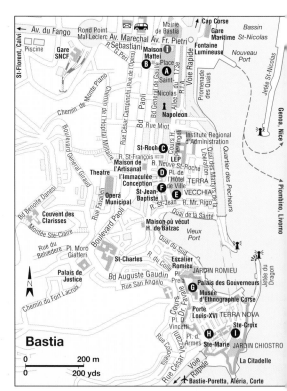

Bastia

0   200 m

0   200 yds

Map on page 196

reprisals that over the following three years ripped through the ranks of the island's paramilitary movement.

Place St-Nicolas

To get to know Bastia the best place to begin is the **place St-Nicolas** , right in the centre of town. The 300-metre (328-yd) long square, built on a terrace overlooking the port, is shaded by palm and plane trees.

Together with its cafés and shops on the landward side, it is strongly reminiscent of squares on the Italian mainland. And there's a lot going on here, particularly in the evenings: young people, fashionably dressed, go strolling up and down, past the bandstand and the marble statue of Napoleon, indulging in the age-old ritual of flirtation.

The older and wiser ones take up their observation positions on the benches around the square where they have a good view of the Corso while discussing everything under the sun. One subject of lively debate is the game of *pétanque*, usually played by the older men in various parts of the square. In the afternoons, the Place St-Nicolas is bathed in a warm, soft light that is typically Mediterranean.

The **statue of Napoleon** – depicted with a flattering washboard stomach, Roman toga and gilded laurel-leaf crown – is not the work of a Corsican, but of the Florentine sculptor Lorenzo Bartolini. It is the only reminder the inhabitants have of the erstwhile Emperor of France. At the bottom of their hearts they've never really forgiven him for choosing Ajaccio as the island's capital instead of Bastia.

It's certainly worth making a short detour at this point to the shop on the western side of the square called **Maison Mattei** , where Corsican products of all kinds can be purchased. There is the fortified wine flavoured with quinine known as Cap Corse Mattei, for example, and also candied citrus fruits, myrtle or cedrat liqueur, olive-wood sculptures, ceramics

BELOW: view of the port.

and several different types of honey. The particular attraction of this shop, apart from its excellent assortment of genuinely Corsican products, lies in its interior, which has not been altered since the business first started around the turn of the 20th century. There is also a Tourist Information Office on the north side of the square, opposite the Centre Administratif; the main Syndicat d'Initiative is on the Boulevard Paoli, between rue Abatucci and rue Miot.

Anyone keen on rummaging through old junk and knick-knacks should definitely take a stroll across the place St-Nicolas on a Sunday, when the **flea market** takes place. It's at this time that the numerous bars and street cafés along the boulevard de Gaulle do particularly good business.

Sitting down here for an aperitif or a coffee is not only an excellent way to wind down, it also provides a very good opportunity to crowd watch. Parallel to the boulevard de Gaulle is the boulevard Paoli, a shopping street that is usually one enormous traffic jam, with all the accompanying exhaust fumes.

Terra Vecchia

Immediately south of the place St-Nicolas, the atmospheric old quarter of **Terra Vecchia** – a complex labyrinth of narrow streets and passageways flanked by dilapidated 16th- to 18th-century buildings – is a lot more romantic than the more modern area to the north. It can most easily be reached by following rue Napoleon from the bottom (southwest) corner of the square. Dominating this approach to the Vieux Port, on the east side of the road, is the sumptuously baroque **Oratoire St-Roch** ⑥, built around 1604 as an act of gratitude after the dreadful plague epidemic of 1589 had come to an end. The interior is Florentine in style and features a magnificent organ, gifted to the church by wealthy local merchants in 1750. A couple of blocks further down the same road, the **Oratoire de l'Immaculée**

BELOW: houses in the Terra Vecchia.

Map on page 196

Conception **D**, built in 1611 by the Confrérie de la Conception, was given its noble interior in the 18th century. The walls and pillars are hung with crimson damask and velvet, lending added intensity to the works of art inside the building.

These include a copy of Murillo's *Immaculate Conception* above the main altar, an 18th-century Genoese crucifix, and the Statue of the Holy Virgin, which is given its annual airing on 8 December when it is carried to the church of St-Jean Baptiste. So grand is the interior of the chapel that it was used by Sir Gilbert Elliot for the first meeting of the Anglo-Corsican Parliament in February 1795.

Forming the commercial heart of Terra Vecchia is the **place de l'Hôtel de Ville** (Town Hall Square) **E**, otherwise known as the **place du Marché**. A food market is held here every morning except for Sundays and public holidays. Farmers from the surrounding countryside sell fresh fruit, vegetables, meat, cheese, honey and *maquis* herbs. Since Bastia has no market hall, the seafood here is sold in the open air. In the afternoon the whole commotion suddenly stops as if by magic, and the square is eerily deserted once more.

The **Eglise St-Jean Baptiste** (church of St-Jean Baptiste) **F**, down by the Vieux Port (Old Harbour) is the largest church in Bastia. Its ornate 17th-century baroque façade, with its two striking towers, has become a symbol of the town. The interior – gilded stucco, Corsican polychromatic marble – dates from the 18th-century. St Roch, protector of plague victims, gazes down at passers-by from several houses down at the harbour.

The tradition whereby each sea captain greeted the saint and prayed for a safe return before setting sail has, however, long since been forgotten. If you take a seat in one of the numerous restaurants around here, which serve all kinds of different seafood dishes, you'll find it a good place from which to observe the colourful fishing boats and the busy harbour.

BELOW: fishing boats.

The Terra Nova (Citadel)

Photographers should really walk across the quai du Sud as far as the harbour mole (Jetée du Dragon) in order to take in the whole of the Vieux Port. The best place to take a comprehensive photograph of the entire Old Harbour is from the top of the flight of steps known as **L'Escalier Romieu**, which leads from the quai du Sud up to the citadel. The view from up here extends across the broad expanse of the New Harbour, where the large ferries dock, all the way to the mountains of Cap Corse.

Today the citadel, surrounded by a defensive wall, and referred to by the Genoese as the **Terra Nova** to distinguish it from the older harbour settlement, is another "Old Town" all on its own. It covers a relatively small area and is strikingly different from the rest of Bastia: the streets are narrow, short and easy to walk along thanks to the absence of cars.

At the top of the steps on the right, the first building you see is the 14th-century

Palais des Gouverneurs ⑥. The round tower at the right-hand corner is the oldest surviving part of the original Genoese fortifications. It is in a remarkably good state of repair. Today the palais houses a museum, the **Musée d'Ethnographie Corse** (open daily 9am–6pm; entrance fee), which at the time of writing was being extensively refurbished and not expected to re-open until at least the summer of 2004.

The geological, historical and folkloristic collections include the tattered flag once carried by Paoli and his troops in their final battle against the French, a symbol of Corsica's struggle for independence. Tours usually wind up in the complex of dungeons below the main building, where during World War II members of the Corsican Resistance were the latest generation to be tortured here in pursuit of the island's liberation.

Rue Notre-Dame leads to the 15th-century church of **Ste-Marie ⑪**. It served as an episcopal cathedral until 1801, when the status of bishopric was conferred upon Ajaccio instead. The church underwent extension work in the 17th century, when it received its tall campanile. A great deal of marble (from Corsica and from Carrera) was used for its magnificent interior. An 18th-century *Assumption of the Virgin* in silver can be seen behind protective glass; it is carried through the town in a solemn procession on 15 August every year. Some of the paintings, taken from Cardinal Fesch's collection, date from the 17th century; the ceiling decoration is 18th-century.

The **Chapelle Ste-Croix ①** is situated directly behind this church, and its unimpressive exterior belies the magnificence within: a fine baroque interior, with cherubs and gilded stucco everywhere. The sky-blue ceiling is particularly delightful. Legend has it that the black crucifix which gave the chapel its name was found floating in the sea by fishermen in 1428. The fishermen of Bastia still offer up the first catch of the season to Our Lord when this black "Christ des Miracles" is carried through the town every 3 May.

Map on page 196

LEFT: statue in the Chapelle Ste-Croix.

The Trinighellu

Bastia is one of the most important stations along the route of the Trinighellu, also known as the "micheline". For more than a century the "Little Train", as the islanders affectionately call their narrow-gauge railway, has been a Corsican institution.

The railway was inaugurated on 1 February 1888. Experts tend to smile at the precision of the timetable. The nicknames testify to the main problems: the most common are TGV (*Train à Grandes Vibrations* – the "Big-Vibration Train") and TBV (*Train à Basse Vitesse* – the "Low-Speed Train"). "It often happens that the train has to stop to permit the removal of a cow which is unconcernedly grazing between the rails," reports Dumé, who studied in Corte and who became accustomed to the idiosyncrasies of the Trinighellu. She recounts a handful of experiences which make the journey seem even more folkloric: the frequent derailments, the stopping of the train by an FLNC commando unit which decides to distribute pamphlets to the travellers in the middle of nowhere; the engine, which breaks down before it is within eyesight of the next station, and has to be push-started to get it going again; the eternal waits at stations, which aren't proper stations at all; obstacles in the form of vehicles which have got stuck between the barriers at level crossing. Journey times have been significantly reduced since the old 1940s Renault diesel engines were replaced by faster Soulé ones and more modern rolling stock, but the trip across the island can still feel like an adventure.

The route from Ajaccio to Bastia and Calvi runs through one of the loveliest regions of Corsica, much to the delight of the 800,000 passengers who embark each year. The journey from Ajaccio to Bastia takes 3 hours, although the distance is barely 110 km (68 miles). The slow pace, however, is more than compensated for by the magnificent views afforded during this trip across the island. The flocks grazing beside the line are blissfully unconcerned at the squeaking of the wheels on the rails, but for passengers the noise is somewhat disturbing when the train enters one of the 43 tunnels hewn in the solid rock, or chugs onto the impressive Vecchio Bridge after Vivario. The viaduct, designed by Gustave Eiffel, is 140 metres (460 ft) long and spans the mountain torrent at a height of some 100 metres (320 ft). While crossing it, you gain an impressive view of the new *route nationale* road bridge spanning the same gorge at a height of nearly 140 metres (460 ft). Another significant engineering feat, the Vizzavona tunnel, is 3,916 metres (12,848 ft) long. When it was built it was the longest tunnel in Europe.

On the main stretch between Ajaccio and Bastia, the traveller passes through a cross-section of Corsican landscapes. After it has left Ajaccio, the Trinighellu enters the Gravona Valley and climbs up into the mountains, stopping several times, at Bocognano, Vizzavona and Vivario, etc. Then it descends into the centre of the island, the area around Corte. Forest and *maquis* alternate until the train reaches the coast again at Bastia.   ❑

Map on page 206

CAP CORSE

The remote, brilliant blue coast along its northern rim,
studded with watchtowers, is the main attraction, along with
the cape's timelessly pretty villages

The Cap Corse, the northernmost tip of Corsica, is not a cape but a peninsula, pointing at the Italian mainland like an index finger. A range of schist mountains runs along this 40-km (25-mile) long and 15-km (9-mile) wide tongue of land from north to south, dropping steeply down to the sea in the west, and more gently so in the east. The villages here, their houses built from the local grey or green stone, are either hidden along the slopes of the lateral valleys, or situated majestically out in the open with a commanding view. The sea is always close at hand on this slender promontory, and each municipality here has its own small harbour, with fishing boats, from which *capcorsin* products (wine, oil, wood, fruit and fish) were formerly exported.

Magnificent *palazzi,* castle-like villas and elegant mausoleums remind the visitor of the region's former prosperity. Dubbed locally as *"maisons d'Americains"*, many of the most ostentatious homes on the cape were erected by returning emigrants who had made fortunes in the colonies of South America and were keen to impress their compatriots with sophisticated and showy architectural fashions acquired abroad.

From the end of the 19th century onwards, however, the Cap Corse suffered a steady economic decline: trade with Genoa slumped, and the vine louse put an end to almost all wine exporting. Some of the local inhabitants emigrated overseas. These days, however, tourism has offered a new source of income, and the Cap Corse's grapes are producing good wines once more, as well as the island's favourite aperitif, "Cap Corse", a punchy, herb-flavoured fortified liqueur made from sweet muscat grapes and quinine; it was originally devised as a malaria prophylactic.

A day-long excursion around this peninsula, with superb landscape viewing, can be undertaken from either St-Florent or Bastia. The whole trip, along the D80, is only 128 km (80 miles) long, but the road is just as sinuous as most others on Corsica, so if you are planning to make detours into the villages, take a few leisurely photographs and possibly do some hiking too, the best thing is to plan on at least one overnight stay. The harbour at Centuri is an idyllic stopping-off point in this respect, and there are several pleasant, small hotels to choose from. Photographers should proceed anticlockwise around the Cap Corse, because the sun shines on the east coast in the morning and the west coast in the afternoon.

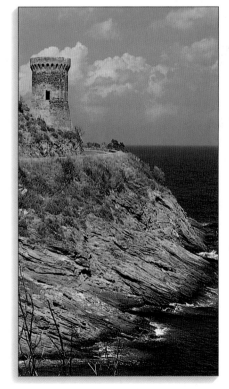

PRECEDING PAGES: the lonely west coast of the Cap Corse.
LEFT: the harbourside of Port de Centuri.
RIGHT: the reserved tower at Losse.

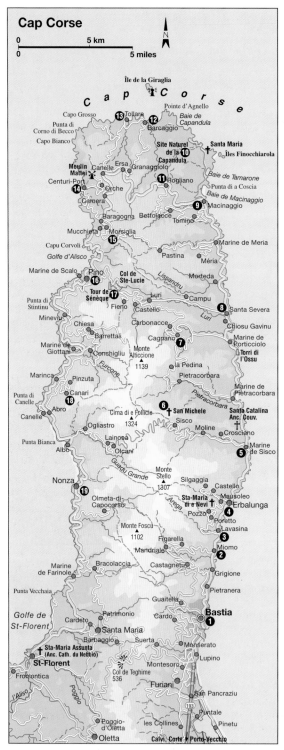

Cap Corse

0 ___ 5 km
0 ___ 5 miles

Île de la Giraglia

c a p   C o r s e

Pointe d'Agnello

Capo Grosso ⑬ Tollare ⑫ Baie de
Punta di   Barcaggio   Capandula
Corno di Becco
Capo Bianco   Site Naturel   Santa Maria
                           de la ⑩
Moulin Canelle Ersa Granaggiolo   Capandula Îles Finocchiarola
Mattei ⚒ Orche   ⑪ Rogliano
Centuri-Port   Baie de Tamarone
⑭ Camera   Punta di a Coscia
                                           Baie de Macinaggio
Baragogna Bettolacce ⑨ Macinaggio
                        Tomino
Mucchieta Morsiglia ⑮
Capu Corvoli   Marine de Meria
Golfe d'Alisco   Pastina   Méria
Marine de Scalo Pino Col de   Morteda
⑯   Ste-Lucie
Punta di   Tour de ⑰ Luri   Campu
Stintinu Sénèque Fieno Castello   ⑧ Santa Severa
Minevia   Chiesa   Carbonacce   Chiosu Gavinu
         Barrettali   Marine de
Marine de   Cagnano ⑦ Porticciolo
Giottani Conchigliu Monte   Torri di
Marinca   Alticcione   l'Ossu
                   ▲1139 la Pedina
         Pinzuta   Pietracorbara
Punta di Canari   Marine de
Canelle ⑱ Abro   Pietracorbara
Canelle   Cima di e Follice San Michele Santa Catalina
            Ogliastro 1324   Sisco   Anc. Couv.
Punta Bianca Lainosa   Moline
       Albo   Olcani   ⑤ Crosciano
                               Marine
                   Monte   de Sisco
Nonza   Stello Silgaggia
⑲   Olmeta-di- ▲1307   Castello
           Capocorso   Mausoleo
                    Sta-Maria Erbalunga
Monte Foscù di e Nevi † ④
  ▲1102   Figarella   Pozzo Poretto
       Mandriale   Lavasina ③
Marine   Bracolaccia Castagnetu Miomo ②
de Farinole   Grigione
Punta Vecchaia   Pietranera
          Guaitella
Golfe de   Patrimonio Cardo **Bastia**
St-Florent Cardeto   ①
       Santa Maria   Monserato
    Barbaggio Suerta
Sta-Maria Assunta   Montesoro Lupino
(Anc. Cath. du Nebbio)
St-Florent   Col de Teghime
Fromontica   536   Furiani
l'Aliso   San Pancraziu
                      193
            Poggio- les Collines Puntale
            d'Oletta   Pinetu
              Oletta Calvi, Corte Porto-Vecchio

The eastern cape

The first beach after leaving **Bastia** ❶ is at the little fishing port of **Miomo** ❷: it is strewn with pebbles, and dominated by a well-preserved Genoese watchtower. Right next to it is a small chapel, built in 1780, with touchingly naive stucco work in its interior. The church of **Notre Dame des Grâces** in the neighbouring hamlet of **Lavasina** ❸ is more than a century older, but has unfortunately been provided with an ugly modern concrete campanile, surmounted by a white statue of the Virgin that can be seen for miles around. On 8 September, Corsicans make the pilgrimage here to the *Madonna of Lavasina*, an altar painting darkened with age. The picture is credited with miraculous powers and is thought to be a product of the school of Perugino (16th century).

A favourite subject for landscape painters is **Erbalunga** ❹, situated on a schist promontory jutting out into the sea. A Genoese tower, now in ruins, once protected access to the tiny fishing harbour. Many of the buildings seem to rise directly out of the water because of the limited space available. The small marina here can be observed from a square filled with snack bars, cafés and pizzerias. The balcony of the gastronomic restaurant called "Le Pirate" affords a particularly fine view.

Anyone interested in observing the whole of the Cap Corse from its second highest peak, **Monte Stello** (1,307 metres/4,300 ft), can travel along the D54 from Erbalunga as far as the hamlet of **Pozzo**, from where the ascent takes around 3 hours to complete. Since clouds usually bubble up over the high ridges by noon and obscure the views, the earlier one starts the better.

A couple of kilometres inland from Erbalunga on the D54 (which starts south of the village centre), in the hamlet of **Castello**, stands a chapel that should not be overlooked by anyone with an interest in early medieval history. Built in the 10th century when the peninsula was under the sway of Pisa, **Santa Maria di e Nevi** (Our Lady of the Snows) holds the island's oldest fres-

Map on page 206

coes: portraits of saints painted in the 1380s. Unfortunately, the chapel was recently vandalized and is nowadays kept locked, but you can arrange a guided visit through the local Mairie (tours daily in summer; entrance fee for adults; tel: 06 86 78 02 38).

The next small harbour on the route is the **Marine de Sisco ❺**, with its short, greyish-coloured pebble beach. The village itself actually lies several kilometres further inland. It was a metal-forging centre in medieval times, producing weapons, armour and jewellery. Right into the 18th century, Sisco's flourishing crafts and far-reaching trade connections made it one of the richest villages on the Cap Corse. Just behind the marina, a statue of St Catherine of Sisco, wearing a sword, can be seen standing on a rock above the promenade. The relics brought to her by sailors returning from Palestine in the 13th century are no longer housed in the Romanesque **Couvent de Santa Catalina** (church of St Catherine), a former monastery, but are now locked away in local Mairie.

Another Early Medieval Pisan chapel that warrants a side-trip from the main road is **San Michele ❻**, tucked away 7 km (4 miles) west of Sisco on the D32. Built in 1030, it rests on a steep, *maquis*-covered hillside looking down the valley towards the sea. Each year on 29 September, the chapel's saint's day, pilgrims travel here to celebrate Mass.

The route now continues past various other small harbours, with sandy beaches this time, ideal for swimming: the **Marine de Pietracorbara** and the **Marine de Porticciolo**. Five kilometres (3 miles) further inland lies the village of **Cagnano ❼**. According to a recent theory, it was here, and not in Genoa or Calvi, that Christopher Columbus was born. This new angle in the dispute as to his origins has been introduced by Corsican historian Lucien Saladini, and there is a reasonable amount of evidence to substantiate the claim: during his youth, Columbus was apparently called Colombo de Terra Rossa, and he once mentioned that he was not the only admiral in the family. The former manor

known as Terre Rosse is situated in Cagnano, and was built by an admiral in the Genoese fleet roughly 200 years before Columbus was born. So was Columbus really a Corsican from Cap Corse? Wherever he hailed from, he made such a mystery of his origins that the speculation is guaranteed to go on for years.

After passing the well-preserved **Torri di l'Ossu** (so named because a cache of human bones was unearthed beneath it in the mid-19th century), the visitor will arrive at **Santa Severa ❽** with its small port at the estuary of the River Luri. The D180 leads west from here across to Luri and Pino.

The northern cape

Anyone keen on seeing the northernmost point of the Cap Corse should stay on the D80 to **Macinaggio ❾**, which possesses a relatively large marina, several small hotels, restaurants and souvenir shops, a disco, and also one of the Cap Corse's rare petrol stations. The harbour here has cer-

tainly had its share of VIP visitors: it was at Macinaggio in 1790 that Paoli set foot on Corsican soil once again on his return from England; Napoleon visited the harbour only three years later, breaking his trip back from Egypt for a short visit to his homeland; and the Empress Eugénie also arrived here in 1869 from Egypt, where she had attended the opening of the Suez Canal, because a storm forced her ship to seek refuge in the harbour.

North of the village extends one of the island's prettiest coastlines, a wild shore comprising several pristine beaches and coves that are nowadays protected as the **Site Naturel de la Capandula** ❿.

With a car, it is possible to drive to the first of these, the **Baie de Tamarone**, from where a footpath winds northwards to the **Chapelle Santa Maria**, an early-medieval church overlooked by a dilapidated Genoan watchtower.

The coast path then bends westwards, passing a couple of remote, well sheltered beaches en route to Macinaggio via Barcaggio and Tollare, which may be reached in 7–8 hours' walking. During their brief sojourn in the area, Empress Eugégie and her retinue spent a day hiking up to the northern cape's principal settlement, **Rogliano** ⓫; the way was steep and arduous, and Eugénie later had a road built. The latter has since been known as the Chemin de L'Impératrice ("Empress Way").

It's definitely worth making a detour off the D80, which runs inland near Macinaggio, to see the ancient hamlets around Rogliano, with their towers, churches and slate roofs. The ruins of the castle of San Colombano can be seen high on a rocky crag; it was once the seat of the da Mare family, who used to own a large section of the Cap Corse. The landscape up at the northernmost point of the Cap Corse is barren and bleak. If you turn off in **Ersa** you can go on a short, 16-km (10-mile) tour of the area. The D253 leads through the *maquis* to the small fishing harbour of **Barcaggio** ⓬, where a

BELOW: hillside village in the Commune of Rogliano.

Map on page 206

gently curving beach leads to an impressive watchtower, and then on to **Tollare** ⓭. Greenish, shimmering serpentine rocks stand at Corsica's windy "Land's End" from where you can get a good view of the Ile de la Giraglia offshore, with its mighty lighthouse.

Back on the D80 you then arrive at the **Col de la Serra** (365 metres/1,200 ft), from which a footpath leads to an old ruined windmill, the **Moulin Mattei**. From here the panorama extends across the west coast of the Cap Corse.

The picturesque **Centuri-Port** ⓮ lies directly below. Boswell's first port of call in 1765, the village, with its grey schist houses grouped around a tiny harbour, makes perfect backdrop for a meal of delicious seafood – lobster is *the* local speciality, as proven by the myrtle-wood pots stacked on the quaysides.

The western cape

Beyond **Morsiglia** ⓯, which extends up from the sea on a series of terraces, the road rises to quite a height, curving its way along the jagged, steep rocky coastline. Pretty **Pino** ⓰, the next sizeable village, is surrounded by lush, almost tropical vegetation: plane trees provide refreshing shade, and olives, figs and oranges grow on the terraced slopes. The baroque façade of the church of Ste-Marie is painted a welcoming white. Down at the harbour, the village's old Genoese tower and its former Franciscan monastery stand opposite one another.

From Pino the D180 climbs to cross the cape's watershed at the Col de Ste Lucie, from where signposts point the way to the **Seneca Tower** ⓱ (Tour de Sénèque), connected to the pass via a badly potholed track. The famous Stoic is said to have lived here during his exile from Rome between AD 41 and 49.

The tower itself could hardly have provided Seneca with shelter considering that it was only built in the 15th century, but it does stand on the site of an earlier structure.

BELOW: Nonza clings to a rocky crag.

Map
on page
206

"Inhospitable" and even "horrible" were just two of the words Seneca used to describe the island on which he involuntarily spent eight years of his life, far from the *dolce vita* in Rome. "Where else is there anything as bare, as overwhelmingly grim as this rocky land?", he wondered.

The Corsicans avenged themselves for this unfriendly description of their homeland with an uncomplimentary little tale about Seneca: apparently the philosopher had his evil way with the daughter of a Corsican shepherd. When her brothers discovered the hanky-panky they massaged Seneca's bare buttocks with a particular variety of stinging-nettle that still grows in the vicinity of the tower. The Corsican name for this species of nettle is a reminder of the whole scandalous affair: Ortica di Seneca.

Back on the corniche, a spectacular stretch of steeply shelving hillsides and cliffs have to be negotiated before the scattered hamlets of **Canari** ⓲ come into view. The village is worth visiting for its two splendid churches. The elder of the pair, **Santa Maria Assunta**, is a very good example of 12th-century Pisan Romanesque: its cornices have curious human and animal faces. The baroque church of **St-François**, formerly part of a Franciscan monastery, contains 15th-century altar paintings depicting St Michael subduing the dragon and weighing human souls, and also Christ dressed as a penitent. A Cap Corse noblewoman, Vittoria di Gentile, holding her child, is depicted on a 16th-century tombstone in front of the choir.

A grey wasteland and old, dilapidated buildings and machinery are all that remain of an asbestos mine on the coast road, which was abandoned in 1965. The overburden has created a beach of black sand that extends as far as **Nonza** ⓳. It forms an ideal surface on which to draw and write using white pebbles, overlooked by near vertical cliffs.

The imposing square tower perched on top of them was defended singlehandedly against the French in 1768 by the resourceful Corsican lieutenant Casella. Using just one cannon, and several flintlocks, Casella delivered such an incredible show of strength that the besiegers did not dare storm the tower. They eventually offered everyone inside it safe passage, and were amazed and very embarrassed when, instead of the whole team they had expected, the cunning old trooper limped out alone.

The church in Nonza is consecrated to St Julie. She was actually martyred in Carthage around AD 300, but legend has shifted her death to Nonza. A double fountain (Fontaine Ste-Julie) is supposed to have sprung up at the place where the stubborn young Christian apparently had both her breasts severed from her body.

Shortly after the town of Nonza, the Golfe de St-Florent comes into view, and the vineyards of the Patrimonio region begin. To get back to Bastia, the D81, which borders the Cap Corse to the south, first has to climb over the Col de Teghime (536 metres/1,750 ft). From the summit of this pass there is a fine view of both coasts. ❏

LEFT: spectacular stretch of road on the Cap Corse. **RIGHT:** the pretty mountain village of Pino.

Map on page 216

AROUND THE EAST COAST

The chief appeal of the flat, fertile east coast lies in off-track wandering through sleepy hill villages, combined with the pleasures of a virtually unbroken white-sand beach and the ruins of Aléria

Along the 100-km (60-mile) stretch from Bastia to Solenzara, Corsica's eastern coastal plain is one long sandy beach, ideal for holidaymakers from spring to autumn. Tourists familiar with Corsica consider the region rather monotonous, however. This is hardly surprising when you consider how much tourism has flourished. The broad coastal plain is fringed with incongruous-looking holiday villages and campsites.

The N198 – the main road from Bastia to Bonifacio – runs in a straight line along much of its length. Being the only straight road on the island it is also the most dangerous, because the Corsicans take ample advantage of it to race their cars; even the speed traps set by the Gendarmerie don't seem to provide much of a deterrent. The villages along this road are devoid of character – the older settlements on the island were all moved up to the eastern mountain slopes centuries ago to provide protection against foreign invaders, mosquitoes and malaria.

Viticulture

The coastal plain itself, up to 15 km (9 miles) wide in places, is used predominantly for agricultural purposes, and (since the 1960s) mostly by French colonists from North Africa. Over 16,000 so-called *pieds noirs*, forced to leave the newly-independent countries of Morocco, Tunisia and Algeria, arrived on Corsica between 1962 and 1966. The former colonial landowners introduced viticulture to the east coast on a large scale. More recently, citrus fruit has also been successfully cultivated here with the aid of irrigation.

Relations between the *pieds noirs* and indigenous Corsicans were strained from the start, and degenerated as the east coast's agricultural revolution gathered pace. For many locals, the fact that their island was fast becoming synonymous with inferior quality wine – being churned out in vast quantities by the *caves* around Aléria – was a source of shame.

Matters came to a head in 1975, when it emerged that one of the largest *pieds noirs* producers had been illegally lacing his wine with sugar to boost its alcohol content. Seizing on the scandal as a pretext to voice their opposition to the French government's North African resettlement programme, a team of nationalist commandos occupied the offending grower's cellar. Two gendarmes were killed in the ensuing shoot-out before the militants surrendered. The siege marked the first of many armed encounters between the French state and Corsican nationalists,

PRECEDING PAGES: Castagniccia, takes its name from the chestnut *(castagna)* forests.

LEFT: fishing nets hung out to dry.

RIGHT: watch out for cows when you're driving around bends.

The East Coast

0   5 km

0   5 miles

N

inspiring the formation of the FLNC (Fronte di Liberaioine Naziunale di a Corsica). Such drama, however, these days seems a world away from the peaceful (and respectable) vineyards and fruit orchards striating the eastern plain, whose back roads and mountainous hinterland offer vivid glimpses of the island's past.

Bastia to Cervione

Anyone arriving in Bastia by ferry who leaves the town and heads south will probably gain a rather poor initial impression of Corsica. The N193 – all four lanes of it – runs in a straight line through an ugly industrial area, which only comes to an end 20 km (12 miles) further on at **Casamozza**, where the N198 to Porto-Vecchio and Bonifacio has branches off to Corte and Ajaccio.

There is, however, a neat way of avoiding the ugly industrial sprawl of Bastia entirely: 5 km (3 miles) south of the town there is a side-road (D107) on the left, signposted to "Bastia-Plage". Follow this inconspicuous-looking sign and you'll soon find yourself in an entirely different world. The road runs past villas, hotels, campsites and sometimes just sand-dunes, along the tongue of land between the **Etang de Biguglia ❶** and the sea. The lagoon is rich in fish and is particularly famous for its eels.

The beach behind the row of flat sand-dunes is easily accessible from just about everywhere and only tends to get relatively full at weekends, when *Bastiais* come here to relax. Anyone planning to stay here for any length of time, though, should bear in mind that **Bastia-Poretta airport** is not far away.

The road comes to an end rather abruptly, at a T-junction. The left turn leads to the **Plage de Pineto** and the right one takes you back to the N193. Before reaching it, however, you will pass the church of **La Canonica ❷** standing at a bend in the road. Those in a hurry can also reach it directly from the N193: turn off towards Bastia-Poretta airport in Lucciana and then turn right again immediately on to the D107. The church of La Canonica appears in the middle

Map on page 216

of the coastal plain and is visible for miles around on clear days. It was here, 100 years before the birth of Christ, that the Roman general Gaius Marius founded the military colony of Mariana for war veterans who had remained loyal to him. The small town that soon arose on this site was a useful starting point for the further colonisation of Corsica, and the Roman emperor Augustus had a harbour built here.

Nevertheless, Mariana was never as prosperous as other Roman settlements. In the 4th century, the town received a basilica and a baptistry. Both were destroyed during raids by the Vandals and the Lombards in the 5th century, and then later covered by a layer of sediment when the Golo River flooded. The foundations of several brick houses at Mariana have been unearthed during excavations.

The remains of the early Christian basilica and also the baptistry, each of them paved with mosaic floors, were also discovered. The church of La Canonica as we know it today was built in the 12th century on foundations dating back to the 5th century, and was consecrated by the Archbishop of Pisa in 1119.

The sheer size of this church makes it clear how important it was in medieval times – it was the seat of the Bishop of Corsica. Despite suffering extensive damage in the 15th and 16th centuries, La Canonica remains one of the best examples of early Pisan Romanesque architecture on the island. The building style of this period is characterised by simplicity of ornamentation. A frieze with animal sculptures can be seen in the church's west façade, above the entrance.

A few hundred metres away to the south-west, stands the beautifully-proportioned church of San Parteo, surrounded by meadows. It is not much older than La Canonica and is also early Pisan Romanesque in style. The fields have been excavated to reveal a cemetery, which was used from pagan right up to medieval times.

Those with time to spare can make a quick detour inland through the villages of the **Casinca** micro-region, perched on natural balconies high above the plain. Smothered in olive and chestnut trees, **Vescovato ❸**, only 3 km (2 miles) off the *route nationale* on the D237, is the most populous, with the majority of its inhabitants travelling to work in Bastia. Its name means "bishopric", referring to the time in the 13th century when the bishop's seat was transferred here from nearby Mariana to escape the malaria that was rife around the swampy coastal lowlands.

The church of **San Martino**, just north of the village's lively square, was renovated and enlarged during the Genoan era of the mid-15th century, and retains its original fittings, including a marble tabernacle of the Resurrection showing two Roman soldiers asleep against the tomb. Vescovato's most famous son was the naval Captain Luc Julian Joseph de Casabianca (1762–98), killed when his ship, the *Orient*, was attacked by Nelson in the battle of Aboukir. His 12-year-old son was on board at the time and insisted on remaining with his father as the vessel

sank, inspiring Felicia Heman's famous poem which begins "The boy stood on the burning deck". A succession of French naval vessels have been named after the family, most notably the submarine *Casabianca*, which provisioned the nascent Resistance in Corsica in 1942–43. From Vescovato the most scenic onward route is to take the winding D237 around the mountain to neighbouring **Venzolasca** ④, another pretty schist village of tall houses clustered around a slender campanile, from where the D37 drops back to the *route nationale*.

Continuing southwards along the N198, **Moriani-Plage** ⑤, 20 km (12 miles) beyond Casamozza, is just one more of the faceless communities strung out along this main road: a handful of ugly, prefabricated modern hotels, several shoddy-looking buildings dotted along the roadside and – almost making up for it all – a magnificently broad sandy beach. Strange as it may seem, this place is also of historical significance: Paoli sailed into exile from here with his father in 1739, and Napoleon also landed on the beach en route to Paris from his exile on Elba in 1815.

Only a short distance further inland, along the eastern flank of the mountains, several far less touristy villages can be reached by taking the D34 from Moriani-Plage. The Corniche de la Castigniccia (D330) runs along the eastern slope of Monte Castello between the villages of San-Nicolao and Cervione. It affords fine views far out to sea, all the way to Elba and Capraia. The road has been hewn out of the rock for part of the way: it runs through two short tunnels and crosses a noisy mountain stream.

San-Nicolao ⑥ has a grand 17th-century parish church with vibrant interior decor and *trompe l'oeil* painting. But the largest village in the area is **Cervione** ⑦, which even has its own 16th-century cathedral, built when the village was a bishopric for a brief period. King Theodore used the episcopal palace as his summer residence from April to Novem-

BELOW: free-range pork.

Map on page 216

ber in the year 1736. Today it houses a folklore museum, giving visitors an idea of what everyday life in the region must have been like all those years ago.

Between Moriani-Plage and Aléria there are several large holiday villages situated between the main road and the sea. At the **Etang de Diane**, the seafood is excellent, especially the oysters, farmed in the lagoon since the time of the Romans (an islet just off shore is made up of a centuries' old midden of discarded shells). An ideal place to sample them is the Pieds Dans l'Eau restaurant.

Castagniccia and around

The name *Castagniccia* translated means "small chestnut grove", but the region that bears this name is in reality a huge forest of sweet-chestnut trees, covering an area of more than 150 sq. km (58 sq. miles). At one time the local inhabitants lived from the chestnuts: the fruits were ground to flour and the wood was used for heating and building. But these days

most of the groves are no longer tended; as a result of urban migrations only the older generations have remained behind in the villages.

The route outlined below enters Castagniccia from the southeast, via Cervione, and follows its principal artery – the D71 – northwest, to join the *route nationale* at Ponte Leccia. Having rounded the mountainside beyond Cervione, the main road penetrates the 22-km (14-mile) long **Alesani Valley**, whose history of invasion and resistance mirrors that of the whole island.

The valley is also extremely beautiful; sharp contrasts in relief force the D71 up and down continually, and around a whole series of hairpins. The ruins of former watermills that once produced chestnut flour can be made out in several places on the main valley floor. The central area of the Alesani Valley is devoid of human habitation, because the mountain flanks are so close to each other at this point that the river has cut a ravine deep into the land. The Alesani River has been dammed

BELOW: view across the Castagniccia.

up to form the Barrage de l'Alesani Reservoir shortly before it enters the coastal plain, and the 11 million cubic metres (2,900 million gallons) of water here have been used to irrigate the lowland areas since 1970.

A garland of mountain villages clings to rocky outcrops, beneath vertiginous rock-faces, in the mighty basin at the end of the valley An example of the settlement pattern typical of this region is provided by the municipality of **Felce**. This type of scattered settlement had its reasons, the main one being the inhabitants' need to protect themselves against enemies from outside, though continuous feuds between rival families also played a part. These often used to end in bloodshed. In the course of time this led to an isolated existence for many people inside clan settlements, where – in accordance with the code of honour of the vendetta – only members and relatives of a single large family were allowed to live.

The layout of the buildings within these clan settlements is almost fortress-like. The German geographer Friedrich Ratzel, who travelled through Corsica in the 19th century, gives us a telling description: "Clustered together, their grey backs turned towards us, they are reminiscent of a crowd of close friends who have a great deal to tell each other – and absolutely nothing to tell the outside world."

But there is still a lot that is picturesque about these communities, with their tall buildings, vaulted passageways, twisting staircases, white window-frames set into unplastered slate walls, and flower-filled niches. The surrounding forest is like something straight out of a fairy-tale, with its huge and ancient chestnut trees, many of them struck by lightning, its moss-covered rocks, bubbling springs and little stone houses overgrown with lianas – an idyll that has largely been spared any outside interference.

Approaching Castagniccia from the east, it's worth turning off the D71 on to the D271 at Valle d'Alesani for the short

BELOW: valleys and mountain peaks.

Map
on page
216

detour down to the **Couvent d'Alesani** , below the hamlet of Casella. Long a political and spiritual centre, the Franciscan monastery has been extensively restored. High on the wall of a side-chapel one can admire a 15th-century Virgin and Child painted on wood, known as the *Madonna with the Cherry*. Since 1983 a copy has replaced the original, which was painted by Sano di San Pietro from Siena, and is notable for its gentle use of colour and its Renaissance charm.

The monastery is more closely connected with the German baron Theodor von Neuhoff, a rogue and adventurer. At a gathering here in the year 1736, after he had brought weapons, money, grain and clothing to the rebels fighting the Genoese, he was appointed Corsica's first and only king. The spontaneous joy quickly evaporated into impatient anger 200 days later. When the provisions were all used up it was clear that far too few replenishments were going to arrive. Disguised as a priest, von Neuhoff escaped from the island and died penniless in London in 1756. Pressing westwards on the D71, the next landmark encountered is the **Col d'Arcarotta**, the watershed between the Fium'Alto and Alesani river systems, where you could pull over at the aptly named Auberge des Deux Vallées.

This area is where the famous green marble known as Verde di Corsica comes from; it was used in the construction of the Paris Opera and the Medici chapels in Florence.

Once across the pass, you enter the true heartland of Castagniccia, a huge basin draped in lush chestnut canopy, dominated by the distinctive profile of Monte San Petrone. The main village in the canton is **Piedicroce** , which has around 200 full-time residents and is situated at the crossroads formed by the D71 and the D506, above the Fium'Alto.

It's certainly worth taking a look at the baroque church of **St-Pierre et St-Paul**, which dates from 1761, and has a magnificent interior which includes the oldest

BELOW:
many schist
hamlets are
almost
deserted.

organ in Corsica, built in the 17th century and now wonderfully restored. Regional specialities prepared from ewe's cheese *(brocciu)* and roast sweet chestnuts *(fasgiole)* can be sampled at the hotel restaurant "La Refuge".

A couple of kilometres downhill from Pedicroce on the D506 brings you to **Stazzona**, whose former prosperity derived from its gun workshops and, later, the naturally fizzy mineral water produced by the springs just below it at **Orezza** . By the 19th century, "les eaux d'Orezza" attracted streams of health tourists from as far afield as the French Asian colonies and, in spite of its unpleasantly metallic taste, the bottled mineral water became one of the island's major exports. After a four-year pause in production in the mid-1990s, the plant, at the end of an avenue of plane trees on the far side of the river, was re-opened by the local municipality. These days the bubbly water is far more palatable than it used to be, its iron content and fizziness being reduced before it is bottled. Back on the D71 again, heading northwards from Pedicroce, the first landmark you pass is the ruins of the former Franciscan **Monastery of Orezza**. The building was once used as an assembly point by Corsican freedom fighters but was destroyed by the Germans in World War II after local Resistance partisans were found to have hidden an arms cache inside it.

The Conca d'Orezza

Above the monastery, at an altitude of roughly 650 metres (2,100 ft), numerous villages form a semicircle at the end of the Fium'Alto valley: the Conca d'Orezza. They united in medieval times to form a so-called *pieve*, a cohesive political and economic unit, and it still survives today as a cantonal administration.

One of the prettiest among them, **Campodonico** ⓫, reached via the first turning left off the road after the monastery of Orezza, marks the start of the popular ascent of **Monte San Petrone**. The sum-

BELOW: small hamlet buried in the mountains.

Map on page 216

mit can be reached after a roughly 3-hour-long walk along a well marked and cleared mule path. From the 1,767-metre (5,800-foot) high peak one can enjoy a breathtaking view: the whole of the Cap Corse to the north; all the way to the mountains of the Fium orbo to the south; eastwards, the entire coastal plain from Bastia to Solenzara; and to the west, Corsica's entire central range of mountains rising up from the Corte basin. It is truly a unique panorama. At your feet, like a green carpet, are the chestnut forests in the Fium'Alto and Alesani valleys, with all their tiny villages. This is definitely the place for an incredible, bird's-eye view of the whole of Eastern Corsica.

If you follow the D71 from Piedicroce in a northwesterly direction, the road passes through **Campana**, with its picturesque campanile, and **Nocario**, where chestnut flour is still produced, before reaching **La Porta ⑫**. This village, with a population of roughly 500, lies at the bottom of a lateral valley of the Fium'Alto,

and since 259 BC has served as a centre of resistance against the Romans, the Vandals, the Byzantines, the Lombards, the Saracens, the Genoese and the French right up to the present day. The main attraction of La Porta, if not of the entire region here, is the richly-adorned church of **St John the Baptist**, designed by a Milanese architect and built in 1648. Its magnificent campanile, dating from (1702), is considered to be the finest baroque bell tower on the whole island.

The church, with its polychromatic ceiling, contains a 17th-century figure of Christ painted on wood, an 18th-century painting of the Beheading of John the Baptist, and a very fine Italian organ. The latter was restored in 1963 by a Paris music teacher named Jacques Chailley, and it now plays an integral role in the concerts held here in the summertime. The *franghju*, or oil press, at La Porta has also recently been restored as part of the government's attempt to stimulate a revival in olive oil production. The D71

BELOW: Morosaglia is the birthplace of Pascal Paoli.

continues on to the 985-metre (3,200-ft) high **Col de Prato**, from where you can also approach the summit of Monte San Petrone on foot. Just below the col, **Morosaglia** ⑬, perched on a mountain slope 800 metres (2,600 ft) above sea level, is synonymous with Pasquale Paoli, the Corsican national hero *(see page 49)* who was born here in 1725. The small **museum** (open 9am–noon, 2.30–7pm, closed Tues; entrance fee) in the hamlet of **Stretta** is regarded as a national monument. Apart from a series of contemporary Corsican books and the first ever Corsican newspaper, the most striking sight here are two white silk flags displaying the mysterious moor's head, one with the symbols of slavery dating from the period before Paoli and the other with its headband pushed up and no earrings, symbolising the liberation that Paoli brought. Paoli's remains are also buried here, in an adjacent chapel, having been transferred to his native village from England in 1889, 82 years after his death.

Ponte Nuovo

From Morsiglia, you can either backtrack along the D71 to the east coast or press on downhill for another 15 km (9 miles) to **Ponte Leccia**, where the D193 crosses the Golo River. From there, the high-spec N193 highway cuts due south towards Corte, while the D197 "Balanina" route veers northwest towards Calvi. Alternatively, head along the main Bastia highway from Ponte Leccia to Casamozza on the eastern plain.

This latter option takes you past one of the island's most politically charge historic monuments, **Ponte Nuovo** ⑭. Contrary to what the name might imply, the bridge is in fact very old and dilapidated. It was built during the Genoese occupation of the island, and was the scene of the last great battle for Corsican independence. In the spring of 1769, the French army, which had been so crushingly defeated by Corsica one year previously near Borgo, marched once again against the Corsican troops under their leader

BELOW: the region was a bastion of support for the independence movement.

Map on page 216

Pasquale Paoli. On 8 May 1769 Paoli had 2,000 of his men cross the Golo River and advance northwards. The attack was repulsed, and the Corsicans fled in the direction of the bridge, which had meanwhile been taken by a group of German mercenaries. Trapped between the advancing French army and the banks of the Golo River, the Corsicans were completely wiped out. After this defeat, Paoli gave up the struggle and left Corsica. A memorial at the roadside stands as a reminder of these historic events.

Ancient Aléria and hinterland

Situated on a small rise, **Aléria** ⑮ is an inconspicuous sort of place these days. In antiquity, though, it was one of the most important ports for seagoing traffic in the Western Mediterranean. The town was founded by the Phocaeans around 500 BC. They named it Alalia, and made use of it as a base for their fleet as well as a trading post. The Romans took Alalia in 250 BC, and it was from here that they began their colonisation of the island. After the Corsican population had been subdued, the town enjoyed a long period of prosperity.

Alalia became one of the most important trading centres of the Western Mediterranean. The Roman emperor Augustus had an amphitheatre, an aqueduct and several defensive walls built here. At that time the Etang de Diane served as a naval base, and the trading vessels would anchor in the Tavignano estuary. Alalia's prosperity ended, however, with the fall of the Roman Empire.

In the 5th century, after it was sacked and burned by the Vandals, the town was abandoned once and for all. The entire area surrounding the Tavignano estuary then degenerated into swampland, and was an ideal breeding-ground for malaria mosquitoes until as recently as World War II. Spraying the area with DDT put an end to the mosquito plague after 1947. The swamps were then successfully drained, the area newly populated and

BELOW: pathway from the Roman excavations to the Genoese town at Aléria. **RIGHT:** Roman town excavations.

the land cultivated once more. Excavations at the old Roman town of Alalia have revealed its former greatness once more. Only certain sections of it have been uncovered so far, including the Forum, a temple, the hot springs and also the Praetorium, official seat of the Roman governor of Corsica.

Archaeological finds from the town are on display in the **Musée Jérôme Carcopino** (open daily 8am–noon, 2–7pm; entrance fee). These include magnificently painted earthenware goblets of Etruscan origin. The 2nd-century marble bust of Jupiter Ammon, found near the Forum, and the finely-worked Etruscan bronze statues are also of particular interest. The museum is situated on the ground floor of the Fort de Matra, built by the Genoese in the 16th century.

Several valleys run inland between Aléria and Ghisonaccia, the largest and widest being the **Tavignano Valley**, whose villages are dotted along high ridges overlooking it. Here, just a short distance away from the busy east coast, you can experience the remoteness and tranquillity of Corsican mountain settlements. One of the most easily accessible is **Piedicorte-di-Gaggio** ⑯, on the northern side of the valley on the D14. The finest of its views are to be had from the ruins of a medieval castle directly above the square – the former seat of the de Gaggio clan who ruled this region in the 13th century.

On the opposite side of the Tavignano, **Antisanti** ⑰, 20 km (12 miles) west of Aléria on the D43, is a 1,000-year-old village with a matchless panorama out over the eastern plain to the distant Tuscan Islands. Its single street was the only one to have survived a retributive attack by the French during Paoli's insurrection in 1753. The road that leads inland from the east coast to Ghisoni presents a totally different aspect of the landscape. It runs through two narrow ravines: the **Défilé de l'Inzecca** ⑱ and the **Défilé des Strette**. The rocky walls here, through which the river and the road

BELOW: drinking vessel (480 BC) on display at the archaeological museum in Aléria.

Map on page 216

wind their precarious way, are often no more than a few yards apart. Winding through the gorges to **Ghisoni** (see page 245), offers one of the most direct routes to the interior mountains.

The foothills rippling south in parallel with the plains from the Défilés comprise the micro-region of **Fiumorbo**, a mountainous area, thickly overgrown with maquis and chestnut forests. Small hamlets and villages keep popping up quite unexpectedly. Long a hotbed of revolution and resistance against the French, who ruthlessly suppressed a series of uprisings here in the 18th and 19th centuries, the region was a favourite hiding-place for bandits until World War II, since when it has remained a remote and little visited area.

An appropriately spectacular approach to the Fiumorbo cuts south from the mouth of the Défilé de l'Inzecca via the D44, which twists through open maquis to **Poggio-di-Nazza** and eventually **Pietrapola-les-Bains ⑲**, whose sulphur springs have been in use since Roman times. People still come here to take the waters. The façade of its church, Santa Maria, encorporates a pillar taken from the ruins of a Jupiter-Saturn temple found nearby.

From Pietrapola, follow the D45 back uphill to the hamlet of Acciani, and from there descend via the D45 to the Fiumorbo's main village, **Prunelli-di-Fiumorbo ⑳**, from whose fortified church there are more wonderful views over the coastal plain and mountains.

The local Mairie houses a small **museum** (open Mon–Fri 9.30am–noon, 3–5.30pm), with Roman artefacts and World War II memorabilia. From Prunelli, a short downhill drive on the D345 takes you back to the coastal highway just south of Ghisonaccia.

The Côte des Nacres

In the course of the past 20 years, **Solenzara ㉑** has developed from a sleepy and dilapidated little coastal village into a full-blown beach resort. Hotels, campsites, discotheques, boutiques and a seemingly endless sandy beach stretching away to the north are all here to attract the tourists. The **Côte des Nacres** (Mother-of-Pearl Coast) begins south of Solenzara.

The steep rocky coast, easily accessible from the main road which runs directly next to the sea, is a real diver's paradise, broken up now and then by romantic bays with fine sandy beaches. There are modest tourist facilities available in Tarcu and Fautea. In Solenzara, a turn off the N198 leads to one of the most varied mountain routes in all Corsica: the D268 up to the Col de Bavella.

It starts off by following the course of the Solenzara River, then the very narrow road (no caravans) begins winding its way up pine-covered slopes to the **Col de Larone**. From up here there is a superb view of the Forêt de Bavella down in the valley basin below, and of the fantastic rocky landscape surrounding it. From the **Col de Bavella** (1,218 metres/4,000 ft) there is a particularly good view of the steep and jagged Aiguilles de Bavella.   ❏

RIGHT: the region suffered massive depopulation after World War I.

CORTE AND ITS HINTERLAND

Maps:
Town 232
Area 233

Framed by a wall of high peaks, Corsica's university town – a charismatic jumble of Genoese buildings spilling below an old citadelle – brings together the old and new aspects of the island's national identity

Corte has been considered the "secret capital" of Corsica since Pasquale Paoli ruled his democratic island-republic from here. Unlike the fortress-towns along the coast it was not founded by the Genoese, and it lies right at the heart of the island at the confluence of two rivers – the Restonica and the Tavignano – and at the junction of several major traffic arteries, including the main road from Ajaccio to Bastia and the road from Aléria to Porto.

Corte ❶ is at its most imposing visually if you arrive from the direction of Ajaccio, via the Vizzavona Pass. Surrounded by barren mountains, the impressive citadel sits high up on a rocky outcrop, towering above the 400-metre (1,300-ft) high valley basin like the prow of an enormous ship. The older part of the town clings to this crag with its protective fortress, while the more modern sections are sprawled out at its feet.

The name "Corte" derives from the Cortinchi family, who ruled this valley in the early Middle Ages. In the 13th century, Corte fell into the hands of the Genoese, and in 1419 Vincentello d'Istria occupied it in the name of the King of Aragon, and began building the citadel. The town has been regularly fought over throughout Corsican history. The Genoese settled here once again, but the Corsicans managed to snatch the fortress away from them on several occasions: Sampiero Corso took it in 1553, and Gianpetro Gaffori stormed it in 1746. From 1755 Corte was the capital of independent Corsica for 14 years until the town was finally forced to surrender to the French.

An important event in the town's history was the foundation of a university here by Pasquale Paoli, who wanted to provide his people with access to higher education. Since 1981 Corte, with its population of around 6,700, has been a university town once more, and the students, of whom there are now about 3.500, have given the town a new lease of life. Alongside subjects such as law and economics, the Corsican language is also taught here, and corsitude is held in high regard. It really is no wonder that the island's students have become the predominant driving force behind its independence movement. But from spring until autumn, this small provincial town up in the mountains is also popular with tourists – it is a rendezvous point for hikers, climbers, anglers and canoeists.

Corte: the town

The **cours Paoli** in Corte is the equivalent of Ajaccio's cours Napoléon: it is the

PRECEDING PAGES: Corte is one of the cultural centres of the island. **LEFT:** view over Corte's old town. **BELOW:** the town's citadel dates back to the 13th century.

main shopping street, albeit somewhat narrower and less cosmopolitan. Hunting and fishing supplies can be seen alongside the usual souvenirs in the shop-windows here, and rucksacks can be filled with provisions. Evening is the busiest time for the restaurants, cafés and bistros. The street ends at the **place Paoli** 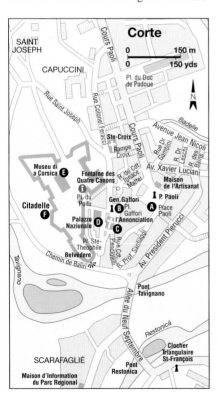, with its bronze statue of Corsica's most famous freedom-fighter. From here we mount the broad steps of the rue Scoliscia and enter the labyrinthine Old Town.

In the **place Gaffori** there is a statue of the famous general. His arm out-stretched, he seems to be giving the command to storm the citadel – he did so despite the fact that the Genoese had taken his son hostage. Gaffori Junior survived the onslaught, however. There is also a memorial tablet on the statue's plinth to Gaffori's spirited wife, Faustina. A relief depicts her holding a lighted torch over an open barrel of gunpowder, recalling the occasion when she barricaded herself inside her own house during the Genoese

siege of the town in 1750. The Genoese planned to kidnap Gaffori's wife in his absence, in order to blackmail him. Just as her friends and helpers were on the point of acceding to the Genoese demands, Faustina threatened to blow the entire house sky-high, thus managing to hold out until Gaffori came to her rescue. The **Gaffori House** was subjected to a hail of bullets, and the holes they made are still there to this day.

The town's **Eglise de l'Annonciation** also stands in this square; though it dates from 1450, it was given a new façade in the 17th century. The church contains a finely-carved pulpit, once the property of the town's former Franciscan monastery, plus a baroque crucifix.

The street climbs steeply to the **place du Poilu**. House No. 1 is the ancestral home of the Arrighi de Casanova family. Napoleon's parents lived here when Carlo Buonaparte was a supporter of Paoli. A plaque above the doorway announces that their first son Joseph, later to become king of Naples and Spain, was born here in 1768. To the left stands the **Palazzu Naziunale**, the seat of the independent Corsican government from 1755–69; today, fittingly enough, it houses the university's Institute of Corsican Studies.

The citadel, which was used as a barracks by the Foreign Legion, is also due to become a lively centre of Corsican culture now that the restoration work on it has been completed. Once referred to as "Corsica's Acropolis", it now houses the **Museu di a Corsica** (open daily 10am–8pm; entrance fee) which houses a huge ethnographic collection and galleries showing temporary exhibitions.

The best view of the 100-metre (300-ft) high rock with its **Citadelle**, and also of the slate and brick roofs of the Old Town, is definitely to be had from the appropriately-named **Belvédère**.

To get there, follow the signs along the rue Balthasar Arrighi. Below, the Restonica and Tavignano valleys emerge from their respective gorges, and in the distance rise the impressive peaks of the central highlands. Another view of the entire picturesque town panorama can be had if

Maps:
Town 232
Area 233

you drive out of town over the Restonica Bridge (Pont-Neuf) and take the second turning right towards the Ferme Auberge Albadu.

The Corte hinterland

The **Tavignano Valley** ❷, stretching northwest of Corte into the heart of the mountains, is a paradise for hikers. You don't need any great mountaineering talents to cover the marked route from Corte to **Refuge A Sega** and back, but plan for a 6–7-hour hike. You leave Corte from the Chapelle Ste-Croix, along the Rue St-Joseph. The cable bridge over a section of the Tavignano makes an ideal photograph. Here, and by the Sega refuge, there are some fine river-beds for swimming. Instead of returning to Corte one can also continue on towards Calcuccia or the Lac de Nino.

Running roughly parallel to the Tavignano Valley towards the high peaks of the watershed, the **Gorges de la Restonica** may be accessed by what many regard as the island's most dramatic road. Upgraded and widened in 2001, the route no longer suffers from the horrendous traffic jams that previously occurred in high summer, but it still gets extremely crowded, so try to make an early start if you intend to follow it all the way up the valley.

Soon after leaving Corte, the stylish and traditional Auberge de la Restonica comes temptingly into view. The trout here are, of course, fresh: they come straight from the mountain torrents nearby. Now the valley gets narrower; its steep rocky walls here are as popular with mountain climbers as they are with mountain goats, and the ravine is a favourite haunt of kayak and river-rafting enthusiasts.

After winding its way across 17 km (10 miles) of pine forest, the small road finally comes to an end at the **Bergerie de Grotelle** ❸. When you reach these stone huts belonging to the region's friendly shepherds you should definitely put your climbing shoes on and hike off to the two finest glacial lakes in all Corsica. The **Lac**

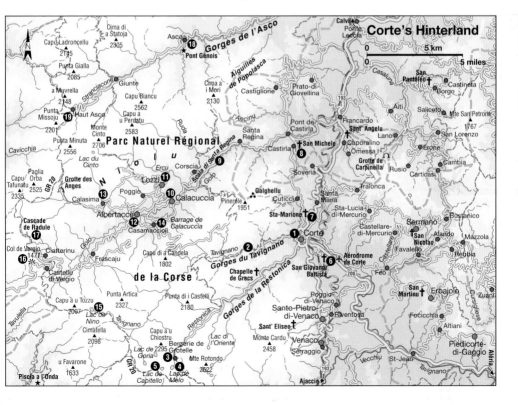

Two Shepherds

On a high plain, far from the bustle of the coastal cities, an encounter with two shepherds. The pattern of their lives is governed by the seasons and by trans-humance, the seasonal migration of flocks. In summer, they live with their goats and sheep in the mountains, but before winter comes they lead them down to the coastal grazing lands.

These shepherds, who are brothers, are following in their father's and grandfather's footsteps. They look forward to their return to the coast, for in September they will stop at the Niolu annual fair. Here the men assemble for the Festival of the Santa, joining together in the polyphonic songs handed down orally since the very dawn of time. They are songs which tell of love, of death and of the earth; songs which move the listener to tears. The shepherds softly hummed one of the beautiful melodies. Then they suddenly burst out laughing as they saw a young goatherd chasing his animals.

"Look," said the elder of the two gently, "That is a boy who went to school to learn how to be a shepherd. We have been tending our flocks since we were children. No teacher in the world can teach you how to become a shepherd." Working to the same harmonious rhythm, the two shepherds whittled away at an olive branch with their fine, sharp knives. It is a common occupation in the country, allowing concentration on intellectual matters.

They were reluctant to speak of their mother, whom like all Corsicans they revered. Pointing heavenwards, Paulo Andria said in a quiet voice full of emotion, "God rest her soul. We should leave her in peace. It is wrong to disturb the spirits." His words sounded like superstition, but did the pair also believe in God? The question surprised them. Their answer was, "We live in the *macchia*, but we're not savages. Look at the Holy Cross above the fireplace, and the branches of olive and palm trees which were blessed last year on Palm Sunday." Paulo Andria leapt to his feet and pointed to a brightly-coloured picture of the Virgin Mary, but not before he had carefully wiped it with his sleeve to remove the layer of dust. The two men crossed themselves, as if such a question might leave its evil mark on the stone walls of their hut.

Two rifles were also hung on the wall. "Don't think that they are there to protect us from bandits. Unfortunately we're the only ones left in the *macchia*. But have you ever seen a Corsican who wasn't armed?" Their grandfather taught them to shoot. "When he pulled the trigger of his old rifle, you had the feeling that the recoil might dislocate his shoulder," they recalled. Did they regret their lonely lifestyle? "Never! Our father taught us to master our fear by taking us with him into the mountains. When we were only eight years old, transhumance was like a fascinating adventure. And we still enjoy it."

A mist descending from the mountains brought our conversation to a close. Paulo Andria pulled the peak of his cap down over his face. The flocks on the mountainside felt the approaching storm as clearly as we did and retreated into their stall. Before we departed we all drank to each other, raising our glasses in a toast. They were filled with a remarkable schnapps, which smelled of the *macchia* and warmed both body and soul. ❑

LEFT: shearing sheep the old-fashioned way.

Map on page 233

de Melo ❹, at 1,710 metres (5,600 ft) above sea level, is about one hour away, and the **Lac de Capitello** ❺ (1,930 metres/6,300 ft above sea level), set into magnificent rocky scenery, is another hour's walk from there. When the bathing season is at its height in June down on the beaches there are still large chunks of ice floating around these mountain lakes.

The Restonica Valley is also a good starting-point for a fascinating day's hike across Corsica's second-highest peak, **Monte Rotondo** (2,622 metres/8,600 ft). If you find the difference in altitude of 1,622 metres (5,300 ft) too much to cope with you should still go up as far as the **Lac di l'Oriente** (2,061 metres/6,700 ft above sea level), with its green, grassy islands, where the Restonica River has its main source. "This incomparable source possesses such sharpness that it cleans iron as bright as a mirror in a very short space of time, and protects it from rust", wrote the historian Gregorovius, who undertook the walk across Monte Rotondo

with a guide and a mule in the year 1852. During Paoli's time the Corsican fighters are said to have placed their rusty flint-locks in the waters of the Restonica in order to clean them.

Early churches around Corte

The ruins of three early Christian churches are hidden in valleys. To reach the first and closest to town, the 9th-century church of **San Giovanni Battista** ❻, take the N200 (towards Aléria) and follow the fork to the right after 1.5 km (1 mile); the chapel stands on a patch of open hillside just beyond the railway line. Only the apse of the basilica remains, and pieces of Roman tile can be seen in its walls – an early example of recycling. Both the church and the adjacent baptistery may have been built on the site of a Roman village.

The twin apses of the **Eglise Santa Marione** ❼ can be seen above the N193, roughly 2 km (1¼ miles) north in the direction of Bastia. Although the church

now stands in ruins, it is still possible to get an idea of its former glory. The third Pisan church, the pre-Romanesque chapel of **San Michele** , lies some 10 km (6 miles) north of Corte on the D18, on the outskirts of the picturesque village of **Castirla**. Its apse contains some fine 15th-century frescoes, recently restored: one of them depicts Christ in majesty, surrounded by symbols of the Evangelists and Apostles. Next to it there is an Annunciation. Before proceeding up the path towards the chapel don't forget to ask for the key at the village hall.

The Niolu Valley

Framed by the mightiest mountains on the island – the 2,706-metre (8,900-ft) high Monte Cinto and the Paglia Orba to the north, and the 2,622-metre (8,600-ft) high Monte Rotondo to the southeast – the mountain basin of **Niolu** can certainly be said to lie at the very heart of Corsica. This huge valley at the upper part of the Golo River, a massive granite basin

roughly 900 metres (3,000 ft) above sea level, used to be one of the most remote districts of the island.

The only access to it is through the daunting ravine known as the Scala di Santa Regina to the east, or via the highest mountain pass in all Corsica, the 1,477-metre (4,800-ft) high Col de Vergio, to the west. The roads over the pass and through the ravine were only built towards the end of the 19th century. Before that time, the Niolu could only be reached along mountain paths, and during the wintertime was completely cut off from the outside world.

In the autumn transhumance, herds of sheep and goats were driven over the high passes into the milder coastal regions – through the Fango Valley, for instance, to the Gulf of Galeria, or through the Scala di Santa Regina to the east coast – and they only returned in springtime after the snows had melted.

The Niolu is full of mountains, valleys, meadows, forests and lakes. The region is

BELOW: the valley is a good natural habitat for lizards.

Map on page 233

very poor: the people here are usually simple shepherds, and their pastures lie around the Lac de Nino, on the upper reaches of the Golo River and beneath Monte Cinto. The local inhabitants have only very recently begun to reap some profit from the tourism industry, especially from visitors who come up here in the summer months to escape the heat of the beaches and enjoy the refreshing, cool mountain air.

If you approach the Niolu from either Ponte Leccia or Corte you will travel through one of the wildest pieces of landscape on Corsica: the **Scala di Santa Regina ⓿**. The barriers of red granite on the eastern side of the valley basin forced the Golo River to dig a huge trench for itself here, managing a drop of 555 metres (1,800 ft) within the space of just 21 km (13 miles). The road passes excitingly beneath rocky overhangs and over arch bridges. The old mule route can still be glimpsed now and then. It leads through the gorge like a staircase *(scala)* hewn out

of the rock. At one point it is possible to walk right down into the ravine and join it, though the road is so narrow that there are not that many suitable stopping-places.

Around Calacuccia

A good base for excursions in this area is the capital of the Niolu, **Calacuccia ⓾**. This village, with its 400 or so inhabitants, possesses a handful of hotels, restaurants and supermarkets, as well as a pharmacy and a post office. The Barrage de Calacuccia, completed in 1968, is a recent tourist attraction. It contains 25 million cubic metres (6,600 million gallons) of water, and the power station here provides the island with much of its electricity. Though the lake is picturesque, it has caused some controversy in recent years, with environmentalists claiming the water has altered the valley's climate and ecology.

The wooden crucifix hanging above the altar in the church in Calacuccia is a fine example of the Niolu woodcarving tradition, as is the statue of St Roch in

BELOW: the reservoir at Calacuccia.

Casamaccioli. The village of **Lozzi** , 1,050 metres (3,400 ft) up on the hillside above Calacuccia, is the starting point for any ascent of **Monte Cinto**. A track has been made here which almost reaches as far as the Bergerie d'Ercu, making the ascent of Corsica's highest mountain a lot shorter. Start the expedition by taking the D84 from Calacuccia in the direction of Albertacce and then take the turn-off to Lozzi.

After passing through the main part of the village, the track then branches off towards Monte Cinto (7 km/4 miles). A marked route then leads from the end of the track to the Bergerie d'Ercu (1,650 metres/5,400 ft above sea level).

The peak can be scaled in 3 hours, but be sure you start out early because the morning sun shines straight on to the mountain. In good weather the whole of Corsica is visible from the summit, and sometimes even Elba and Sardinia too. Visibility does tend to get hazy from midday onwards, though. The mountains of the central massif all around the peak, such as Paglia Orba, Capu Larghia and Monte Rotondo are all extremely impressive as well.

The village of **Albertacce** ⑫, to the southwest of Calacuccia, boasts one of the area's best restaurants and a well-equipped *gîte d'étape* serving walkers who pass through on the Mare a Mare Nord long-distance trekking route. A road and footpath also lead from from Albertacce to **Calasima** ⑬, the highest village in Corsica at 1,095 metres (3,600 ft). There is a fine hiking route from here that leads under the jagged peaks of the Cinque Frati (Five Brothers) through the Viro Valley and then on to the Refuge Ciottuli di i Mori, beneath the peaks of the Paglia Orba and the Capu Tafunatu.

Only very few villages lie scattered across the Calacuccia basin. South of the reservoir is **Casamaccioli** ⑭, where an annual singing contest and fair take place between 8 and 10 September to mark the festival of La Santa du Niolu. The "young

BELOW: a shepherd and his flock.

Map on page 233

shepherds in good voice" here have become rather more elderly recently, but the tradition is still kept alive. The high point of the festivities is the procession on 8 September, when the statue of the Santa du Niolu is carried through the village *(see page 91).*

Forêt de Valdu-Niellu

If you drive up the D84 towards the Col de Vergio, you pass through the largest area of forest on the island, the **Forêt de Valdu-Niellu.** This region comprises 4,638 hectares (11,460 acres) in total, and 70 percent of it consists of Corsican black pine, also known as Laricio pine, as well as deciduous trees such as beech and birch. Thin alder scrub can be seen along the tree line. The forest of Valdu Niellu possesses the finest stands of pine on Corsica: some of the trees are 500 years old and can grow to a height of about 40 metres (120 ft). In the centre of the forest, at an altitude of 1,076 metres (3,500 ft), lies the Maison Forestière de Popaja, the

starting point for hikes to the Lac de Nino. The route, marked with yellow paint flashes, first leads through tall pine trees and small forests of birch, and then alongside the small Colga River. An hour later you will reach the stone buildings of the Bergerie Colga, and it takes another hour to get to the **Bocca a Stazzona** (1,762 metres/5,800 ft) at the top of the pass leading to the grazing land by the Lac de Nino.

At the top of the pass there are several large and unusual-looking rocks strewn about, which, according to an old Niolu legend, are the petrified oxen of the devil. The Niolu is the scene of many stories concerning St Martin and the devil, some of which date right back to the dawn of Christianity. When the devil discovered that St Martin, in his role as a shepherd, was successfully converting a large number of people, he decided to disguise himself as a farmer and teach the local population a lesson. He created enormous valleys in the mountains with a huge ploughshare. St Martin coolly observed

BELOW: the Forêt de Valdu-Niellu is the largest area of forest on the island.

these attempts, and then made fun of the devil, wondering why his furrows were so full of bends and asking him why he was unable to plough in a straight line. In a sudden burst of anger, the offended devil threw his ploughshare away as far as he could. It flew straight through a rock, forming the huge hole that can still be seen today – Capu Tafunatu. According to the legend, the devil's oxen were then immediately turned to stone by St Martin to prevent any further mischief.

It takes 15 minutes to make the journey from Stazzona Pass to the **Lac de Nino** ⓯. The landscape here is bathed in bright, clear light, cattle, horses and pigs graze away, and there is a marvellous tranquillity about the place.

The marshy meadows with their meandering streams here are called *pozzines* (from *pozzi*, the Corsican word for spring), and are the remnants of lakes that were filled up with sedimentation after the last Ice Age. The Lac de Nino, 1,743 metres (5,700 ft) above sea level, is the source of the Tavignano River. There is a wonderful 8-hour-long route back to Corte from here along its banks.

On the **Col de Vergio** ⓰, 1,477 metres (4,846 ft) up, the snow can sometimes be as deep as 1.5 metres (5 ft) deep, although for the past few years the winters have been very mild and snowfall scant. A mountain hotel and various ski-lifts cater for winter sports enthusiasts (on those rare occasions when there is enough snow to coat the slopes), while from June until late-September, streams of hikers pour through on the GR20.

Roughly 200 metres (650 ft) below the pass there is a good view of the Calacuccia Valley basin, and of the huge hole in the rock in Capu Tafunatu to the north. If you cross the pass here and go through the forests of Aitone you can then get back to Evisa and the Golfe de Porto on the West Coast.

From the pass, sections of the (orange waymarked) Mare a Mare Nord and (red-and-white waymarked) GR20 long-

LEFT: snow can fall until May on the Col de Vergio. **BELOW:** the Golo, still a mountain stream in the Niolu.

Map
on page
233

distance footpaths wind north through an idyllic forest filled with pine and birch towards the **Bergeries de Gradule**. Nestling in the middle of some unbelievably romantic rocky scenery, the shepherds huts can be reached in less than half an hour. Dangling copper pots and handmade signs indicate to visitors that freshly-prepared cheese can be purchased here. After leaving the the bergeries it is necessary to descend a steep slope in order to arrive at the **Cascade de Radule ⑰**, a popular picnic spot where the Golo flows through a series of deep blue pools, situated picturesquely at one end of a ravine.

If you continue following the red-and-white signs for the GR20 even further up the Golo River at this point, you will find plenty more nautral bathing pools and little cascades in which to have a bracing dip. From here it is still another two hours' hike to get to the refuge **Ciottulu di i Mori**, the starting-point for ascents of Paglia Orba and Capu Tafunatu.

The Asco Valley

Separated from the Niolu basin by the mighty Cinto massif, the **Asco Valley** possesses a higher, wilder and more rarified atmosphere than any other region accessible by road on the island. Aside from being enclosed by Corsica's highest ridges, it is also barely populated, with only one village and a scruffy ski station that sees a lot more through traffic in the summer hiking season than in winter – thanks to the scarcity of snow these days.

The sole approach to the valley is via **Ponte Leccia**, from where a good metalled road winds southwest beneath a succession of spectacular cliffs to **Asco ⑱** village. Beehives scattered around the hillside terraces give a clue as to the settlement's traditional source of income, but visitors stop less often to taste the famous herb-scented honey than to drop to the river, where a handsome old **Pont Génois** (Genoese packhorse bridge) spans a popular swimming spot. The path from its far side scales a wild side valley, grazed by wild boar, which can be followed for a couple of hours in fine weather. The landscape grows increasingly grandiose as you

progress up the main valley, with stands of Laricio pine and birch spread beneath the towering snow peaks. **Haut-Asco ⑲**, a desultory ski station at the road's end, comes as an anticlimax, but its hotel and café provide a convenient platform for forays into the wonderfully rugged terrain looming around it.

The 4½-hour ascent of **Monte Cinto** (2,706 metres/8,878 ft) from this face of the massif presents no technical challenges, but is relentlessly strenuous and involves crossing large nevés at an altitude above 2,000 metres (6,560 ft), where changes in weather conditions can be sudden and treacherous at any time of year. Only adequately equipped and experienced hikers should attempt the route.

Less demanding walks in the area include the streamside ambles along the approach path to Monte Cinto and neighbouring Punta Minuta, up the Tighjettu Valley, where you may catch a glimpse of the rare Corsican nuthatch (*Sitta whiteheadi*), scampering up the pine trunks. ❑

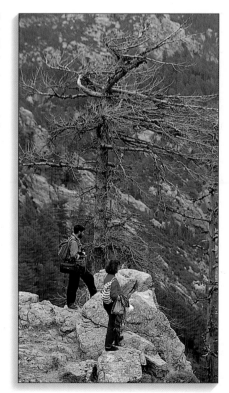

IGHT: the ∃co Valley is 'ime walking ∍untry.

Map on page 244

CORTE TO AJACCIO

The Laricio pine forest between Corte and Ajaccio divides Corsica into two. This chapter covers two routes, the first takes in the Monte d'Oro massif, while the other travels through charming off-track villages

Between Corte and Ajaccio, the island's watershed forms a wall of granite and mountains dense with Laricio pines, smothered most afternoons in thunderous cloud. This natural barrier has for thousands of years divided the island into two separate halves – a division mirrored by the present *départements* of Haute-Corse and Corse-du-Sud. It can be traversed via two different routes. The first and most direct, keeping to the N193, winds in tandem with the Bastia–Ajaccio train line, and may be covered comfortably in a couple of hours.

The second is a more convoluted itinerary crossing the range further south at Col de Verde and then dropping down to the coast through the head of the sparsely populated Taravo Valley. Both have their relative merits. Route one provides views of the awesome Monte d'Oro massif, while the second route penetrates wilder, better watered countryside, with a string of off-track villages to stop at along the way, where you can enjoy the vistas of the surrounding peaks over coffee on sleepy squares.

The Col de Vizzavona route

Grandiose views across the Tavignano Valley accompany the start of the route south from Corte on the N193. Walkers should consider pulling over at the village of **Santo-Pietro-di-Venaco ❶**, which lies near the trailhead for one of central Corsica's classic hikes – the pilgrimage path to the **Chapelle Sant'Eliseo** (1,555 metres/5,102 ft).

Sat astride a high bluff against the massive bulk of Monte Cardu, the tiny chapel is dedicated to the patron saint of shepherds, which explains why it is still the object of a mass pilgrimage in August, when Venachesi from across the Corsican diaspora gather to make the 2½-hour climb. The well waymarked

route starts from the end of the forestry track winding uphill out of the village.

Aside from the excellent Restaurant de la Place on the main square, **Venaco ❷**, the next village straddling the *route nationale*, holds little to detain visitors, although you may be tempted to pause at the impressive **Pont du Vecchiu**, 5 km (3 miles) further south, where both the road and railway line cross a deep ravine by means of two separate bridges. Dating from 1825, the elder of the pair was designed by Gustave Eiffel (of tower fame); its neighbour was constructed in 1999 and reaches a height of nearly 140 metres (459 ft).

Once across the gorge, the route swings up to **Vivario**, on whose outskirts stands

the derelict **Fortin de Pasciolo** ❸, a French watchtower that was used in Napoleonic times to incarcerate troublesome rebels from the Fiumorbo region. Facing a vast sweep of pale grey mountain, the fort, built in the late 18th century, is most easily reached from a car park 2 km (1¼ miles) beyond the village on the N193.

From here on, the route climbs steadily through thick pine forest towards the watershed, which the train ducks under via a gigantic 4-km (2½ mile)-long tunnel. The N193, meanwhile, skirts past the station and hiking centre of **Vizzavona**, a waystage on the GR20 and the best base for ascents of **Monte d'Oro**, to crest the ridge at the **Col de Vizzavona** ❹. It's worth stopping here to visit the wonderful Hotel Monte d'Ori, a vestige of the *grande époque*, with an evocative interior recalling the era when this was a popular retreat for British aristocrats fleeing the heat of Ajaccio.

One of their favourite picnic spots, and still a popular walk from the road, are the **Cascades des Anglais**, a series of exquisite pools and falls surrounded by mature Laricio pines; the path to it begins 200 metres (219 yds) north of the hotel (heading back in the direction of Corte).

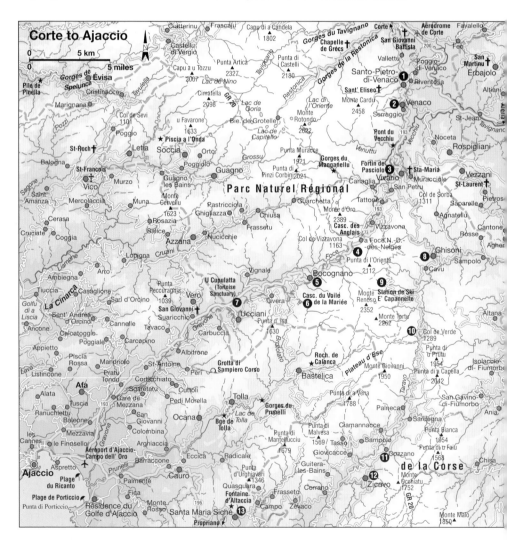

Map on page 244

Bocognano ⑤, the first village reached after crossing the pass, will forever be associated with the names of Antoine and Jacques Bellacoscia, two of Corsica's most infamous bandits. The brothers were born here in 1817 and 1832 respectively, taking to the *maquis* in 1848 after Antoine murdered the mayor. Over four decades of violent crime ensued before they surrendered in 1892 at Vizzavona station – an event attended by the national press.

Set on a natural balcony above the valley, amid a swath of lush chestnut groves looking out to the summit of Monte d'Oro, Bocognano also boasts some of the region's finest waterfalls: the **Cascade du Voile de la Mariée ⑥** (Bride's Veil falls), where the River Gravona crashes 150 metres (492 ft) through the forest. The approach to them follows the D27, beginning on the western edge of the village.

The tree cover thins out and the *maquis* takes over definitively as the road and railway twist from Bocognano down the widening Gravona Valley. Only 17 km (10½ miles) outside Ajaccio, the tortoise sanctuary of **U Cupulatta ⑦** (open daily 9.30am–7pm; entrance fee) is the last worthwhile stop before the capital – and an essential one for children. No less than 125 different species of tortoise from five continents are bred at this 2.5-hectare (6-acre) site, foremost among them local Corsican strains which are under perennial threat of extinction in the wild.

The Ghisoni route

From Corte as far as Vivario the road to follow is the N193 in the direction of Ajaccio. On a right-hand bend you will suddenly see a turn-off: the D69 to Ghisoni. This road leads through attractive forest scenery up to the **Col de Sorba** (1,311 metres/4,300 ft). From the top of the pass on the west side, in clear weather, the view takes in Monte d'Oro and the Vecchio Valley and extends as far as the Corte basin. On the other side you can make out the Etang d'Urbino over on the east coast, glittering in the far distance and framed by the steep rock walls. From the Col de Sorba it takes a good hour to reach the 1,565-metre (5,100-ft) high **Punta**

Muro to the northeast, via a stony forest path. There is an all-round panoramic view from the summit.

The route from the Col de Sorba leads through tall forests down to **Ghisoni ⑧**. A large amount of forest was destroyed by fire in this region in 1985. Ghisoni lies at the foot of the massive towering rocks known as the **Punta Kyrie-Eleison** (1,535 metres/5,000 ft). In front of the main peak, in the middle distance, that particularly impressive jagged rock formation, the **Rocher Christe-Eleison**, can be seen towering steeply out of the valley.

There is a legend attached to the names of these mountains: the last few supporters of the Giovannali, a reformist sect founded in 1530 in Carbini (near Levie), persecuted as heretics by the Inquisition, are meant to have fled to Ghisoni. They were captured here and, having been accused of communistic tendencies, indulging in superstitious sacrificial practices and nighttime debauchery in the church, were condemned to death. It is

said that the Giovannali were burnt alive on a huge funeral pyre in the village, but the ash rising from the pyre then turned into a white dove. While the villagers were chanting the words of the requiem Mass, the dove slowly flew up towards the mighty rocks above. The sound of the chant is said to have re-echoed back from the mountains. Ghisoni has another peculiarity too: above the village fountain there is a large statue of Neptune, killing a sea-monster with his trident. It reminds us of the proximity of the sea, and of the harbour at Aléria which was once the largest on Corsica.

If you drive from Ghisoni to the east coast you will pass through two of the finest ravines of the Fiumorbo, a region known for its turbulent history and the independent and recklessly brave nature of its people. The first one is the **Défilé des Strette**. Then comes a small reservoir, and after a short tunnel one suddenly finds oneself in the steep, rocky gorge known as the **Défilé de l'Inzecca**.

The road to **Col de Verde** (D69) runs southwards from Ghisoni through the huge **Forêt de Marmano**, and weaves its way uphill between mighty pine, oak and chestnut trees. One turn-off leads up to the dilapidated ski station of **E'Capannelle ❾**, and it's definitely worth following it a short way. After a few kilometres the forests start to get brighter, and then there is a magnificent view of the Ghisoni Valley basin and the mountains surrounding it. At the end of the road one reaches the *station*, where a large herd of sheep can be seen grazing in the summertime.

The *Gîte d'étape* and bar-restaurant at E'Capanelle is the favourite starting-point for ascents of **Monte Renoso**. The route, partly marked, leads past a small mountain lake, the **Lac de Bastiani**. After around 3½ hours' walk you will find yourself at the summit. On clear summer mornings Monte Renoso provides an utterly breathtaking view that takes in the entire southern part of the island. In wintertime, on those rare occasions when

BELOW: a typical farmhouse of the region.

Map on page 244

there is adequate snow, the Bergerie de E'Capanelle is a skiing destination, and there is a chairlift up to 1,960 metres (6,430 ft). People who come up here tend to favour long-distance cross-country skiing tours.

The Col de Verde route

At **Col de Verde ❿** (1,289 metres/4,200 ft), from which this route – the Route du Col de Verde – also gets its name, the D69 intersects with the GR20 long-distance hiking trail. There are several footpaths on either side of the head of the pass leading off into lonely forest areas. From Col de Verde, the road winds its way around countless bends, through the **Forêt de San-Pietro-di-Verde**, and then the **Forêt de St-Antoine**. A few kilometres past the head of the pass, the view suddenly opens out down into the thickly-wooded Taravo Valley. The first hamlet to be reached along here is **Cozzano ⓫**. In the large village square, the old men sit in the shade of the trees, waiting either for something to happen or for the weather to get cooler towards evening.

The next village is **Zicavo ⓬** (Zacava). Its inhabitants can look back proudly on an illustrious past: during the Corsican War of Independence, their ancestors were among the very last to surrender to the military might of the French troops. It is only when you drives down into the valley that you notice how the village houses cling tightly to the mountain slope. It's possible to make a short detour from Zicavo to **Guitera-les-Bains**. The sulphur springs in this shallow valley basin have been famous since Roman times. A small hamlet has grown up around them, and some of the buildings – the Hôtel des Bains, for instance – have a melancholy charm, reminding us of the village's erstwhile ambitions as a spa town.

Shortly before joining the main Propriano–Ajaccio *route nationale*, N196, the D83 winds through one of the few villages in Taravo Valley that's still well populated. **Sta-Maria Siché ⓭** is closely associated with the memory of Sampiero Corso *(see page 38)*, a Corsican mercenary who fought for the French against the Genoese in the mid-16th century, and who later led a Corsican insurrection against the island's continental overlords.

Dubbed "the most Corsican of Corsicans", Sampiero is vividly described in Ferdinand Gregorovius' historical sketches: all the typical Corsican attributes were apparently combined in "this man of primeval granite: a wild daring, an unshakeable tenacity, a glowing love of freedom and of his native land, penetrating insight, indigence and modesty, ruggedness, a hot temper, and truly volcanic passion", as well as a strong vengeful streak which eventually led him to strangle his young wife, Vannina, whom he suspected of having been in league with his hated enemies, the Genoese.

The murder was avenged in typically Corsican fashion by her brothers, who ambushed Sampiero in 1567 and killed him. The couple's house, the Palazzo Sampiero, still stands at the bottom of Sta-Maria Siché, 500 metres (550 yds) beyond the church. ❑

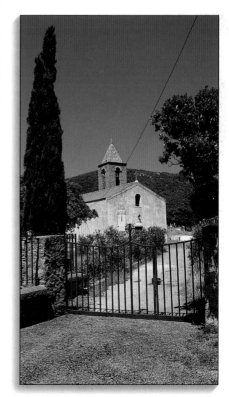

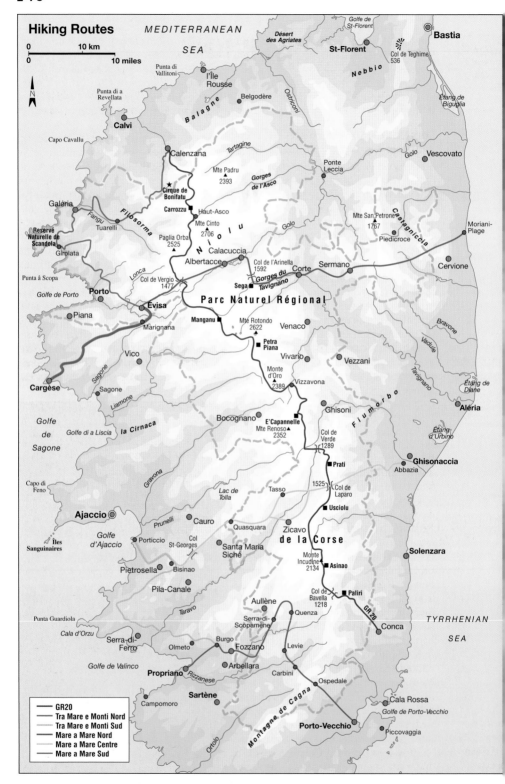

Hiking Routes

0 |—————| 10 km
0 |—————| 10 miles

GR20
Tra Mare e Monti Nord
Tra Mare e Monti Sud
Mare a Mare Nord
Mare a Mare Centre
Mare a Mare Sud

Map on page 248

HIKING

In addition to the famous GR20, regarded by many as Europe's top route, Corsica offers a first-class infrastructure of paths and refuges, catering for walkers of all abilities and set in relentlessly dramatic scenery

The Parc Naturel Régional de la Corse covers 354,000 hectares (875,000 acres), and is one of the finest nature conservation areas in Europe. It incorporates the central Corsican mountain chain, which runs across the island from northwest to southeast. Planning work began on the project in 1963, and in 1969, just in time for Napoleon's 200th birthday, the park was established.

The main aims were to create a harmonious balance between conservation, folkloric tradition and tourism. On the conservation side, the most important task is to protect rare species of plant as well as to preserve the habitats of animals facing extinction. Instructing people about the dangers of forest fires is also especially important. In addition to its mountainous interior, part of Corsica's rocky coastline between Galéria and the Calanche has also been incorporated into the park. Old villages and traditional structures such as bridges, mills and shepherds' huts are being restored and preserved – and not just for the purposes of tourism.

The GR20

When the Parc Naturel was still only in the planning stage, work had already begun on a long-distance Alpine hiking trail that has now become internationally famous and attracts thousands of walkers annually: the **GR20**. This is just one of the many long-distance paths in France – another is the equally famous GR10 in the Pyrennees – created and organised by Le Comité National des Sentiers de Grande Randonnée. Approximately 140 km (87 miles) in length, the GR20 is the best way for hikers to get acquainted with the remoter parts of the island. Fitness and stamina are essential, though. The trail starts at **Calenzana**, near Calvi, and ends 10 to 15 hiking days later at Conca near the Golfe de Porto-Vecchio. Just as is the case with all the other French *grande randonnées*, the route is completely marked in the distinctive stripes of white above red, painted on rock faces, boulders, walls, tree trunks and specially-erected posts and cairns when no other feature is available. These signs are usually no more than 50 metres (160 ft) apart. The "Alpine variants" – the detours leading over more challenging territory – are usually coloured yellow.

The best season to tackle the GR20 is from the beginning of June to the end of September. Before then some stretches may still be snow-covered, and only passable with ice-picks and crampons. The section referred to as GR20 Nord, from Calenzana to Vizzavona, requires both

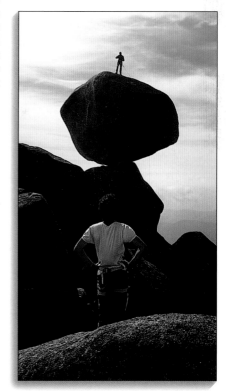

RIGHT: the Homo di Cagna is a prominent landmark.

firmness of foot and a head for heights in several places, while the GR20 Sud, from Vizzavona to Conca is easier going than its northern equivalent.

Walking the GR20

The main problem faced by hikers here is how heavy their rucksacks should be. Outside the main season, when the mountain pastures are still empty and the mountain hotels closed, extra provisions need to be packed. The total weight of equipment, clothing, food and water should not exceed 15 kg (33 lb) for men or 10 kg (22 lb) for women. The self-catering huts do contain stoves, but it's best to take along a medium-sized aluminium pan, a drinking flask, a bowl, cutlery, matches and a knife. Those not sleeping inside the huts (a fee is charged) can pitch their tents on the nearby campsites.

At the start of the GR20, there's a 1,600-metre (5,250-ft) ascent, from Calenzana up to the **Refuge de l'Ortu di u Piobbu**. If you survive the first day, you'll be more than rewarded on the second by the unforgettable view down into the **Bonifatu Basin**, before reaching the idyllically situated **Carrozzu** refuge the same afternoon. The third day begins with a crossing of the Spasimata River – over a cable bridge – and then the trail leads on through a rocky region to the 1,985-metre (6,500-ft) high **Bocca a i Stagnu** before descending again 563 metres (1,800 ft) to the **Hotel Le Chalet** on the Plateau de Stagnu at Haut' Asco. This descent became necessary after the refuge at Altore was destroyed in a fire. The hotel is also a starting point for climbers tackling the north side of Monte Cinto.

The next day, the route leads 600 metres (1,970 ft) up from the Plateau de Stagnu at Haut' Asco to the ruins of the Refuge d'Altore and then on to the 2,183-metre (7,200-ft) high **Col Perdu** (aka the Bocca Tumasginesca). Now fixed ladders, stanchion cables and chains are needed as you descend into the **Cirque de la Solitude** (Solitude Basin). Here, the hiker is con-

BELOW: rest stop at Col de l'Arinella.

Map on page 248

fronted by fascinating rock formations – and firmness of foot and a good head for heights are essential. After scaling the Bocca Minuta (2,218 metres/7,200-ft) you then descend to the newly refurbished refuge at **Tighiettu** (Tighjettu).

On the fifth day the trail leads round the base of **Paglia Orba** before reaching the refuges known as **Ciottuli di i Mori** (Ciottulu a i Mori), the starting point for ascending the 2,525-metre (8,300-ft) high peak. As you begin your ascent there is a good view of the huge hole in the rock over to the left – **Capu Tafunatu**. Anyone who decides against an ascent of the mountain can spend the day continuing their journey to **Col de Vergio** along the lovely banks of the Golo River.

The attraction of the following day is the countryside surrounding the **Lac de Nino**. The next section of the route takes us from the **Refuge de Manganu** up to the 2,225-metre (7,300-ft) high **Brèche de Capitello**. Beyond this pass comes one of the most delightful sections of the entire GR20. Along the length of the ridge leading to **Bocca a Soglia** there is an enchanting view of the **Lac de Capitello** and the **Lac de Melo**. The pleasant **Refuge de Petra Piana** at the end of this strenuous day's tour lies at the foot of **Monte Rotondo** (2,622 metres/8,600 ft), one of the highest mountains in Corsica.

The next day provides enough time for a bit of dawdling, along the banks of the Manganello, though after the midday rest-stop in the idyllic **Bergerie Tolla**, the 500-metre (1,600-ft) ascent to the **Refuge d'Onda** can be really tough going. After eight to ten days' hiking, with **Monte d'Oro** and the marvellous **Agnone Valley** behind us, we reach the summer mountain resort of **Vizzavona**. The island railway runs to Ajaccio and Corte from here.

Those wishing to continue along the GR20 will now be starting on its southern section. Over the next two days the route mostly runs through pine forests, beneath the **Monte Renoso** massif. After ascending from **Col de Verde** to the

BELOW: one of the highlights of the GR20 – Lac de Nino.

Refuge de Prati you then proceed directly southwards along a long mountain ridge that provides you with your first views of the nearby east coast. The mountains gradually get lower now, with the last really big one, **Monte Incudine** (2,134 metres/7,000 ft), causing no problems, and then you suddenly plunge right back into the fascinating mountain world of Corsica as the rocky spires of the **Bavella** come into view.

Even after the **Bavella Pass**, the landscape, with its reddish rocks, is still as impressive as ever. Now the *maquis* starts to get more widespread as the GR20 comes to an end near **Conca**. If you want to spend a couple more days by the sea after the 170-km (105-mile) crossing of Corsica you can relax at the adequate beach at **Fautéa** or in **Pinarello**.

Tra Mare e Monti

For hikers who think they're going to find the mainly mountainous GR20 too strenuous, the long-distance trail known as **Tra Mare e Monti** is definitely to be recommended. It takes eight to ten days, and runs from **Calenzana** to **Cargèse**. The well-marked route (waymarks are in orange) leads through the foothills along the central part of the west coast, and provides opportunities for a refreshing swim in the sea or a creek. The daily route takes between 3 and 6½ hours, and at the end of each section there are *gîtes d'étape*, providing dormitory accommodation and three-course cooked meals. Equipment should be kept to an essential minimum on this route as well.

The Tra Mare e Monti gives an entirely different impression of the natural scenery Corsica has to offer. It includes typical coastal vegetation: *macchia*, with rockroses, strawberry trees and myrtle and juniper bushes. Villages and hamlets with ancient chestnut groves are strung out along the route. The trail however can get strenuous, and the height differences covered daily should not be underestimated.

BELOW: crossing the Spasimata River.

Map on page 248

Mare a Mare Nord

Alongside these two long-distance hiking trails which run vertically down the island, the park administration has laid out new trails in the past few years that run east–west across the entire island, with overnight accommodation available on each leg of the journey. A large network of trails has thus been built up, and individual sections can, of course, be combined to form discrete routes. The east–west trails run through various different regions of the island: the *macchia* landscape down by the coasts, the Corsican forests and also the mountains in the central range.

There are three hiking trails running from coast to coast, *da mare a mare*. All of them are marked with blobs of orange paint. The **Mare a Mare Nord** begins at the church of San Nicolao, just inland from the east-coast town of **Moriani-Plage** and takes you on a ten-day march to **Cargèse** on the west coast. The first two sections wend their way through the **Castagniccia** at between 200 and 1,090

metres (650–3,575 ft) over to its western side, the Boziu, at **Pianello**. The next two days via **Sermano** to **Corte**, at altitudes of between 400 and 900 metres (1,300–3,000 ft), offer a splendid view up to the highest peaks such as the Monte Cinto (2,706 metres/8,878 feet).

On the fifth day the route gradually ascends the magnificent **Tavignano Valley**, and then passes through a marvellous pine forest to reach the **Refuge a Sega** (1,190 metres/3,900 ft). This is a good place for a swim in the river. The Niolu is reached on the following day. The route ascends to the **Bocca de l'Arinella** (1,692 metres/5,550 ft) and then leads back down to **Calacuccia** and along the banks of the reservoir of the same name to **Albertacce**. The next section of the trip proceeds from here through the extensive area of Laricio pine forest known as the **Forêt de Valdu Niellu** up to the highest mountain pass crossed by a road in Corsica, the **Col de Vergio** (1,477 metres/4,800 ft).

BELOW: walking the GR20.

On the next day the markers for the route begin next to a statue at the mountain hotel Castel di Verghio and lead the hiker through the **Forêt d'Aïtone**, then over the **Bocca a u Saltu** in the direction of Évisa. The nearby **Cascades d'Aïtone** are a superb place for a bathe. The route then passes through a chestnut forest on the way down to **Évisa**. From here it is still another 2½ hours' hiking before the *Gîtes d'Étape* in **Marignana**. The final stages of the journey then follow the route of the Tra Mare e Monti, finally ending up on the west coast at the town of **Cargèse**.

Mare a Mare

The long-distance hiking trail which runs from near **Ghisonaccia** to near **Porticiccio** – the **Mare a Mare Centre** – takes six strenuous days to complete. It begins in **Abbazia**, a few kilometres southwest of Ghisonaccia. From there it follows a road briefly as far as **Acquacitosa** (Sualellu). The first exhausting section up to **Catastaghiu** involves an ascent of 900 metres (2,900 ft) in 5 hours. The second day is just as arduous: a 6-hour-long slog that proceeds from an altitude of 523 metres (1,700 ft) above sea level right up to the **Col de Laparo** (1,525 metres/5,000 ft) and then down to **Cozzano** (727 metres/2,400 ft). The third stage leads via **Tasso** to **Guitera-les-Bains**, with its sulphur springs. If you like you can also reach Guitera by hiking from Cozzano via **Zicavo** – a very pleasant route through chestnut forests. The fourth stage of the journey ends in **Quasquara**, where a simple mountain hut provides refuge for the night. Day five sees you cross the last pass on this trail, the **Col St-Georges**, through which the N196 also passes. **Ajaccio**, is just a brief car ride from here – or, if you still feel like it, another seven gruelling hours on foot.

Another coast to coast route, this time through Corsica's south, is the **Mare a Mare Sud**, which leads from near **Porto-Vecchio** to **Propriano**. It starts at **Alzu di Gallina**, roughly 10 km (6 miles) from Porto-Vecchio. The best way to get there

BELOW: the Ladrocellu ridge, on the GR20.

Map on page 248

is to take a cab from Porto-Vecchio along the D159 to **Muratellu**, and then walk northwards: the markings begin on the other side of the bridge across the Bola River. On the first section the route starts off steeply, rising to a height of 1,020 metres (3,300 ft) above sea level, and leads on to **Cartalavona** and **Ospédale**, which provides a breathtaking view of the entire Golfe de Porto-Vecchio. The height gained on the first day gets lost on day two, however. The route descends via **Carbini** to an altitude of just 260 metres (850 ft), then ascends again to **Levie** (610 metres/2,000 ft). The third section leads through forests via **Zonza** to **Quenza**. This is a good place to plan a detour to the Torréen fortress at **Cucurruzzu**. The landscape gets more barren here. The fourth stage of the trip is mostly *macchia*, and takes us to **Serra di Scopamène**, where there is a renovated windmill. The fifth stage leads through oak and chestnut forests to **Ste-Lucie de Tallano**. And on the sixth day you'll end up in **Propriano**, on the Golfe de Valinco.

The "Sentiers des Douniers"

Three new coastal walks have been opened in Corsica. Based on routes first created by Genoan coastguards, hence their popular name, the *sentiers des douniers* (customs officers' paths), they provide access to the island's more remote shorelines. At the far northern tip of **Cap Corse**, a two-day route from **Macinaggio** leads to Centuri-Port, via the Site Naturelle de la Capandula. Accommodation is available at **Barcaggio**, roughly the midway point, but otherwise the terrain is deserted and wild, save for the hamlet of **Tollare**. Maps outlining the path are available at local tourist offices.

The same applies to the two-day hike along the far southwestern **Sartenais coast**, from **Campomoro** to **Roccapina**. Crossing even rougher country in two days, the path frequently disappears into *macchia* and walkers attempting it should be self-reliant, with adequate food and water to reach the halfway mark at **Tizzano**. The reward is a succession of extraordinary beaches that remain deserted except in high summer. The most recent of the three coastal footpaths, and one that again requires a degree of determination and experience, is the one traversing the **Désert des Agraites** in northwest Corsica, between **St-Florent** and the **Plage de Perajola** at the mouth of the Ostriconi Valley. Here too, few water sources and facilities are available along the way, besides a campsite at Saleccia beach and a refuge-*gîte d'étape* at **plage de Guignu**. Most walkers divide the route into three stages, but it is possible to cover the distance in two days. For more advice on this path, which skirts some of the finest coastal scenery in the entire Mediterranean, contact the tourist office in St-Florent.

With all three *sentiers des douaniers*, it is essential to be prepared for hot sun from April onwards: wear a hat and drink plenty of fluid. Sun stroke can be life threatening if you run out of water a long way from a spring or stream – which can happen on any of these routes. It is also advisable to take along the relevant IGN map of the area covered in order to better plan your itinerary and rest stages. ❏

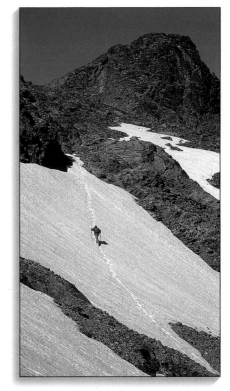

RIGHT: making the approach to Monte Cinto.

INSIGHT GUIDES

Travel Tips

✴ INSIGHT GUIDES Phonecard

One global card to keep travellers in touch. Easy. Convenient. Saves you time and money.

It's a global phonecard

Save up to 70%* on international calls from over 55 countries

Free 24 hour global customer service

Recharge your card at any time via customer service or online

It's a message service

Family and friends can send you voice messages for free.

Listen to these messages using the phone* or online

Free email service - you can even listen to your email over the phone*

It's a travel assistance service

24 hour emergency travel assistance – if and when you need it.

Store important travel documents online in your own secure vault

For more information, call rates, and all Access Numbers in over 55 countries, (check your destination is covered) go to www.insightguides.ekit.com or call Customer Service.

JOIN now and receive US$ 5 bonus when you join for US$ 20 or more.

Join today at

www.insightguides.ekit.com

When requested use ref code: **INSAD0103**

OR SIMPLY FREE CALL
24 HOUR CUSTOMER SERVICE

UK	0800 376 1705
USA	1800 706 1333
Canada	1800 808 5773
Australia	1800 11 44 78
South Africa	0800 997 285

THEN PRESS ⓪

For all other countries please go to "Access Numbers" at www.insightguides.ekit.com

* Retrieval rates apply for listening to messages. Savings based on using a hotel or payphone and calling to a landline. Correct at time of printing 01.03

(INS001)

powered by

"The easiest way to make calls and receive messages around the world"

CONTENTS

Getting Acquainted

Nationality: French.
Location: 41° north, 9° east.
Area: 8,800 sq. km (3,352 sq. miles), the third largest island in the Mediterranean.
Distance from France: 180 km (113 miles).
Distance from Italy: 83 km (52 miles).
Distance from Sardinia: 12 km (7.5 miles) across the Straits of Bonifacio.
Length: 183 km (115 miles), Cap Corse to Capo Pertusato.
Width: 83 km (52 miles), Capo Rosso to Bravone.
General characteristics: a mountain range rising from the sea. There is a coastal plain on the east side.
Coastline: 1,000 km (625 miles).
Highest point: Monte Cinto, 2,706 metres (9,055 ft).
Population: 260,000.
Capital: Ajaccio.
Départements: Corse du Sud, Haute-Corse.
Official language: French, though recent census figures report that 27 percent of the population regard themselves as fluent in Corsican.
Religion: Roman Catholic.
Currency: Euro.
Electricity: Generally 220/230 volts, but still 110 in a few areas.
Weights & Measures: France uses metric for all weights and measures.
Time zone: Greenwich Mean Time + 1 hour, Eastern Standard Time + 7 hours. In summer the time is advanced by one hour.
Dialling code: International access (00) + France (33) + Corsica (495). From elsewhere in France: 0495.

Geography

The topography of Corsica resembles a skeleton. The backbone of the island is linked by more than 20 mountains over 2,000 metres (6,562 ft), including the impressive Monte Cinto. As the main watershed, this great ridge of mountains, often as little as 30 km (18 miles) from the coast, runs from the northwest to the southeast, dividing the island into two halves of approximately the same size.

The high mountains, which make up no less than 47 percent of the island's total area, are broken by only four passes: the Col de Verghio, Col de Vizzavona, Col de Verde and Col de Bavella. Corsica's mountain landscape is characterised by rugged peaks, jagged ridges, steep slopes and deep valleys. The mountains in the northeastern part of the island are less rugged than those of the main central massif. While tourism booms along the sandy beaches of the east coast, the north and west coasts are far more dramatic. Corsica's interior is stupendous with the valleys of the Niolo and Asco dominated by Monte Cinto and closely tracked by the epic GR20, Europe's toughest and most spectacular hike.

People

Forty-two percent of the island's population resides in the two principal towns of Ajaccio and Bastia. Members of established Corsican families, who have lived on the island for centuries, still make up the majority of the residents, despite the emigrations. Ever since the Genoese first arrived, many young Corsicans have gone to the mainland. These emigrants often return after retirement to spend the twilight of their lives on their native soil.

The Corsicans are an island folk whose history has left an indelible mark on the present. The result of continual settlement by other peoples is a deeply-rooted distrust of just about everything that comes from across the sea. Corsica also has a tradition of immigration: 200 years ago Greek Orthodox refugees finally settled in Cargèse. After World War II Italians came as agricultural workers and they adapted fairly quickly to life on the island. The settlement of about 17,000 French colonists from North Africa, so-called *pieds-noirs*, in 1962–66, caused political conflicts and finally led to the formation of different "nationalist" and even underground movements.

Today, around 22,000 (or 8 percent of the island's total population) are manual labourers from North Africa, employed mainly in agriculture and construction.

Family Life

Family life in Corsica centres on the traditional clan which holds together through thick or thin. The head of the family has great importance. Familial structure is still strictly patriarchal, especially in isolated valleys. Personal connections are important, particularly in the more rural areas. People who do business with Corsicans or who are simply looking for a hotel room for one night during the peak tourist season will be surprised to find out how the acquaintance with a certain *patron* can make the impossible possible.

As a result of the rapid development of tourism, especially in areas near the coast, Corsican hospitality has taken quite a beating. However even today in the island's interior, visitors can generally count on finding a friendly reception.

Economy

A good third of the gainfully employed population in Corsica is occupied in some sort of agricultural pursuit (although most of them are immigrant workers from North Africa). Nevertheless, the agricultural products which are imported from the mainland are on the whole cheaper to buy than those produced on the island itself. As a result, more and more small farming businesses are having to cease operations and agriculture now lags well behind tourism in

Climate

Summer: long, hot, reaching 36°C/96°F on the coast.
Winter: wet and moderately cool.
Average annual temperature: 12°C (54°F).
Rainfall: 95 days a year, mostly falling between November and May.
Climatic conditions vary greatly from region to region, depending upon elevation. For instance it may well be possible to bask in the sunshine on the coast in April while there is still snow in the mountains, which may remain into June. During the summer the temperature in the high mountains is pleasant. **Storms** are more likely to occur on the west coast and in the mountains than anywhere else. The prevailing **winds** are from the southwest. The *Scirocco* is a hot southeasterly wind which may blow sand from the Sahara Desert onto the island. The cold *Mistral* from the northwest can also reach Corsica. The *Libecciu* blows in from the west to southwest, often in conjunction with the *Mistral*, and is characterised by gusts and large fluctuations in temperature. The *Libecciu* blows particularly strongly on the east coast of Cap Corse, where it can quite suddenly sweep over the coast road with hurricane-like force.

terms of its overall economic importance, generating a mere 1–2 percent of GDP. In order to try to halt this decline existing structures are being changed to make home produce more competitive. Farms are becoming larger and different methods of production and cultivation are being introduced. The cultivation of fruit is increasing in importance. Particularly in the east, there are large orchards of apples, cherries and plums. Large-scale irrigation has enabled the cultivation of citrus fruits. Olives and chestnuts are cultivated for local consumption. In the area around Porto-Vecchio, cork production from cork oaks is also significant. Various regions on the island are involved in viticulture. High-quality Corsican wines are above all produced on Cap Corse (Rogliano) in the Nebbio (Patrimonio) and in the areas around Ajaccio, Sartène and Figari. The vineyards along the east coast – some of which have now been abandoned – were laid out in the 1970s by the new French-Algerian arrivals. Livestock breeders in Corsica raise cattle, sheep, goats and pigs. The latter are generally allowed to run about freely and root for food in the forests. Bee-keeping is also of some significance on the island. Coastal fishing does not contribute markedly to the economy. Agriculture may be widespread and diverse in Corsica, but it would not be viable without subsidies. Around 500 million euros of national aid and 1.32 billion euros from Brussels pours in to the island each year, making it the most heavily subsidized region of the EU.

Unemployment is virtually nil during the summer, but off season soars to nearly 10 percent; sickness and invalidity benefits also account for a significant proportion of the islanders' gross income.

Since the 1980s, tourism has been Corsica's main source of revenue, accounting for between 10 and 12 percent of GDP annually. Industry is by comparison of negligible importance; with the exception of a few medium-sized businesses in greater Ajaccio and Bastia, there are hardly any large factories in Corsica. Of the 15,000 businesses registered on the island, only one percent of them employ more than 50 people.

Government

Corsicans have never liked the idea of being governed from Paris and since the late-1960s a regional movement has been increasingly involved in combating the central French power. The movement's militant armed wing, the FLNC (Front de Libération Nationale Corse) and its various spin-off groups, demand greater autonomy and is not afraid of using violent means when the interests of the Corsican people are thought to be under threat.

In 1975 Corsica's administration was divided into two *départements*: the Corse du Sud (Ajaccio Prefecture) and the Haute-Corse (Bastia Prefecture). Taken together these two *départements* make up the Région Corse (with its headquarters located in Ajaccio), which has been given a certain amount of authority in making governmental decisions. Following the election of the Socialist François Mitterrand to presidency in May 1981, the Région Corse received a statute of autonomy, granting – at least on paper – extensive authority to the 61-member regional government. In the wake of the outbreaks of violence and strikes in 1991 and subsequent elections in 1992, another even more extensive statute of autonomy was established. Subsequent discussions about allowing the island the state of a "Territoire d'Outre-Mer" (TOM) like French Polynesia and New Caledonia were rejected, as was the more recent Matignon Process – a far-reaching package of devolutionary measures proposed by the socialist government of Lionel Jospin, which were ditched when the Gaullists returned to power under Jacques Chirac in 2002.

In a referendum held on 7 July 2003, Corsicans narrowly rejected an offer of limited autonomy from France. It is assumed that the result will mean the continuation of the campaign for full independence. Opinion polls show that most Corsicans want to remain French. Given that 40 percent of Corsicans are French government employees, many may have concluded that without this economic motor Corsica would be left to support itself on tourism alone.

Planning the Trip

Citizens of countries belonging to the European Union, or from the rest of western Europe, Canada, the US, Japan and New Zealand do not need a visa to visit France. All other nationals should contact the visa section of their local French embassy or consulate. Children under the age of 16 must be in possession of their own passport, or must be included in the passport of one of their parents.

Extended stays: Visitors wishing to stay longer than 90 days in France are no longer considered tourists and are obliged to apply for a *carte de séjour* (residence permit). Further information regarding extended visits can be obtained from the residence permit authorities responsible for the district you wish to remain in. These officials are also responsible for processing applications.

Customs

Tourists arriving directly from the French mainland, whether by boat or by plane, are free to set off in any direction immediately after reaching the island. Since the Schengen Convention between members of the European Union has been adopted, there is no more customs and passport control when arriving from Italy. But there may be spot checks by customs officers; even carrying small portions of hashish can cause a lot of trouble.

EU Customs Regulations

All personal effects may be imported into France without formality (including bicycles and sports equipment). It is forbidden to bring into the country any narcotics, pirated books, weapons and alcoholic liquors that do not conform to French legislation. In theory, there are no customs barriers within Europe for alcoholic drinks and tobacco. However, there are still recommended allowances, shown below.

The following quantities can be exceeded, provided proof is shown that the goods bought are for personal consumption (for example, a family wedding) and not for resale. If in doubt, check with your local customs office. In the UK, contact HM Customs and Excise, tel: 0845-0109000.

Customs allowances for each person over 18 years of age are:
- 10 litres of spirits or strong liqueurs over 22 percent vol.
- 20 litres of fortified wine
- 90 litres of wine (of which no more than 60 litres may be sparkling wine)
- 200 cigars, or 400 cigarillos or 3,200 cigarettes or 1 kg tobacco
- 110 litres of beer

Non EU-visitors can bring in €7,600 in currency. For goods from outside the EU (note that this applies to Andorra, which is outside the EU), the allowances are: 200 cigarettes or 100 small cigars, 1 litre of spirits and 2 litres of wine, and 50g of perfume.

Health

IAMAT

The International Association for Medical Assistance to Travellers (IAMAT) is a non-profit-making organisation that anyone can join free of charge. Benefits include a membership card (entitling the bearer to services at fixed iamat rates by participating doctors) and a traveller clinical record (a passport-sized record completed by the member's own doctor prior to travel). A directory of English-speaking IAMAT doctors on call 24 hours a day and advice on immunisation is published for members. IAMAT is at:
US: 417 Center Street, Lewiston, NY 14092, tel: 716-754 4883. Canada: 1287 St Claire Avenue, W. Toronto, M6E 1B9, tel: 416-652 0137 or 40 Regal Road, Guelph, Ontario, N1K 1B5, tel: 519-836 0102; www.iamat.org.

EU Citizens

EU nationals should check before leaving home that they qualify for subsidised treatment in France under EU rules. Most British nationals do – check with the Department of Health and ask for the E111 form from the post office. The E111 does not cover the full cost of treatment, so you may find it worthwhile to take out private insurance as well.

Money Matters

The euro (€) is available in 500, 200, 100, 50, 20, 10 and 5 euro notes, and 2 and 1 euro, 50, 20, 10, 5, 2 and 1 cent coins.

Changing Money. Banks displaying a Change sign will exchange foreign currency and, in general, give the best rates; you will need to produce your passport in any transaction. If possible, avoid hotel or other independent bureaux de change, which may charge a high commission.

Credit cards are widely accepted. Visa is the most common. Access (MasterCard/Eurocard), Barclaycard and Diners Club are also widely accepted; American Express is not very popular.

Credit and debit cards from many European banks can be used in French cash machines. Check the validity of your card with your bank before departure. You will need to know your PIN number for both debit and credit cards, not just for use in cash machines but for use in some shops, restaurants and filling stations, which use the PIN number rather than a signature for identifcation. If your cash withdrawal card carries the European Cirrus symbol, withdrawals in euros can be made from bank and post office automatic cash machines bearing the same symbol. The specific cards accepted are marked on each machine, and most give instructions in English. Credit card companies charge a fee for cash advances, but rates are often better than bank rates.

Note that French credit cards often have a chip (or *puce*) rather than the more common magnetic strip, and therefore foreign cards are not always easily read by French card reading machines. Most retailers understand this, but if you have difficulties explain that your card is valid and that you would be grateful if the transaction is confirmed by phone: *Les cartes internationales ne sont pas des cartes à puce, mais a bande magnétique. Ma carte est valable et je vous serais reconnaisant d'en demander la confirmation auprès de votre banque ou de votre centre de traitement.*

Travellers' Cheques (available in euros) are a popular way to take money on holiday. Most banks accept travellers' cheques, but may be reluctant to accept personal cheques with a cheque guarantee card, which is not widely used in France.

Value Added Tax

In France a value added tax *(TVA = Taxe Valeur Ajoutée)* of 20.6 percent is added to most articles. For certain services it may not be necessary to pay the value added tax. It is possible to apply for a reimbursement of the value added tax on larger purchases which are intended for export.

Getting There

Faced with the alternative of a complicated (and potentially more expensive) land and sea journey, the vast majority of visitors to Corsica from the UK and Ireland travel by plane. Flights are at least ten times faster and invariably work out cheaper than covering the comparable distance by ferries and trains. That said, since the advent of low-cost airlines such as Ryanair and Easyjet, it has been possible,

with some careful forward planning, to save time and money by opting for a combination of both surface and air travel.

BY AIR

There are no direct flights to Corsica from the UK or Ireland, but Air France and British Airways – in conjunction with their domestic French partners – can get you there from a choice of different departure points around Britain and Ireland. This involves a change of planes in Paris or one of the Mediterranean ports (Marseille and Nice) – a lot more hassle than it sounds if you happen to arrive and depart from airports on different sides of the city.

The overall cost of flying scheduled rarely works out less than a fare on a direct charter flight – by far the quickest, most convenient and cost effective way to reach Corsica. From May until the end of September, a handful of charter airlines fly weekly from Heathrow, Gatwick, Birmingham and Manchester. Tickets tend to be block-booked by package holiday firms, who sell any they have left over as "flight onlys"; such companies are best approached by phone. Alternatively, contact Holiday Options, the UK's largest consolidator of charter flights to Corsica, who may offer fares from as low as £125 depending on demand and the time of year.

Bear in mind whoever you book through that the closer to your desired date of departure you purchase your charter flight, the less expensive it is likely to be, but also that your chances of finding a fare decrease the later you leave the booking.

None of the UK's low-cost airlines fly direct to Corsica, but you can travel with Easyjet to Nice or Marseille and then pick up a scheduled French domestic flight (with Air Liberté, Compagnie Corse Mediterannée or Air Littoral) from there. In addition, Ryanair fly to Alghero in Sardinia, a 4-hour bus ride away from the northern port of

Santa Teresa di Gallura, from where regular ferries sail 12 km (7½ miles) across the straits to Bonifacio.

BY LAND AND SEA

Travelling by surface transport to Corsica involves a complicated combination of ferries and trains, all bookable through the agency Rail Europe in London. For the first leg to Paris, Eurostar's 3-hour train service via the Channel Tunnel competes with Hoverspeed's cheaper rail and ferry link from Waterloo. From Paris Gare de Lyon, SNCF can get you with the superfast TGV Mediterranée train to Marseille in under 4 hours – a far smoother option than the regular train service, which takes double the time and costs around the same.

The final leg by ferry to Corsica invariably poses the most problems when it comes to booking. Demand on these services is high, especially during school holidays, and reservations should be made as far in advance as possible.

Ferries (operated by SNCM Ferryterranée and Corsica Ferries) run year round to Nice and Marseille, and between April and September from Toulon. The shortest crossing is via Nice, from where you have a choice of NGV hydrofoils (2hr 45min) to Calvi, L'Île Rousse, Bastia or Ajaccio, or a slower overnight service (7–10hr) that costs the same.

It is also possible to reach Corsica through the Italian ports of Genoa (with Corsica Marittima or Moby Lines), La Spezia (Happy Lines), Livorno (Corsica Ferries, Corsica Marittima or Moby Lines), Piombino (Moby Lines) and Savona (Corsica Ferries).

MOTORAIL

As an alternative to driving your own car to the ferry terminal there are several SNCF motorail services that you might want to consider, not only those departing from Paris, but also the direct overnight connections between Calais and Nice. Putting your car on the train is much more relaxing and also saves you time; it might also save you money when you consider the cost of the extra overnight stays otherwise involved. French motorail schedules are partially synchronised with ferry departure times. Both information and reservations for all the above services are available from:

Rail Europe, Tel: 0870-584 8848.
Rail Europe Inc., 226–230 Westchester Avenue, White Plains, NY 10604, Tel: 914-682 2999.
Frenchrail Inc., 1500 Stanley Street, Suite 436 Montréal, Québec H3A IR3, Tel: 514-288 8255.
In Australia and New Zealand details are available from **Thomas Cook** offices.
SNCF has a central reservation office in Paris, Tel: 08 36353535 (they speak English).

Package Tour Companies

IN THE UK

Club Med
Tel: 0700-007 007 007 or 0700-258 2633, www.clubmed.co.uk
Packages in purpose-built resort campus on the west coast.
Corsican Affair
Tel: 020-7385 8438,
www.corsicanaffair.co.uk
Hotel and villa packages.
Corsican Places
Tel: 01424-460046,
www.corsica.co.uk
Hotel and villa packages, plus tailor-made holidays.
Cresta Holidays
Tel: 0870-161 0900
Hotel and villa packages.
French Expressions
Tel: 020-7794 1480,
www.expressionsholidays.co.uk
Upscale hotel packages.
Mark Warner
Tel: 020-7761 7100,
www.markwarner.co.uk
Watersports-based holidays in beachside hotels.
Simply Corsica
Tel: 020-8541 2205 or 8995 9323, www.simply-travel.com

The UK's largest operator, offering a correspondingly wide portfolio of properites and good provision for kids.
Voyages Ilena
Tel: 020/7924 4440,
www.voyagesilena.co.uk
Hand-picked villas, hotels and country cottages across the island.

IN THE US

Adventure Centre
Tel: 1-800/228-8747
www.adventure-centre.com
Offers hiking and "soft adventure" holidays to Corsican villages.
Butterfield & Robson
Tel: 1-800/678-1147
www.butterfield.com
Luxury tours of the island staying in four-star hotels with gourmet meals.
Infohub
www.infohub.com
Eleven-day guided cycle tours of the island.
Vacances en Campagne
Tel: 1-800/327-6097
Specialises in hiring of luxury châteaux and country houses.
World Expeditions
Tel: 1-800/567-2216
www.worldexpeditions
Self-guided trekking holidays.

Maps

The best map for drivers is the yellow-covered Michelin sheet NO. 90 (scale 1:200,000), which includes all the island's roads and highlights the most scenic routes – or *parcours pittoresques* – with green lines.
Recommended for hiking are the Institut Géographique National (IGN) Séries Bleues maps drawn to a scale of 1:25,000, which cover the island in a total of 20 sheets. Extracts relevant to the PNRC's long-distance walks are compiled in the Topoguides published by the Fédération Française de la Randonnée Pédestre (FFRP).

Where to Buy Maps

In France, most good bookshops and Maisons de la Presse should

have a range of maps, but they can often be bought more cheaply in supermarkets or service stations.

Stockists in the UK are:
Stanfords International Map Centre, 12–14 Long Acre, Covent Garden, WC2E 9LP, tel: 020-7730 1354, www.stanfords.co.uk
The Travel Bookshop,
13 Blenheim Crescent, London W11 2EE, tel: 020-7229 5260, www.thetravelbookshop.co.uk
Map World Direct (mail order service), 25 Saltesford Lane, Alton, Staffordshire ST10 4AY, tel: 01538-703042, fax: 01538-702019, www.map-world.co.uk
A French travel centre offering information, books and guides is at the French Government Tourist Office, 178 Piccadilly, London W1J 9AL, tel: 09068-244123 (calls charged at 60p per minute; lines open Mon–Fri 9am–7.30pm), fax: 020-7493 6594, e-mail: info@mdlf.co.uk, www.franceguide.com

Children

Corsica is a great place to take the kids on holiday. The water at most of the island's sandy beaches is relatively shallow and the breakers are small. However, it is best to avoid the beaches along the rugged part of the west coast, where the water often becomes deep quite suddenly and the undertow can be dangerous.
There are few recreational or entertainment facilities specifically for very young visitors to Corsica, although there is a Go-Cart track located in Sarrola (near Ajaccio) for people over 12 years of age and the Aqua Cyurne Gliss in Porticcio. Close to Ajaccio, the tortoise sanctuary 'U Capulatta' *(see page 245)* is also certain to please little ones. Among UK tour operators, Mark Warner and Simply Corsica *(see left)* also make special provision for kids.

Practical Tips

prohibited, doing so only increases the risk of a possible theft.

Drivers should realise that their vehicles are not safes; car boots are frequently broken into. Car radios or other items of value, such as cameras, present relatively easy targets for experienced car thieves.

Medical Services

For minor ailments it may be worth consulting a pharmacy (recognisable by its green cross sign), which have wider "prescribing" powers than chemists in the UK or US. They are also helpful in cases of snake or insect bites and identifying fungi.

If you need to see a doctor, expect to pay around €20 for a simple consultation, plus a pharmacist's fee for whatever prescription is issued. For EU citizens, the doctor will provide a feuille des soins which you need to keep to claim

Security & Crime

Tourists are the targets of thieves the world over, and Corsica is no exception. In the busy towns pick-pockets and purse-snatchers are often at work, but theft also occurs in more rural areas as well as on nearly empty beaches.

You should deposit money and valuables in the safe at your hotel reception or campground. Apart from the fact that camping wherever you feel like it (including in a caravan or trailer) is strictly

Emergency Numbers

Ambulance 15
Police 17
Fire 18
Sea Rescue 04 95 20 23 63
Mountain Rescue 04 95 30 36 32 or 04 95 29 18 18

Even in areas lacking network coverage, it should be possible to reach the emergency services via a **mobile phone** by dialing 112.

back the majority of the cost (around 75 percent) under the EU agreement. The pharmacist will attach to the *feuille* the little sticker *(vignette)* from any medicine prescribed to enable you to claim for that too. Refunds have to be obtained from the local Caisse Primaire (ask the doctor or pharmacist for the address).

In cases of medical emergency, either dial 15 for an ambulance or call the Service d'Aide Médicale d'Urgence (SAMU) which exists in most large towns and cities – numbers are given at the front of telephone directories.

The addresses of chemists open for emergency service nights and weekends *(Pharmacie d'urgence)* are posted in chemist shop windows. You can also find out the address of the nearest chemist which is open by calling telephone information (tel: 12), or the police.

Some chemists' in Ajaccio and Bastia remain open until 8pm each day during the summer season.

Tourist Offices

In addition to local tourist offices across the island, information on Corsica can be obtained at the French tourist information offices outside France.

Corsica
Ajaccio
Place du Marché, Tel: 04 95 51 53 03, www.tourisme.fr/ajaccio
Bastia
Place St-Nicholas, Tel: 04 95 54 20 40, www.bastia-tourisme.com
Bonfacio
Rue Fred Scamaroni, Tel: 04 95 73 11 98
Calvi
Quai Landry, Tel: 04 95 65 16 67
Corte
Citadelle, Tel: 04 95 46 26 70
Porto
Marina, Tel: 04 95 26 14 25
St-Florent
Route de Patrimonio, Tel: 04 95 37 06 04

Outside Corsica
Australia
25 Bligh St, 22nd Floor,

Sydney, NSW 2000. Tel: 02-9231 5244. Fax: 9221 8682. E-mail: ifrance@internetzy.com.au
Britain
178 Piccadilly, London W1V 0AL. Tel: 09068-244123. Fax: 020-7493 6594. E-mail: picadilly@mdlf.co.uk
Canada
1981 av McGill College, Suite 490, Montréal QC H3A 2W9. Tel: 514-288 2026. Fax: 845 4868. E-mail: mfrance@attcanada.net
Ireland
10 Suffolk St, Dublin 1. Tel: 01560-235235. Fax: 679 0814. E-mail: frenchtouristoffice@mdlfr.com
USA
New York: 444 Madison Ave, 16th Floor NY 10022-6903. Tel: 212-838 7800, Fax: 838 7855. E-mail: info@francetourism.com
Los Angeles: 9454 Wilshire Blvd, Suite 715, Beverly Hills, CA 90212, Tel: 310-271 6665, Fax: 276 2835. E-mail: fgtola@juno.com
Chicago: 676 North Michigan Ave, Suite 3360 IL 60611-2819. Tel: 312-337 6339

Business Hours

Business hours in France are fairly flexible. **Shops** in Corsican cities and small towns generally open 9am–noon and 3–7pm, including Saturdays. **Supermarkets** open 8.30am–7pm. In peak season they remain open even during lunch time. Many shops in **tourist areas** are also open on Sunday, at least until noon. Fashion boutiques often stay open until midnight. **Banks** normally conduct business 8.45–11.45am and 2–5pm Monday–Friday.

Tipping

A service charge is usually included in hotel and restaurant prices *(service compris)*. It is customary for satisfied guests to leave an additional tip amounting to about 10 percent of the total bill. Taxi drivers and tourist guides also expect tips of around 10 percent.

Religion

Although Corsicans are mostly Catholic, pre-Christian elements surface in local customs and celebrations. Christian festivals are often lavishly celebrated. In Cargèse, where the descendants of 17th-century Greek immigrants live, the congregation is Greek Orthodox.

Media

PRINT

Corsica's only daily newspaper is *Corse Matin*, the local edition of *Nice Matin*. There are purely Corsican weekly and monthly magazines, too. All of them, dailies and periodicals, have some articles written in Corsican.

RADIO

In addition to the national French stations, there are several local and regional ones, broadcast mainly on FM. They host for the most part music programmes and phone-ins, occasionally in Corsican.

TELEVISION

The six French television networks are part privately and part publicly operated. FR3 is a regional programme for Corsica. On the east coast, Italian television stations can be received. Many hotels have satellite TV and you can count on a good reception for broadcasts from southern Europe and north Africa.

Public Holidays

Corsica enjoys a total of 12 national holidays *(jours fériés)*, when many, although not all, shops, businesses, museums and restaurants close.
1 January New Year's Day
Easter Sunday
Easter Monday
Ascension Day (forty days after Easter)
Pentecost (seventh Sunday after Easter, plus the Monday)
1 May May Day/Labour Day
8 May Victory in Europe Day
14 July Bastille Day
15 August Assumption of the Virgin Mary
1 November All Saints' Day
11 November Armistice Day
25 December Christmas Day

Postal Services

Post offices (PTTs) in villages close at noon. Those in cities and beach-resorts remain open 9am–noon and 2.30–5pm. Postcards and letters weighing up to 20 grams destined for other EU countries are treated as domestic mail. Stamps may be purchased in the *Bureaux de Tabac* as well as in post offices.

Telecommunications

The French telephone network is extremely modern and since a ten-digit code has been introduced there are no longer connection problems between the island and the mainland or other countries. All telephone numbers start with 0 when calling from within France.
Calling from abroad: First dial the international code (00 from the UK), followed by 33 for France and then, skipping the 0, start with 495 for Corsica, and the remaining digits.
From within France: For telephone connections within France start with the dialling code 0495.
On the island: There are a large number of telephone booths on the island, some even in small mountain villages. But only a few accept coins (50 centimes, 1, 2 or 5 francs). If you don't have a Télécard which you can buy in post offices and tobacconists, there are telephones in bars and other public places under the sign of "Point Phone", which still take coins.
Calling abroad: First dial the international access code 00, then the national code (44 for the UK, 61 for Australia, 1 for the US and Canada).
Reverse charge calls: Dial 0 800 99 (free of charge) and then the national code to get in touch with an operator:
UK: 0044 (BT)
Canada: 0016
United States: 0011 (ATT).
In most kiosks you can also receive a call; you will find the number of that particular telephone posted on the information board inside the kiosk.
Fax: There are public telefax machines *(Publifax)* for sending faxes at all larger post offices.
Mobile phones: Most networks in the UK provide coverage in Corsica, although you'll probably have to pay extra for the privilege. Supplementary charges are also made for incoming calls.
Internet access: Corsica has been slow to embrace the worldwide web, and Internet cafés are few and far between, limited to the main towns. Internet and email access is more generally available to guests at hotels.

Embassies & Consulates

Australia: 4 Rue Jean-Rey, 75015 Paris, tel: 01 40 59 33 00.
Canada: 35 Avenue Montaigne, 75008 Paris, tel: 01 44 43 29 00.
Ireland: 4 Rue Rude 75016 Paris. tel: 01 44 17 67 00.
UK: 16 Rue d'Anjou. BP111-08, 75353 Paris Cedex 08, tel: 01 44 51 31 02.
US: 2 Rue St-Florentin, 75001 Paris, tel: 01 43 12 47 08.

Getting Around

BY BUS

With the exception of those operating along a few major traffic routes, bus connections in Corsica are not particularly good. For the most part there are several buses a day which travel along the major roads between the larger settlements and Ajaccio, Bastia, Porto-Vecchio and Corte. Buses destined for smaller towns and the more remote valleys run just once a day or even less, with services drastically scaled down (and sometimes cancelled completely) over the winter when demand falls off; frequently those that do run out to more isolated villages don't return to town until the following day.

Reliable timetable information can be difficult to obtain as each route is run by a different company. In theory, local tourist offices should have copies of current schedules, but this isn't always the case.

BY RAIL

Running across the mountains from Ajaccio to Basita via Corte, with a branch line veering northwest to

Railway Stations

Recorded timetable information is available (in French only) on Tel: 04 95 32 80 60, otherwise call the stations direct:
Ajaccio Tel: 04 95 23 11 03
Bastia Tel: 04 95 32 80 61
Calvi Tel: 04 95 65 00 61
Corte Tel: 04 95 46 00 97

Calvi, Corsica's narrow-gauge railway – le Chemin de Fer Corse (or CFC) – provides a dependable all-weather link between the island's main towns. A recent upgrade of the diesel engines and rolling stock have decreased journey times significantly, but this is still a relatively sedate way to travel, commendable mainly for its scenic and novelty value.

The "Micheline" or "Trinighellu", as the train is affectionately known, takes a little over 3 hours to cover the distance between Ajaccio and Bastia; services run between two and four times daily, with reduced schedules on Sundays and in winter. Only two trains per day continue up to Calvi from the junction at Ponte Leccia. However, the branch line along the coast between L'Ile Rouse and Calvi boasts its own summer service, Le Tramway de la Balagne, which shuttles up to ten times daily in season.

Private Transport

BY TAXI

In addition to the cabs in the main towns there are also taxis in many smaller towns. For passengers wanting to hire a taxi for a longer journey or excursion, it's best to agree on the price with the driver beforehand. Rates tend to increase after 8pm and at weekends, even on runs to and from the airports, which in the case of Calvi Ste-Catherine and Figari (in the far south) can only be reached by taxi.

CAR HIRE

In addition to the large car hire agencies such as Hertz, Avis, Budget and Europcar, there are local rental companies in many places. During the summer it's a good idea to reserve a car well in advance. It is possible to do this prior to your expected arrival in Corsica by phone or email. Local tourist offices can supply you

with details. Agencies usually require that you present a credit card as security when hiring a car. The minimum age to hire a car is 21.

Car Hire Companies in the UK
Autos Abroad
Tel: 0870/066 7788,
www.autosabroad.co.uk
Avis
Tel: 0870/606 0100,
www.avisworld.com
Budget
Tel: 0800/181 181,
www.budget.co.uk
Europcar
Tel: 0845/722 2525,
www.europcar.co.uk
National
Tel: 0870/5365 365,
www.nationalcar.com
Hertz
Tel: 0870/844 8844,
www.hertz.co.uk
Holiday Autos
Tel: 0870/400 00 99,
www.holidayautos.co.uk

Car Hire Companies in the US
Auto-Europe
Tel: 1-800/223-5555
www.autoeurope.com
Avis
Tel: 1-800/331-1084
www.avis.com
Budget
Tel: 1-800/527-0700
www.budgetrentacar.com
Dollar
Tel: 1-800/800-4000
www.dollar.com
Hertz
Tel: 1-800/654-3001
www.hertz.com
Thirfty
Tel: 1-800/367-2277
www.thrifty.com

Car Hire Companies in Corsica
ACL Rent-a-Car
Tel: 04 95 51 34 45,
wwww.rentacar.fr
Avis
Tel: 04 95 23 56 90,
www.avis.fr
Budget
Tel: 04 95 35 05 04,
www.budget-en-corse.com

Citer
Tel: 04 95 70 16 95,
www.corse-auto-rent.fr
Europcar
Tel: 04 95 30 09 50,
www.europcar.com
Hertz Locasud
Tel: 04 95 23 57 04,
www.hertz.fr

MOTORCYCLE HIRE

Corsica's dependably dry weather and spectacular scenery make for some memorable motorcycle touring. For those arriving from abroad without their own vehicle, several firms rent bikes, although due to a recent hike in insurance premiums this has become an expensive way to get around. Rates for a 50cc moped range from €30–35 per day, rising to €50–60 per day for a 125cc trials machine. To undertake a full tour of the island you'd be best off shelling out €70–80 per day (or €360–375 per week) for a 500–600cc bike.

A clean car licence and your credit card are all you'll need to hire anything up to 125cc, but more powerful bikes require full motorcycle licenses. Helmets are included in the price.

DRIVING IN CORSICA

On the Road
Despite the fact that major roads in Corsica are relatively new and well maintained, most of the island's roads are narrow and have an abundance of sharp bends. Pot-holes are no rare occurrence either and you should be aware that honking before driving into a blind curve is mandatory. It is quite possible that the road you're on suddenly becomes blocked by a herd of cows or pigs. When organising a longer journey, plan on a maximum average speed of about 40 kph (25 mph). Filling stations can only be found in larger towns. Drivers of large caravans and trailers should be well-practised in manoeuvring their vehicles in the

mountains. Passing places are few and far between.

Rules of the Road
• The minimum age for driving in France is 18.
• Britons must remember to drive on the right: extra care should be taken when crossing the carriageway or when emerging from a junction – when it is easy to end up on the left side without thinking.
• Full or dipped headlights must be used in poor visibility and at night; sidelights are not sufficient unless the car is stationary. Beams must be adjusted for right-hand-drive vehicles, but yellow tints are not compulsory.
• The use of seat belts (front and rear) in cars, and crash helmets on motorcycles is compulsory. Children under 10 are not permitted to ride in the front seat. Babies are permitted in the front only if it is

Give way to the right

On main roads, traffic on the major road normally has priority, with traffic being halted on minor approach roads with one of the following signs:
Cédez le passage – give way
Vous n'avez pas la priorité – you do not have right of way
Passage protégé – no right of way.
But care should be taken in towns, and in rural areas where there may not be any road markings (watch out for farm vehicles), in which case you will be expected to give way to traffic coming from the right. If an oncoming driver flashes their headlights it is to indicate that he or she has priority – not the other way around. Priority is always given to emergency services and also to vehicles from public utility (e.g. gas, electric and water) companies. A yellow diamond sign indicates that you have priority; the diamond sign with a diagonal black line indicates you do not have priority.

fitted with a rear-facing safety seat.
• The French drink-driving limit is 50 mg alcohol per 100 ml of blood. This can mean that just one glass of beer can take you up to the limit.

Insurance
You should always carry your vehicle's registration document and valid insurance – third party is the absolute minimum and a green card from your insurance company is recommended, but not obligatory. Additional insurance cover, which can include a get-you-home service, is offered by several organisations including the British and American Automobile Associations and Europ-Assistance, Sussex House, Perrymount Road, Haywards Heath, West Sussex RH16 1DN, tel: 01444-442211, fax: 01444-455026, www.europe-assistance.co.uk

Information
FFAC (Fédération Française des Automobiles Club et des Usagers de la Route), 8 place de la Concorde, 75008 Paris, tel: 01 56 89 20 70, fax: 01 67 20 37 23. Co-ordination with Automobile clubs from other countries, mainly assistance with breakdown. They don't hire out cars but can give local numbers, etc.

Roads in France
Motorways *(Autoroutes)* are designated "A" roads, National Highways *(Routes Nationales)* "N" or "RN" roads. Local roads are known as "D" routes.

Web Information
www.mappy.fr provides maps and itineraries for journeys throughout Europe. www.autoroutes.fr suggests routes on French motorways and gives information on tolls, weather, safety, etc. www. bison-fute.equipement.gouv.fr provides up-to-date information on road conditions.

Petrol
Leaded petrol is no longer on sale at French petrol stations, having been replaced by a substitute

unleaded petrol than can be used in leaded fuel vehicles. Petrol on the autoroutes is the most expensive; most French drivers prefer to fill up at supermarkets.

BOAT TOURS

For those visitors wishing to get to know Corsica by boat, but who do not own their own ocean-going vessel, tour agencies offer a number of opportunities in the form of organised cruises or yacht voyages. Boat excursions present a relatively inexpensive means by which to explore the Corsican coastline. The following trips are possible:

Ajaccio to the Iles Sanguinaires, or longer cruises to Giroala and Bonifacio, with Nave Va (Tel: 04 95 51 31 31).

Bonifacio to the Grotte du Sdragonato and other caves in the sea cliffs, as well as to the islands of Lavezzi, Baïnzo and Cavallo. A dozen or more companies run these excursions continually throughout the day; tickets can be purchased shortly prior to departure from the counters on the quayside.

Calvi to Girolata and Ajaccio, with Colombo Line (Tel: 04 95 65 32 10)

Porto to the Calanche of Piana, or to Giroalata and Scandola, with Porto Linea (Tel: 04 95 26 11 50) or Nave Va (Tel: 04 95 26 25 26).

Cargèse/Sagone to Girolata and Scandola, with L'Ancura (Tel: 04 95 28 02 66).

Propriano to the Sartenais coast, with Big Blue (Tel: 04 95 73 43 15).

BY BICYCLE

Riding a bicycle in Corsica requires above all that you be in good physical shape. Lengthy and steep ascents are no rarity but the tenacious rider will be rewarded with fantastic views and, of course, a painless descent. Cyclists can experience the varied landscape and vegetation contained in a small area more intensely than car passengers. Traffic is especially

light along minor roads in the island's interior. A good map is indispensable for bike touring. **Hire**: It is also possible to hire bicycles in Corsica – usually mountain bikes (VTT in French) – by the hour, day or week. Rates start at €15 per day or €80 per week.

Bicycle hire firms in Corsica
Ajaccio
BMS Location, Port Tino Rossi,
Tel: 04 95 21 33 75 or 04 95 24 56 55
Corse Évasion, Montée St-Jean,
Tel: 04 95 20 52 05,
www.corsicamoto.com
Locacorse, 10 av Beverini-Vico,
Tel: 04 95 20 71 20, Fax: 04 95 20 44 52
Rout'Evasion, 10 av Noel Franchini,
Tel: 04 95 22 72 87, Fax: 04 95 22 46 69
Bastia
Objectif Nature, rue Notre-Dame-de Lourdes,
Tel: 04 95 32 54 34
Calvi
Location Ambrosini, rue Villa-Antoine,
Tel: 04 95 65 02 13
Porto
Porto Location, opposite Spar supermarket,
Tel: 04 95 26 10 13
Propriano
TCC Sarl, 25 rue Général-de-Gaulle,
Tel: 04 95 76 15 32
Location Valinco, 25 av Napoléon,
Tel: 04 95 76 11 84

Where to Stay

Places to Stay

Nearly 2 million people holiday in Corsica each year, yet the island holds few large-scale developments – a consequence of nationalist resistance to non-traditional architecture, and France's strict environmental laws. Prices, too, are on the whole restrained, as long as you avoid peak season in July and August – the *Grandes Vacances* – when half of France and Italy descends on the Mediterranean.

Most of the accommodation on offer is in hotels costing under €65 for a double room, and pricier privately rented cottages or villas. You're also rarely out of range of a campsite, and dozens of hill villages have hostels for hikers with a choice of dormitory beds or individual rooms.

Wherever you stay, advance booking is essential, particularly over the summer months when vacancies are few and far between. Demand for beds tends to be less intense away from the coast, but it is always a good idea to phone ahead to check the establishment you're aiming for has vacancies. Generally, a verbal agreement should suffice to secure a reservation; in some cases, however, you may be asked to pay a deposit by credit card or postal order.

Tariffs quoted usually apply to two people sharing, although many places also offer half-board *(demi pension)* which, especially in high season, may even be obligatory. Standards of *demi pension* vary greatly, with some hotels limiting your choice of food to set dishes, but as a rule of thumb opting for half board will invariably save you some money.

Hotels

By British standards, Corsican hotels represent extremely good value. Even those at the bottom end of the range are nearly all impeccably well maintained, efficient and clean. In common with the rest of the France, a star-rating system is used to categorise them, starting at one star for the more basic places to four stars for establishments boasting pools, gardens, private access to the sea and mod cons in the rooms. The island also has a good number of non-starred hotels offering a choice of rooms with or without en-suite bathrooms.

Prices fluctuate according to the season, with the highest tariffs reserved for August and the lowest for April and October. Only a handful of hotels remain open through the winter, and in such cases even lower off-season rates tend to apply. The exact dates when room tariffs change vary from place to place. Breakfast may or may not be included in the room rate (in starred hotels it nearly always is).

Houses, villas and gîtes ruraux

Private houses and villas account for the bulk of accommodation bundled together with flights and sold in northern Europe as package holidays. Companies in the UK vie to secure the most appealing places at the most competitive prices, leaving little choice for visitors who try to save money by booking independently through local tourist offices (where leaflets giving a full rundown of private properties for rent in the area are handed out free). Basically, unless you've plenty of time and the necessary language skills, it's much easier to choose from the range offered in the holiday companies' brochures; for a list of package operators, *(see page 262).*

An alternative would be to book a *gîte rural.* Ranging from simple cottages to more luxurious villas with pools, these are fully equipped holiday residences – more often than not in remote rural locations inland – promoted through national organisations such as the Relais Régional des Gîtes Ruraux (77 cours Napoleon, 20000 Ajaccio Tel: 04 95 10 54 30; www.gîtes-corsica.com). Reservations can be made by post or via the internet: two more websites worth a browse include: www.guidevacances.com/gites/corse.html and www.mylinea.com/gites.

Gîtes d'étapes and refuges

Not to be confused with *gîtes ruraux, gîtes d'étapes* are essentially hikers' hostels, offering simple dormitory accommodation, cooking facilities and set meals for walkers following Corsica's trail network. Nearly every village featured on the routes has its own *gîte d'étape,* run either by a local couple or the council. Some are larger and smarter than others, with en-suite double rooms and parking space in addition to four and six-bed dorms, but rates are a standard €10 (plus extra for bedding if you don't bring your own sleeping bag).

Meals are invariably offered to guests, charged on a half-board basis of around €30 for bed, breakfast and three-course supper. Again, standards vary from *gîte* to *gîte,* but most wardens are keen to promote their *cuisine régionale* and it's rare to be served a meal that's not freshly home cooked with traditional ingredients, copious and accompanied by unlimited quantities of local *vin de pays.*

Once again, advance booking is strongly recommended, even in spring and autumn (which are busy trekking seasons in most areas). On the more frequented routes you'll be expected to pay some kind of deposit.

Up in the mountains, well beyond the reach of the island's roads, *refuges* provide very basic shelter for walkers. Built by the Parc Naturel Régional Corse (PNRC) to service high-altitude trails such as the GR20, most are converted shepherds' huts with bunk beds (€9) and a simple kitchens. Conditions inside can be cramped and stuffy, and many walkers prefer to camp or bivouac outside instead (€5). From June until the end of September on the GR20, the *gardiens* of the *refuges* supplement their income from the PNRC by cooking up stews and selling simple provisions (at inflated prices due to the effort involved in getting them up the mountain to the huts).

Bed and Breakfast

B&B – or *chambres d'hôte* as it's known in French – is a relatively new phenomenon that's fast catching on in Corsica, particularly in remoter hill villages. Unlike in the UK, this is not the cheapest accommodation option, with most places charging between €50 and €70 per double, but it does offer more in the way of personal contact with local people. The rooms themselves tend to be fully en suite in newly converted or constructed annexes, separate from the family home; and there's normally a communal terrace on a patio outside where breakfast is served.

Ferme-auberges are similar to *chambres d'hôte,* but the accent is more on the cuisine. Guests come primarily to eat and drink quality local fare at a typically French pace, in an unspoilt rural setting. The accommodation offered will be comfortable and invariably very good value, but *la restauration* forms the heart of the business. If you opt to stay, half-board (normally €50–60 per head) is always obligatory and a notch pricier than hotels offering comparable levels of comfort because the food will be fine *cuisine du terrior,* using organically grown ingredients directly from the farm or local producers.

Camping

The overwhelming number of summer visitors who come to Corsica spend their holidays on campsites. Deterred by the prospect of two ferry crossings and a long drive across France, few British tourists follow the example of their German counterparts and travel in recreational vehicles, but by bringing along a tent to stuff in the boot of your hire car you can save a lot on hotel bills and venture off the roads more easily.

Sites range from simple one-star camp grounds with few facilities beyond the *blocs sanitaires*, to sprawling three-star places boasting pools, pizzerias and direct access to the beach. The farther from the coast you travel the cheaper they tend to be; you'll be charged per head, per tent and per vehicle, which in the swisher sites can easily add up to the equivalent cost of a budget hotel.

Tourist offices keep listings for camp sites in their area. Note that most only open between mid-June and mid-September, and that wild camping is strictly forbidden within the bounds of the national park. (For campsite listings *see page 275*.)

Hotel Listings

Hotels are grouped according to the order of chapters in the book. Locations are listed in alphabetical order. Prices are indicated by the following codes:
€ = Budget: under €55
€€ = Moderate: €55–100
€€€ = Expensive: €100 and up
All price codes refer to the cost of a double room. Credit cards are accepted unless otherwise stated.

AJACCIO

Du Golfe
5 bd du Roi-Jérôme
Tel: 04 95 21 47 64
Fax: 04 95 21 71 05
www.hoteldugolfe.com
Comfortable three-star opposite the Place du Marché and ferry port. €€
Kallisté
51 cours Napoléon
Tel: 04 95 51 34 45
Fax: 04 95 21 79 00
www.cyrnos.net

Modern place occupying the third floor of an old Napoleon-era tenement on the main street, with ample off-road parking and helpful young management who speak English. The best mid-range choice. €€
U San Carlu
8 blvd Danielle-Casanova
Tel: 04 95 21 13 84
Fax: 04 95 21 09 99
At the top of this bracket, but easily the most appealing option in the old town, right opposite the citadel and beach. Recommended for disabled travellers. €€
La Pinède
Route des Sanguinaires
Tel: 04 95 52 00 44
Fax: 04 95 52 09 48
Swish four-star on the edge of town, commanding fabulous views over the gulf, with a pool and clay tennis court. One of the few luxury places in Ajaccio that deserves its tariffs. €€€

Price Guide

All price codes refer to the cost of a double room.
€ = Budget: under €55
€€ = Moderate: €55–100
€€€ = Expensive: €100 and up

AJACCIO TO PROPRIANO

Porticcio
Le Maquis
Tel: 04 95 25 05 55
Fax: 04 95 25 11 70
www.lhw.com/lemaquis
Facing Ajaccio from across the bay, this ultra-chic hotel overlooks its own private cove. Each of the 20 rooms are individually styled and both the indoor and outdoor pools make the most of the location. €€€

Côti Chiavari
Le Belvédère
Tel: 04 95 27 10 32
Fax: 04 95 27 12 99
Stupendous panoramas of the Golfe d'Ajaccio and central mountains from luminous rooms in a new hilltop block; and the food is on a par with the views. €€

Porto Pollo
Le Golfe
Tel/Fax: 04 95 74 01 66
Small, unpretentious hotel in a period building – a rarity in this village – slap opposite the marina. Reception is at the café next door. €€

Olmeto
U Santa Maria – Chez Mimi
Place de l'église
Tel: 04 95 74 65 59
Fax: 04 95 74 60 33
Spotless little rooms in a typical Valinco village house, up a winding stone staircase from the church square. Full of Corsican character, as is the indomitable *patronne*, Mme Mimi. €€

Propriano
Bellevue
Av Napoléon
Tel: 04 95 76 01 86
Fax: 04 95 76 38 94
Friendly, inexpensive and perfectly placed opposite the quayside; ask for a front-side room (*côté mer*) for the best of the views. €€
Loft Hôtel
3 rue Capitaine Camille-Piétri
Tel: 04 95 76 17 48
Fax: 04 95 76 22 04
Great value rooms with minimalist modern decor in a converted warehouse, tucked away behind the seafront area. €

THE SARTENAIS

Sartène
Rossi Hôtel (Fior di Riba)
1 km (⅔ mile) west of town on the Propriano road
Tel: 04 95 77 01 80
Fax: 04 95 73 46 67
Simple but smart family-run place looking across the Rizzanese Valley; a short drive out of town and with a small pool that's very welcome in summer. €€

Campomoro
Le Ressac
Tel: 04 95 74 22 25
Fax: 04 95 74 23 43
An attractive modern block of tiled

rooms on two floors, on the edge of the village, with balconies facing the bay or olive groves to the rear, plus a top-notch restaurant. €€

Tizzano
Du Golfe
Tel: 04 95 77 14 76
Fax: 04 95 77 23 34
The only place to stay in this remote coastal village, hence the higher than average prices. Most of the rooms overlook the harbour. €€€

THE ALTA ROCCA

Levie
A Pignata
4.5 km (3 miles) west of Levie, nr Cucuruzzu archaeological site
Tel: 04 95 78 41 90
Secluded *ferme-auberge*, deep in high woodland above the Rizzanese Valley; people come here mainly to eat, but the location is quintessential *Corse profonde*. €€

Zonza
L'Aiglon
Tel: 04 95 78 67 79
Fax: 04 95 78 63 62
In an old granite building on the village's main street, with textiles from around the world decorating the rooms. Some are on the small side and have shared toilets, but there's a gorgeous wood-lined family suite on the top floor. €€

Quenza
Sole e Monti
Tel: 04 95 78 62 53
Fax: 04 95 78 63 88
www.solemonti.com
Part of the Logis de France chain and lacking local character, but the valley views and fine dining more than compensate. €€

Aullène
Hôtel de la Poste
Tel/Fax: 04 95 78 61 21
On the main street just above the square, this 19th-century coaching inn offers traditional Alta Roccan hospitality. The rooms are basic but comfortable. Unbeatable value for the area. €€

Bonifacio
Centre Nautique
The Marina
Tel: 04 95 73 02 11
Fax: 04 95 73 17 47
www.centre-nautique.com
Warm-toned wood walls and nautical bits and bobs set the tone of this stylish hotel on the quayside. Rooms are on two storeys connected by spiral staircases. €€€
Des Étrangers
4 av Sylvère-Bohn
Tel: 04 95 73 01 09
Fax: 04 95 73 16 97
Bonifacio's only real budget hotel, on the main road out of town, has simply furnished double-glazed rooms. €€
A Trama
The Route de Santa Manza
Tel: 04 95 73 17 17
Fax: 04 95 73 17 79
www.oda.fr/aa/trama
Secluded three-star, tucked away behind a wall of Mediterranean vegetation 1.5 km (1 mile) out of town. Ranged around a pool and relaxing garden, the rooms all have private terraces. €€€
Le Roi d'Aragon
13 quai J. Comparetti
Tel: 04 95 73 03 99
Fax: 04 95 73 07 94
The least expensive option facing the marina, with all the usual trimmings of a three star and particularly good shoulder-season discounts. €€

BONIFACIO TO PORTO-VECCHIO

Figari
L'Orcu
Lieu dit San Gavino, nr Poggiale
Tel: 04 95 71 01 27
Off-beat B&B in an old granite hamlet straight out of Marcel Pagnol. Handy for Figari airport, and they serve home-cooked evening meals. €

Cala Longa
Marina di Cavu
6 km (4 miles) east of Bonifacio on the D258
Tel: 04 95 73 14 13
Fax: 04 95 73 04 82

www.marinadicavu.com
Swathed in flowering *maquis* on a slope looking out to the Îles Lavezzi, this isolated luxury hotel boasts a sublime pool and gourmet restaurant. €€€

Santa Manza
Du Golfe
6 km (4 miles) northeast of Bonifacio on the D58
Tel: 04 95 73 05 91
Fax: 04 95 73 17 18
www.corsud.com
Homely two-star perched on the edge of a secluded bay, with shuttered windows and a dependable restaurant on the ground floor. €€

Palombaggia
Roc e Fiori
Bocca dell Oro, 1 km (⅔ mile) inland from Palombaggia beach
Tel: 04 95 70 45 20
Fax: 04 95 70 47 61
www.rocefiori.com
A cluster of exclusive suites and apartments, all painted in fresh Mediterranean pastels and set amid sea-facing, landscaped gardens. €€€

Porto-Vecchio
Goéland
Port de Plaisance
Tel: 04 95 70 14 15
Fax: 04 95 72 05 18
E-mail: hotel-goeland@wanadoo.fr
Pleasantly old-fashioned hotel on the waterside below the citadel – the only one in town with such a desirable location. €€
Modern
10 cours Napoléon
Tel: 04 95 70 06 36
Recently renovated place on the main square. Some of its rear-side rooms are gulf-facing. €€
Panorama
12 rue Jean-Nicoli
Tel: 04 95 70 07 96
Fax: 04 95 70 46 78
Basic *pension*-style hotel of a kind that's fast disappearing in Corsica, run by an elderly couple. Low tariffs are its main selling point, but the rooms are acceptably clean. €
Grand Hôtel de Cala Rossa
Cala Rossa, 4 km (2 miles)

northeast of town, near Lecci di Porto-Vecchio
Tel: 04 95 71 69 24
Fax: 04 95 71 60 11
www.cala-rossa.com
One of Corsica's finest hotels, screened by umbrella pines above its own beach. The driftwood decor and teak decks are delightful, the rooms light and private and the restaurant Michelin-starred. €€€

THE WEST COAST

Vico
Hôtel U Paradisu
Tel: 04 95 26 61 62
Fax: 04 95 26 67 01
Old-established two-star Logis de France place on the edge of the village, with a pool. €€

Sagone
Hôtel Cyrnos
Tel: 04 95 28 00 01
Serviceable modern hotel between the main road and beach that's particularly recommended for scuba divers. €€

Cargèse
Les Lentisques
Plage de Pero
Tel: 04 95 26 42 34
Fax: 04 95 26 46 61
Refreshingly unpretentious three-star, right behind one of the west coast's most attractive beaches. Good low-season discounts. €€

Piana
Les Roches Rouges
Tel: 04 95 27 81 81
Fax: 04 95 27 81 76
Unquestionably the most romantic hotel on the island, dating from the early 20th century. Its views over the Golfe de Porto are sublime, and 1920s Alpine-style architecture and Art Deco decor timelessly elegant. €€

Porto
Le Golfe
Porto Marina
Tel: 04 95 26 13 33
Dependable budget hotel bang

opposite the Genoese watchtower, all of whose rooms are sea facing – a rarity in this bracket. €
Le Belvédère
Porto Marina
Tel: 04 95 26 12 01
Fax: 04 95 26 11 97
A notch up in terms of comfort from Le Golfe, with three stars and even more dramatic views of the marina and surrounding crags. €€

Evisa
La Châtaigneraie
on the Porto road
Tel: 04 95 26 24 47
Fax: 04 95 26 23 11
Well-kept en-suite rooms behind a traditional granite building, smothered in chestnut trees. Perfectly placed for valley walks. €

Galéria
Stella Marina
Tel: 04 95 62 00 03
Fax: 04 95 64 02 29
Sunny rooms with good-sized balconies, set above a flower-filled garden overlooking the bay. €

CALVI AND BALAGNE

Calvi
Cyrnea
Route de Bastia
Tel: 04 95 65 03 35
Fax: 04 95 65 38 46
E-mail: peretti.p@wanadoo.fr
Large modern place on the outskirts, a 20-minute walk from town, but close to the quietest stretch of beach; outstandingly good value for Calvi. €€
Grand Hôtel
3 blvd Wilson
Tel: 04 95 65 09 74
Fax: 04 95 65 25 40
www.grand-hotel-calvi.com

Time-worn but characterful vestige of Calvi's pre-war grande époque, retaining original furniture, fittings and feel. €€
La Villa
Chemin de Notre-Dame-de-la-Serra
Tel: 04 95 65 10 10
Fax: 04 95 65 10 50
www.hotel-lavilla.com
Calvi's – if not Corsica's – top hotel: luxurious Mediterranean-fusion architecture complimenting grandiose gulf views. €€€

Calenzana
Bel Horizon
Tel: 04 95 62 71 72
Simple hotel facing the church, popular mainly with hikers. €
Ferme-Auberge A Flatta
Tel: 04 95 62 80 38
www.aflatta.com
Luxurious rooms with exposed wood beams, stone walls and chiffon drapes, perched on the side of a wild valley 3 km (2 miles) outside Calenzana. €€

Pigna
Casa Musicale
Tel: 04 95 61 77 31
Fax: 04 95 61 74 28
Live traditional music and fine Corsican food are the main incentives to stay in this charming hotel, but its rooms – decorated in Mediterranean pastels – are like something off a film set. €€

Feliceto
Mare e Monti
Tel: 04 95 63 02 00
Fax: 04 95 63 02 01
Granite-floored palazzo, standing in the shade of old cedars, with antique furniture and fine valley vistas. €€

Speloncato
Spelunca
Tel: 04 95 61 50 38
Fax: 04 95 61 53 14
Old family-run hotel, occupying the former mansion of an 18th-century cardinal, just off the square of one of the Balagne's most photographed villages. €€

Belgodère

Hôtel Niobel
Tel: 04 95 61 34 00
Fax: 04 95 61 35 85
Modern but homely place, with
sweeping views over olive groves
down to the coast. €€

Giunssani

Auberge l'Aghjola
Pioggola
Tel: 04 95 61 90 48
Fax: 04 95 61 92 99
A gem of a country *auberge*:
traditional Corsican architecture,
fine *cuisine du terroir* and a pool, at
bargain rates. €

Algajola

Stella Mare
Above the train station
Tel: 04 95 60 71 18
Fax: 04 95 50 69 39
Newest and brightest of this village's
crop of two stars. Light and airy
rooms and a large garden, facing
north over the village to the sea. €€

L'Ile Rousse

Napoleon Bonaparte
3 place Paoli
Tel: 04 95 60 06 09
Fax: 04 95 60 11 51
Originally built in the 1700s, this
grand old *palazzo* is now frayed
around the edges and somewhat
overpriced, but oozes *fin-de-siècle*
grandeur. €€€
Santa Maria
Route du Port
Tel: 04 95 63 05 05
Fax: 04 95 60 32 48
www.santamaria.com
Recently refurbished three star,
near the eponymous red rocks and
ferry dock, with beachside patios
and access to a private cove. €€€

THE NEBBIO

St-Florent

Maxime
Route d'Oletta, just off place des
Portes
Tel: 04 95 37 05 30
Fax: 04 95 37 13 07
Small, impeccably well maintained
and modern place, hidden down a

side road off the plane-shaded
main square. €€
La Roya
Plage de la Roya
Tel: 04 95 37 00 40
Fax: 04 95 37 09 85
www.hoteldelaroya.com
Self-consciously stylish three star on
the outskirts, next to the town beach,
set in extensive gardens and with a
gastronomic restaurant. €€€

Casta

Le Relais de Saleccia
Tel: 04 95 37 14 60
Simple roadside hotel that serves
as a congenial base for forays into
the Désert des Agriates – the
owners have mountain bikes for
hire. €

Bastia

Central
3 rue Miot
Tel: 04 95 31 71 12
Fax: 04 95 31 82 40
www.centralhotel.fr
Bastia's most commendable budget
option, on the first floor of an old
tenement, a stone's throw from
place St-Nicholas. €€
Posta-Vecchia
Quai-des-Martyrs-de-la-Libération
Tel: 04 95 32 32 38
Fax: 04 95 32 14 05
E-mail: hotel-postavecchia@wanadoo.fr
A choice of differently priced rooms
next to the Vieux Port – the only
hotel in this atmospheric area. €€
Les Voyageurs
9 av Maréchal-Sébastiani
Tel: 04 95 34 90 80
Fax: 04 95 34 00 65
www.hotel-lesvoyageurs.com
Very smart, central and well placed
for the ferry terminal, though
lacking views. €€
L'Alivi
3 km (2 miles) north on the Route
du Cap
Ville Pietrabugno
Tel: 04 95 55 00 00
Fax: 04 95 31 03 95
www.hotel-alivi.com
Luxurious three star out on the
city's northern fringe, with gloriously
light, spacious rooms facing across
the Ligurian Sea to the Tuscan
Islands. €€€

Pietracap
Route de San Martino
Tel: 04 95 31 64 63
Fax: 04 95 31 39 00
www.hotel-pietracap.com
This district's other chic three star,
close to L'Alivi, but higher up the
hillside, with more open views and
attractive landscaped gardens. €€€

CAP CORSE

San Martino di Lota

La Corniche
San Martino di Lota
11 km (7 miles) north along the
corniche road
Tel: 04 95 31 40 98
Fax: 04 95 32 37 69
www.lacorniche.com
Modern Logis de France place high
up on the corniche, whose rooms
make the most of the panoramic
views. €€

Erbalunga

Castel Brando
Tel: 04 95 30 10 30
Fax: 04 95 33 98 18
Elegant 18th-century *maison
d'Americain*, framed by palms and
crammed with period furniture and
engravings. One of Corsica's few
genuine heritage hotels. €€€

Sisco

**Hôtel de la Marine ("Chez
Giuseppi")**
Tel: 04 95 35 21 04
Modest chalets set in a garden
between the main road and beach. €

Pietracorbara

Macchia e Mare
Tel: 04 95 35 21 26
Fax: 04 95 35 22 35
www.macchia-e-mare.com
Family-run two star whose bland
modern architecture is offset by
fine views across the bay. €

Macinaggio

U Ricordu
On the south side of the route de
Rogliano
Tel: 04 95 35 40 20
Fax: 04 95 35 41 88
www.hotel-uricordu.com

The northern cape's swishest hotel, set back from the harbourfront with its own pool and tennis court. €€

Rogliano
Auberge Sant'Agnellu
Tel/Fax: 04 95 35 40 59
www.hotel-usantagnellu.com
Former Mairie high above Macinaggio, converted into a welcoming, plush country inn that has more character than most, plus a quality restaurant. €€

Barcaggio
La Giraglia
Tel: 04 95 35 60 54
Fax: 04 95 35 65 92
Right on the harbourfront of Corsica's northernmost village and very comfortable, although a little overpriced – you pay for the location. €€

Port Centuri
Vieux Moulin
Tel: 04 95 35 60 15
Fax: 04 95 35 60 24
Former *maison d'Americain* overlooking the island's most picturesque fishing harbour. Worth booking into just for the run of its lovely stone terrace. €€

Nonza
Auberge Patrizi
Tel: 04 95 37 82 16
A scattering of old schist and granite houses, packed on to the steep hillside above Nonza beach. €€

EAST COAST AND INLAND DETOURS

Moriani
A Casa Corsa
6 km (4 miles) south of Moriani, just north of the D71 junction on the highway
Tel: 04 95 38 01 40
Fax: 04 95 37 07 11
Friendly little B&B off the main Bastia–Porto-Vecchio road, with lovingly decorated rooms and a sunny breakfast terrace. €

Castagniccia
Le Refuge
Pedicroce
Tel: 04 95 35 82 65
Fax: 04 95 35 84 42
Castagniccia's only hotel clings to the steep valley side, surveying a vast spread of chestnut forest and hills. €

Price Guide

All price codes refer to the cost of a double room.
€ = Budget: under €55
€€ = Moderate: €55–100
€€€ = Expensive: €100 and up

Aléria
L'Atrachjata
Cateri
Tel: 04 95 57 03 93
Fax: 04 95 57 08 03
www.hotel-atrachjata.net
Plush three star on the roadside. Hardly the most inspiring location, but comfortable enough and a convenient place to break a journey along the east coast. €€

Solenzara
Maquis et Mer
On the north side of the village
Tel: 04 95 57 42 37
Fax: 04 95 57 46 85
An elegant Riviera-style mansion dating from the 19th century, with traditionally furnished rooms and a serene poolside terrace. €€

CORTE AND ITS HINTERLAND

Corte
La Restonica
2 km (1¼ miles) south of Corte
Vallée de la Restonica
Tel: 04 95 45 25 25
Fax: 04 95 61 15 79
Wood panels, leather furniture and hunting trophies define the feel of this old-style mountain *auberge*. €€
Dominique Colonna
2 km (1¼ miles) south of Corte
Vallée de la Restonica
Tel: 04 95 45 25 65
Fax: 04 95 61 03 91

Sister concern of La Restonica, in a more modern mould, but at the same lovely location beside a mountain stream, surrounded by pine woods. €€
Du Nord et de l'Europe
22 cours Paoli
Tel: 04 95 46 00 33
Fax: 04 95 46 03 40
www.hoteldunord-corte.com
Budget hotel in the heart of town that has retained its 19th century charm without descending into shabbiness (as have most of the competition). Reception at the adjacent Café du Centre. €

Calacuccia
Hôtel des Touristes
Tel: 04 95 48 00 04
Large, no-frills place, little altered since its 1930s heyday, with rooms to suit most budgets and basic dorms for hikers. €

Asco
Chez Ambroise et Nicole Vesperini
Tel: 04 95 47 83 53
Snug rooms and home cooking in an hospitable little *ferme-auberge* run by a couple of bee-keepers. €

CORTE TO AJACCIO

Vizzavona
Monte d'Oro
La Foce
Tel: 04 95 47 21 06
www.sitec.fr/monte.oro
Formerly the preserve of wealthy British aristocrats, this beguilingly old-fashioned hotel near the Col de Vizzavona is locked in a early 20th-century time warp, although it remains well maintained. €€

Ghisoni
Kyrié
Tel: 04 95 57 60 33
Fax: 04 95 57 63 15
Plain but comfortable rooms opening on to the valley: a congenial springboard for walks into the Renoso massif, and the Corsican-speciality cooking is excellent. €€

Zicavo
Hôtel le Florida
Tel: 04 95 24 43 11
Fifteen basic rooms in a
modern annexe in the centre of the
village, above a cosy bar-restaurant.
€

Hiking

GR20
Between its trailheads at Calenzana
in the north and Conca in south,
the GR20 only touches road level at
five places, each of which is served
by a hotel or *gîte d'étape* offering
more comfortable accommodation
than that available up in the
mountains. Elsewhere, *refuges*
provide shelter and basic
ammenities between waystages.
Advance booking is generally
possible for hotels and *gîtes*; *refuge*
beds are allocated on a first-come-
first-served basis.

Calenzana *(see also page 271)*
Gîte d'Etape Municipal
at the bottom of the village
Tel: 04 95 62 77 13
Large, well run *gîte* with four-bed
dorms.
Haut' Asco
Le Chalet
Tel: 04 95 47 81 08
Fax: 04 95 30 25
Simple chalet-style rooms and *gîte
d'étape* dorm beds.
Col de Verghio
Hôtel Castel di Verghio
Tel: 04 95 48 00 01
Run-down ski station offering basic
hotel, *gîte* and *refuge* facilities.
Vizzavona *(see also page 273)*
Resto-Refuge-Bar De la Gare
Tel/Fax: 04 95 47 22 20
Grotty *gîte d'étape* without camping
space.
E' Capannelle
Gîte d'Etape "U Fugone"
Tel: 04 95 57 01 81
Fax: 04 95 56 39 34
Privately run place with bar
and restaurant – far preferable to
the dreadful municipal *refuge*
nearby.
Col de Verde
Refuge San Petru di Verdi
Tel: 04 95 24 46 82

Wooden dormitory huts or shaded
camping places.
Bavella
Auberge du Col
Tel: 04 95 72 09 87
Fax: 04 95 72 16 48
Clean and comfortable *gîte*.
Conca
La Tonnelle
Tel: 04 95 71 46 55
The best set up *gîte* on the route,
with ample camping and a
restaurant.

TRA MARE E MONTI: GÎTES D'ETAPE

Calenzana
Gîte d'étape municipal
Tel: 04 95 62 77 13
Bonifatu
Auberge de la Forêt
Tel: 04 95 65 09 98
Tuarelli
L'Alzelli
Tel: 04 95 62 01 75
Galéria
Chez M. Rossi
Tel: 04 95 62 00 46
Girolata
Le Cabane du Berger
Tel: 04 95 20 16 98
Curzu
Chez M et Mme Sagny
Tel: 04 95 27 31 70
Serriera
U me Mulinu
Tel: 04 95 26 10 67
Ota
Chez Félix
Tel: 04 95 26 12 92
Marignana
Ustaria di a Rota
Tel: 04 95 26 21 21
Revinda
E Case
Tel: 04 95 26 48 19

MARE A MARE NORD: GÎTES D'ETAPE

(For other accommodation along the
route, *see also Cargèse, page 271*)
**I Penti, Santa-Reparata-di-
Moriani**
Luna Piena
Tel: 04 95 38 59 48

Pianello
Gîte Municipal
Tel: 04 95 39 60 74
Sermano
Gîte Municipal
Tel: 04 95 48 67 97
Corte
U Tavignano
Tel: 04 95 46 16 85
Calacuccia
Le Couvent
Tel: 04 95 48 02 73
Albertacce
Gîte Municipal
Tel: 04 95 48 05 60 or 04 95 48
08 05
Evisa
Sarl u Poggiu
Tel: 04 95 26 21 28
Marignana
Ustaria di a Rota
Tel: 04 95 26 21 21
Revinda
E Case
Tel: 04 95 26 48 19
Cargèse *(see page 271)*

MARE A MARE CENTRE: GÎTES D'ETAPE

Ghisonaccia
Hôtel de la Poste
Tel/Fax: 04 95 56 00 41 €
Serra-di-Fiumorbu
Gîte Municipal
Tel: 04 95 56 75 48 or 06 81 04
69 49
Catastaghju
Gîte Municipal
Tel: 04 95 56 70 14 or 04 95 56
10 89
Cozzano
Bella Vista
Tel: 04 95 24 41 59
Tasso
Gîte Municipal
Tel: 04 95 24 52 01
Guitera les Bains
Gîte Municipal
Tel: 04 95 24 44 40 or 04 95 24
42 54
Quasquara
Gîte Municipal
Tel: 04 95 53 61 21
Col St-Georges
Gîte Municipal
Tel: 04 95 25 70 06
Porticcio *(see page 269)*

MARE A MARE SUD: GÎTES D'ETAPE

Burgo
U Fracintu
Tel: 04 95 76 15 05
Fax: 04 95 76 14 31
Ste-Lucie-de-Tallano
U Fragnonu
Tel: 04 95 78 82 56
Fax: 04 95 78 82 67
Serra-di-Scapomène
Gîte Municipal
Tel: 04 95 78 64 90
Fax: 04 95 78 72 43
Quenza
Corse Odyssee
Tel: 04 95 78 64 05
Fax: 04 95 78 61 91
Levie
Bienvenue à l'Alta Rocca
Tel: 04 95 78 46 41
Cartalavonu
Le Refuge
Tel: 04 95 70 00 39
Porto-Vecchio *(see page 270)*

Campsites

The list of campsites below is by no means exhaustive. It notes the island's best, and could be used to form the basis of an island tour.
Bastia: Casanova Miomo, 5 km (3 miles) north of Bastia along the route du Cap, tel: 04 95 33 91 42.
Calvi: Bella Vista 2 km (1¼ miles) along the N197 from Calvi, tel: 04 95 65 11 76.
L'Ile Rousse: Camping Bodri, 2 km (1¼ miles) west of L'Ile Rousse, tel: 04 95 60 10 86.
Porto: Camping Sol e Vista, Vaita, Porto, tel: 04 95 26 15 71.
Piana: Camping d'Arone, 5 km (3 miles) southwest at Plage d'Arone, tel: 04 95 20 64 54.
Ajaccio: Le Barbicaja, 4.5 km (3 miles) west of Ajaccio along the route des Sanguinaires, tel: 04 95 52 01 17.
Propriano: Camping Colomba, 3 km (2 miles) northeast of Propriano along the route de Baracci, tel: 04 95 76 06 42.
Campomoro: Camping Peretto Les Roseaux, Campomorro, tel: 04 95 74 20 52.
Bonifacio: Pian del Fosse, 4 km

Camping Guide

There are 116 campsites in Corsica and they are subject to similar classification as hotels. All of them have to meet certain minimum standards. Campsite facilities can be classified in general from satisfactory to good. Towards the end of the season, however, signs of exhaustion in the campsite personnel can sometimes be detected. With a few exceptions, campsites are situated on the coast, frequently even directly on the beach. Because they are even more dependent on the season than the hotels are, most are only open from May until the end of September.

Campers must stay only on campsites. Wild camping is prohibited and the law is vigilantly enforced.

(2 miles) (north of Bonifacio on the route de Santa Manza, tel: 04 95 73 16 34.
Porto-Vecchio: Arutoli, route de l'Ospédale, 4 km (2 miles) northwest of Porto-Vecchio, tel: 04 95 70 12 73.
Aléria: Marina d'Aléria, Aléria, tel: 04 95 57 01 42.
Corte: L'Albadu, 2.5 km (2 miles) southwest of Corte, tel: 04 95 46 24 55.

Where to Eat

Eating Out

Eating out is a serious business in Corsica. Regarding it as an aspect of national identity, the islanders are deservedly proud of their distinctive local cuisine, and most restaurateurs consider sourcing authentic local ingredients every bit as important an aspect of their *metier* as the preparation itself. This reflects the Corsican emphasis on freshness and natural Mediterranean flavours over the elaborate sauces that predominate across the water in continental France. That said, many resorts these days boast high-gastronomy restaurants, whose chefs seek to infuse traditional island recipes with innovative twists.

Standards of cooking are generally high, although as with most mass tourism destinations, the busy coastal strips in particular have their fair share of fly-by-night restaurateurs churning out formulaic food at inflated prices. By and large, it's best to avoid quaysides, beachside promenades and town squares, where you'll pay over the odds for the location. The finest dining tends to be in country *auberges*, hidden away in the depths of the *maquis*, where the dishes are all derived from home-grown, organic produce and cooked according to tried-and-tested family recipes.

For those on low budgets, Corsica's ubiquitous pizzerias offer tasty, inexpensive meals out. Even on the coast, pizzas tend to be baked in wood-fired ovens, using local ewe's cheese *(brocciu)* and *charcuterie* rather than mozzarella and mass-produced meats.

Regional specialities – such as

cannelloni al brocciu, wild boar, kid stew, veal in olives and stuffed trout – dominate menus of most other restaurants on the island, where you'll be offered a choice between a few *menus fixes* (sometimes called *formules*) and individually priced à la carte dishes. Fresh seafood is available everywhere on the coast, but it can be very expensive, with fish priced per 100g on most menus.

Bills can these days nearly always be settled by credit or debit card, even in remote hill villages – although it's always wise to check first. Service charges will be indicated by the acronym 'SC' on the bottom of the ticket; if it isn't, consider leaving a tip of between 10 and 15 percent.

Restaurants

AJACCIO

L'Aquarium
Rue des Halles
Tel: 04 95 21 11 21
Old-established place tucked away down a narrow alley behind the Place du Marché. A dependable option for inexpensive seafood, with especially good fish soup and *friture du golfe* (pot luck of pan-fried whitebait, calamari and leftovers from the day's catch). **€**

Ariadne
Route des Sanguinaires
Tel: 04 95 52 09 63
Bus No. 5 from place de Gaulle. Lively beach bar-restaurant on the outskirts of town featuring an eclectic mix of dishes from southeast Asia, Africa, South America and the Caribbean. Live World Music from 8.30pm most nights. **€**

Le 20123
2 rue Roi-de-Rome
Tel: 04 95 21 50 05
Ajaccio's quirkiest Corsican speciality restaurant, decked out with old village ephemera (including a 1960s Vespa). The food is definitive mountain cuisine: top-grade charcuterie, pork stews and chestnut-flour desserts. **€€**

Le Floride
Port de Plaisance Charles-d'Oornano
Tel: 04 95 22 67 48
The serious seafood-lover's choice: prime cuts of devil fish, snapper, mullet and bream, served in a smart dining hall fronting the posh end of the marina. **€€**

AJACCIO TO PROPRIANO

Porticcio
L'Arbousier
Hôtel Le Maquis
South edge of village
Tel: 04 95 25 05 55
Chic gourmet food, elaborated from local dishes, in swish surroundings with the lights of Ajaccio twinkling across the bay. **€€€**

Restaurant Prices

€ = Budget under €25
€€ = Moderate €25–40
€€€ = Expensive €40 and up

Coti-Chiavari
Le Belvédère
1 km (⅔ mile) south of the village on D55A
Tel: 04 95 27 10 32
Gulf views don't come much better than the one from this hilltop restaurant, on the far southern rim of the gulf. Phone ahead for the limited *menu fixe* and to book a table on the terrace. Signature dishes include wild boar terrine and guinea fowl with chestnuts. **€€**

Near Filitosa
Auberge U Mulinu
Pont de Calzola
Tel: 05 95 24 32 14
Wild river trout stuffed with local AOC *brocciu* is the speciality of this highly reputed *auberge*, housed in a converted water mill on the banks of the Taravo River. Rooms available if the wine list proves too much of a temptation. **€€**

Le Kiesale
Pont de Calzola
Tel: 04 95 24 35 81 or 04 95 24 36 30

One of the island's finest wines, the Domaine d'Abbatucci's award-winning white, comes from this property, and there's no better way to appreciate it than over a wood-grilled fish supper at their homely little farm restaurant. **€**

Olmeto
U Santa Maria – Chez Mimi
Place de l'église
Tel: 04 95 74 65 59
Old-fashioned Corsican *auberge* off a typical stone square, just down the lane from vendetta heroine Colomba's house. The feisty *patronne*, Mme Mimi, serves succulent regional dishes such lamb with wild Alta Roccan mushrooms. **€€**

Propriano
L'Hippocampe
Rue Jean-Pandolfi
Tel: 04 95 76 11 01
Top seafood from the gulf, served in simple surroundings at reasonable prices – a far safer choice than the row of more scenically situated restaurants lining the marina. **€**

THE SARTENAIS

Sartène
A Tinedda
5 km (3 miles) northwest along the Propriano road
Tel: 04 95 77 09 31
Down-to-earth *ferme-auberge* that offers a single set menu of wholesome local dishes – including *the* local speciality, sweetbreads à la sartenaise – in a snug dining room in winter or on a garden terrace in summer. Advance booking essential. **€**

Campomoro
Le Ressac
Behind the east end of the beach
Tel: 04 95 74 22 25
Unfussy, succulent *cuisine du terroir* (such as *cannelloni al brocciu* and lamb ragout) prepared by a father-and-son duo in the kitchen. Locally caught fish features prominently on the menu – splash out on their sublime boullabaisse,

Corsican seafood stew featuring just about everything that's edible in the waters of Campomorro. €

Tizzano
Chez Antoine
Above the harbour
Tel: 04 95 77 07 25
It's hard to imagine a more perfect spot to savour Sartenais seafood, plucked straight from the jetty just below this restaurant's terrace. Wood-grilled snapper and ray's wing in lemon sauce are among the keynote dishes. €€

ALTA ROCCA

Levie
A Pignata
5 km (3 miles) west of Levie near Cucuruzzu archeological site
Tel: 04 95 78 41 90
Patronne Lily de Rocaserra is the long-time standard bearer of Alta Roccan cooking, served on a gorgeous terrace overlooking the Rizzanese Valley. All the dishes have been handed down through generations and the ingredients come off the family farm. Stay the night and you can enjoy Lily's home-made fig jam at breakfast. €€

Zonza
L'Aiglon
In the centre of the village
Tel: 04 95 78 67 79
Sumptuous mountain cuisine given an inspired gastronomic spin. Their *plat de résistance* is "La Muntanela", featuring a dozen mouthwatering *mezzes*: grilled Alta Roccan liver sausage, walnut and *brocciu* tart, chestnuts marinated in black muscat. €€

Quenza
Sole e Monti
On the Zonza road
Tel: 04 95 78 62 53
M Balesi's flavoursome regional cuisine is served in a leafy garden opposite the hotel. Produce of the nearby Coscione Plateau – organic lamb, creamy *brocciu*, trout and wild herbs – dominate the menu. €€

Aullène
Hôtel de la Poste
Centre of the village
Tel: 04 95 78 61 21
The chestnut forests that engulf this high Alta Roccan village are the secret of the intense flavours of the charcuterie, pork stews and honey-scented desserts served on the stone terrace of this 19th-century coaching inn. €

Bonifacio
Stella d'Oro (Chez Jules)
23 rue Doria, near the church of St-Jean-Baptiste.
This is the place to sample Bonifacio's showpiece dish, *merrizzane* – aubergine stuffed with *brocciu*, tomatoes and herbs, baked in a wood oven. It's offered à la carte, alongside such delicacies a pasta in crayfish sauce. €€
Cantina Doria
27 rue Doria
Tel: 04 95 73 50 49
Simple regional dishes (including particularly tasty lasagna *à la bonifacienne*) served in a suitably rustic vaulted dining room or on little tables out in the alley. Restrained prices for the citadelle, and their wine list features the cream of southern Corsica's output. €
Marina di Cavu
Cala Longa, 6 km (4 miles) out of town
Tel: 04 95 73 14 30
The last word in *haute gastronomie corse*, which you can enjoy in a swish dining hall that's moulded around a huge granite boulder and open fireplace, or on a magnificent poolside facing the Lavezzi Islands. €€€

BONIFACIO TO PORTO-VECCHIO

Palombaggia
Tamaricciu
South end of the beach
Tel: 04 95 70 49 89
Chic beach bar-restaurant made from huge chunks of imported teak, overlooking some of the Med's whitest sand and bluest water. Inexpensive pizzas, mozzarella

salads and bruschettas are on offer, in addition to more copious meat and seafood mains. €€

Porto-Vecchio
Le Tourisme
In the citadelle, opposite the church
Tel: 04 95 70 06 45
Refined French-influenced Porto-Vecchien cooking that's lighter and more imaginatively presented than the competition. Try their pasta dish of the day in mussel-and-pastis or wild asparagus sauce; and for dessert they do a divine chilled myrtle and strawberry "soup". €€
A Cantina di l'Oriu
5 cours Napoleon
Tel: 04 95 70 26 21
The region's finest artisanal charcuterie, cheeses, oils, olives and wines, sampled in various *formules* in a stone-vaulted *cave* in the old quarter. €

Reading the Menu

To decipher what's on the menu, turn to Dining Out in the Language section on page 287

THE WEST COAST

Cargèse
Le Cabanon de Charlotte
In the marina
No phone
Greek-style *taverna* down on the quayside where you can order seafood straight off the boats and authentic Maniote salad with real feta and oregano. €

Piana
Les Roches Rouges
On the Porto road
Tel: 04 95 27 81 81
If anywhere is likely to seduce you into splurging on a *menu gastronomique* it will be this elegant restaurant, whose Art-Deco dining hall exudes 1920s sophistication. Come early for an *apéritif* on their superb west-facing terrace, which affords matchless views of the Golfe de Porto. €€

Porto
Le Sud
Adjacent to the watchtower
Tel: 04 95 26 14 11
Stylish Mediterranean-fusion cuisine, drawing on North African and Spanish as well as Corsican influences: try the lamb tagine with almonds and apricots or pan-fried veal in orange, and be sure to book a seat on their wonderful *terasse panoramique* which surveys the marina and cliffs of Capo d'Orto. €€

Restaurant Prices

€ = Budget under €25
€€ = Moderate €25–40
€€€ = Expensive €40 and up

Ota
Chez Félix
Centre of the village, near the mairie
Tel: 04 95 26 12 42
Walkers with Gargantuan appetites make up most of the clientele of this little village bar-restaurant, whose tiny terrace affords dizzying views across the Spelunca Valley. Local standards such as wild boar stew and wood-grilled veal are prominent on a good-value *menu corse*, and there are usually couscous-based alternatives for vegetarians. €

Evisa
Hôtel du Centre
Centre of the village
Tel: 04 95 26 20 92
You'll have to book days in advance to be sure of a table in this cosy mountain *auberge*, whose wild boar steak in orange and dark chocolate sauce is *the* house speciality. For a starter, they order in oysters fresh each day from the east coast lagoons. No credit cards. €€

Girolata
Le Bel Ombra
On the headland above the beach
No Phone
Lobster fished from the coral-edged cliffs of the adjacent Scandola

peninsula were this remote village's *raison d'être* before tourism took over, and at the teak-lined *Bel Ombra* you can order one straight from the tank. Pricier than usual, but everything other than seafood has to be brought in by boat. €€

Galéria
Stella Marina
At the west edge of the bay
Tel: 04 95 62 00 03
Among the scattering of restaurants in the Balagne's most isolated resort, this is the most welcoming and dependable place to order local crayfish *(langouste)*, rounded off with their perenially popular apple pie flambéed in local *eau de vie*. €€

CALVI AND BALAGNE

Calvi
L'Abri Côtier
Rue Joffre
Tel: 04 95 65 12 76
Eating can be a pricy, hit-and-miss affair on Calvi's quai Landry, but here you're guaranteed value for money, plenty of choice and careful cooking, as well as optimal views of the marina. €€
Chez Tao's
Rue St-Antoine, in the citadel
Tel: 04 95 65 00 73
Established by a White Russian deserter from the Bolshevik war in Crimea (whence the Rasputin-like photos in its vaulted interior), this place has been a legend since the 1930s. Film stars and pop idols flit through in summer for the cutting edge nouvelle cuisine and bird's eye views over the quay. €€
U Famale
Route de Porto
Tel: 04 95 65 18 82
Walk west of town towards the Punta della Revellata to find this refreshingly unpretentious Corsican speciality restaurant. Stock dishes include tasty lamb baked in *brocciu* and white wine and more-ish *fiadone* with *maquis* honey. Both feature on a copious set menu, and they also do less pricy pizzas. €

Bonifato
Auberge de la Forêt
An hospitable *gîte d'étape*, hemmed in by the cliffs of the Cirque de Bonifatu. Try the scrumptious (and vegetarian) *tarte aux herbes* or – if you're here in the autumn hunting season – their famous wild-boar-and-dwarf-bean stew. €€

Calenzana
Le Calenzana "Chez Michel"
7 cours Blaise, opposite the church
Tel: 04 95 62 70 25
By far the best place to eat in the village, not least because of Michel's melt-in-the-mouth suckling lamb, served with wheat-rolled potatoes. And their wood-baked pizzas are delicious too. Popular with GR20 finishers, which ensures a lively atmosphere in season. €

Pigna
Casa Musicale
Tel: 04 95 61 77 31 or 04 95 61 76 57
Matchless panoramas over the olive groves of the Balagne coast and live Corsican folk music serve as a backdrop to the painstakingly traditional cuisine dished up in this ancient stone house on the edge of the village. Opt for half-board and you can breakfast on orange-blossom honey and chestnut biscuits. €€

Feliceto
Osteria U Mulinu
On the Speloncato road
Tel: 04 95 61 73 23
Eccentric *ferme-auberge* in a converted olive-oil mill that's famous as much for the whip-cracking, gun-firing cabaret of its owner as the top quality food. Advance booking essential. $$

Speloncato
Auberge de Domalto
6 km (4 miles) below the village off the D71
Tel: 04 95 61 50 97
Superb *cuisine régionale* from the coast (sea bream in cream of lemon) and valleys (fragrant wild boar terrine), in a remote 18th-century *palazzo*. Tricky to find, but worth the effort. €€

Giunssani
Auberge l'Aghjola
Pioggiola
Tel: 04 95 61 90 48
Variously priced, superb value
menus fixes featuring quails in
cream of mint sauce and veal with
wild forest mushrooms. On fresh
evenings you can dine next to a
blazing fire under exposed beams.
€

Algajola
La Vieille Cave
Next to the citadelle
Tel: 04 95 60 70 09
Inventive cooking and a romantic
venue in a rambling Genoese-era
square. The *plat de résistance* here
is scorpion fish stuffed with *brocciu*
and charcuterie (only available à la
carte). €€

L'Ile Rousse
Les Jardins d'Emma
Col de Fogata, 2 km (1¼ miles)
along the Calvi road
Tel: 04 95 60 49 07
Refined "*gastro-corse*" menu with
house specialities such as spider
crab soup, stuffed seafood and
unashamedly decadent desserts,
served alfresco in a flowery garden.
€€
A Tesa ("Chez Marylène Santucci")
Lozari par Belgodère
Tel: 04 95 60 09 55
Acclaimed Corsican *ferme-auberge*
ensconced amid *maquis profond*
6 km (4 miles) inland from town. In
a converted riverside dairy, the
Santucci family rustle up definitive
Balagne dishes that include
delicate courgette fritters and
quails in honey. Everything comes
from the garden or village farms,
even most of the wines. €€

THE NEBBIO

St-Florent
La Gaffe
On the harbourfront
Tel: 04 95 37 00 12
Classic seafood cuisine, based on
produce from the gulf and restocked
fresh each day. By far the best place
to eat in this bracket. €€

La Rascasse
On the harbourfront
Tel: 04 95 37 06 99
Fashionable terrace restaurant on
the marina with an inventive
gourmet menu dominated by fish
and crustacea: try their cream of
scorpion fish or lobster sautéed in
Nebbio *charcuterie*. €€€
La Roya
Plage de la Roya
Tel: 04 95 37 00 40
Among one of very few restaurants
on the island staking a serious
claim to a Michelin star, hence is
Pantagruelesque *menu prestige*,
with its ultra-fancy takes on local
standards (eg spider crab turnover
with a squirt of Scotch). €€€

Murato
Ferme-Auberge Campu di Monte
3 km (2 miles) below the village
Tel: 04 95 37 64 39
One Corsica's most highly rated
fermes-auberge, hidden away at the
bottom of a valley below Murato
(turn left at *Victor Bar* in the village
and follow the signs). Mme Juillard
modestly attributes her success to
the quality of the local ingredients,
recipes refined over three
generations and the magnificent
location. €€

Bastia
A Casarelle
6 rue Ste-Croix
Tel: 04 95 32 02 32

Delightful Balagne specialities,
among which the *casgiate* (lumps of
fresh ewe's cheese baked in a wrap
of chestnut leaves) have earned the
chef island-wide acclaim. The most
appealing budget option in the
citadelle. €
La Citadelle
6 rue du Dragon, Citadelle
Tel: 04 95 31 44 70
French gourmet restaurant that's a
shade more sophisticated, both in
terms of cuisine and atmosphere,
than the competition, yet offers
genuine value for money. *Magret de
canard à l'orange* is the keynote
dish, available à la carte only. €€€
U Tianu
4 rue Rigo
Tel: 04 95 31 36 67
Bastia holds few restaurants
serving real *cuisine de campagne*
such as villagers would have eaten
in times past – blackbird terrine,
mutton-and-lentil stew and stuffed
sardines – and this is arguably the
best of them, housed in a crumbling
Genoese tenement down a narrow
alley just behind the Vieux Port. €€

CAP CORSE

San Martino di Lota
Auberge San Martino
place de l'église
11 km (7 miles) north of Bastia
Tel: 04 95 32 23 68
Cheap and cheerful village inn run

What to Drink

Water: Corsican spring water,
such as Aqua Corsa, St-Georges
and Zilia, has quite a pleasant
taste. It is also an ingredient in a
number of bottled soft drinks.
Beer: Pietra is a tasty Corsican
beer based on chestnuts. French
brands come from northern France
and Alsace. Beers from Belgium,
Holland and Denmark are popular,
and German beer can also
frequently be found at tourist
centres.
Wine: Corsicans primarily drink
wine. Red, rosé and white wines
are produced on the island as well

as naturally sweet Muscat and
Rappo. There are eight high-quality
districts. Dry and sweet whites are
a speciality of Cap Corse; around
Patrimonio you will find excellent
white, rosé, red and Muscat
wines; the wine from the Ajaccio
region is mostly red and rather
powerful; from the Sartenais in
the southern part of the island
(Figari, Pianottoli) there are
pleasant white, red and rosé
wines. Good wine is made along
the east coast where some of the
grapes are mechanically
harvested.

with uncommon enthusiasm from a characterful 19th-century house, high up on the corniche. The cavernous interior, crammed with old farm implements and antiques, doesn't do justice to the views, but the hospitable atmosphere is ample compensation. **€**

Erbalunga
Le Pirate
Off the square in the old quarter
Tel: 04 95 33 24 20
Cap Corse's flagship seafood restaurant, with a resolutely gastronomic menu that for once caters well for vegetarians. **€€**

Marine de Sisco
A Stalla Sischese
200 m (220 yds) up the D32 towards Sisco
Tel: 04 95 35 26 34
Groaning portions of totally authentic, delicious Cap Corse cooking, on a great value six-course menu; and the wine list features Lina Venturi-Pieretti's prize-winning rosé. **€**

Macinaggio
Les Îles
On the marina
Tel: 04 95 35 43 02
Simple, consistently fresh seafood and home-made pâtisserie desserts, indoors or à la terasse on the marina. **€**

Rogliano
Auberge Sant'Agnellu
Bertolacce
Tel: 04 95 35 40 59
A gorgeous terasse panoramique surveying Macinaggio's hinterland, where you can enjoy genuine hospitality and fine local cuisine, made from produce off the patron's brother's farm. **€€**

Port Centuri
A Macciotta "Chez Sker"
Behind the harbour
Tel: 04 95 35 64 46
Seafood afficionados shouldn't pass up the chance to eat at this tiny restaurant, in a converted fisherman's cottage. Sea bass, sea

anenomes and lobster feature on the showcase menu poisson. **€€**

EAST COAST AND INLAND DETOURS

Cervione
Les Trois Fourchettes
On the village square
Tel: 04 95 38 14 86
Cosy budget restaurant just below a medieval placette, offering a four-course menu of Castagniccian standards at an unbeatable price. **€**

Restaurant Prices

€ = Budget under €25
€€ = Moderate €25–40
€€€ = Expensive €40 and up

Pedicroce
Le Refuge
East of the village centre
Tel: 04 95 35 82 65
Clinging to the side of the valley above a sea of woodland, this is the most obvious pitstop on the route through Castagniccia, at roughly the midway point. Chestnut, free-range pork and game dishes feature on their various menus. **€**

Campana
Restaurant Sant'Andria
Tel: 04 95 35 82 26
Airy, wood-lined family restaurant, fitted with traditional carved furniture, overlooking the heart of the region. The patronne does the cooking herself, with chard, spinach and mint from the garden, pork reared in the local woods and tangy Niolo cheeses; and her chestnut desserts are a dream. **€**

La Porta
Restaurant de L'Ampugnani "Chez Elizabeth"
Centre of the village
Tel: 04 95 39 22 00
More magnificent views and quality Castagniccian food, served in a larger and more impersonal dining hall in the region's main village. **€€**

CORTE AND ITS HINTERLAND

Corte
U Museu
Rampe Ribanelle/rue Colonel-Feracci
Tel: 04 95 61 08 36
Reliable and efficient budget restaurant occupying a glass-sided building and terrace crouched below the citadelle walls. They offer a wide range of inexpensive menus fixes, and à la carte options including an enormous hot goat's cheese salad. **€**
Au Plat d'Or
Place Paoli
Tel: 04 95 46 27 16
The only fine dining restaurant in town: their limited menu features typical cortenais dishes such as stuffed Tavignano trout in Cap Corse liqueur and beef bruschettas with wild morel mushrooms. **€€**

Calacuccia
Auberge du Lac
Sidossi, 3 km (2 miles) up the valley
Tel: 04 95 48 02 73
Sunny dining hall on the shore of the lake where you can sample top-grade cuisine nioline: pungent Niolo cheeses, several kinds of charcuterie and succulent shepherds' stews. **€€**

Albertacce
Restaurant U Cintu ("Chez Jo Jo")
Centre of the village
Tel: 04 95 48 06 87
The ideal antidote to an appetite worked up in the surrounding hills: wholesome home cooking (literally in this case) – from the patron's own figatellu sausage and cheese to madame's divine ravioli brocciu – served in a dining room that doubles as the family lounge. **€**

CORTE TO AJACCIO

Venaco
Restaurant de la Place
Village square
Tel: 04 95 47 01 30
Undistinguished looking place on

the main square, within sight of the highway, but the best spot to eat on the journey between Corte and Ajaccio. Lamb stew, spinach tart, stuffed sardines in filo parcels and walnut flan number among the home-made specialities. €

Ghisoni
Kyrié
Centre of the village
Tel: 04 95 57 60 33
Family cooking that's far more exciting than the bland 1970s decor of this mountain hotel. Try the *patronne*'s own *cannelloni al brocciu* or leek and chestnut fritters. Good value. €

Zicavo
Le Tourisme
Centre of the village
Tel: 04 95 24 40 06
Zicavo's shepherds traditionally spend the summer on the roadless Coscione grasslands a day's walk up the mountain, which accounts for the full-flavoured *charcuterie*, *brocciu* and other regional dishes enjoyed in this family restaurant, patronized as much by locals as visitors. €

Attractions

Cinema

Cinemas in Ajaccio, Bastia, Calvi, Corte, L'Ile Rousse, Porticcio, Porpriano and Porto-Vecchio screen current releases, and open-air theatres pop up in the resorts at the height of the summer season. In both cases, English language movies are nearly always dubbed into French.

Nightlife

Nightlife is tame by the standards of the rest of Europe and although all the towns and resorts on the island have bars that stay open late, there are barely a handful of major clubs. The largest and most sophisticated of them is Via Notte (Tel: 04 95 72 02 12, www.vianotte.com), on the southern outskirts of Porto-Vecchio, a very glitzy place, pitched at rich young tourists from Italy, which hosts internationally famous DJs in the summer.

Traditional Music

Various groups keep the tradition of Corsican music alive. But there is a difference between the folkloric guitar music presented in "Cabarets Corses" and the soul-stirring recitals of plain *lamenti* or the *paghjelle* for several voices. This purely vocal music seemed forgotten at the end of the 1970s but it has had a renaissance since becoming part of the "Corsitude", the awareness of a Corsican identity.

The most famous groups are A Filetta, Canta, Caramusa, E Voce di u Cumune, I Chiami Aghjalese, I Muvrini, Les Nouvelles Polyphonies Corses, Orizonte and Estudiantina Ajaccina. The most outstanding singers are Antoine Ciosi, Petru Guelfucci, Jacky Micaelli, Jean Paul Poletti, Patricia Gattaceca and Patricia Poli.

Festivals and Events

Corsica's festival calendar has traditionally revolved around religious events, particularly Saints' Day celebrations and the more sombre processions of hooded penitents that tend to accompany Easter. Of these, Sartène's U Catenacciu *(see page 139)*, Erbalunga's La Cerca and Calvi's Granitola are the most famous, but you'll encounter similar rituals on a smaller scale across the island if you're here at that time.

To attract summer visitors and entertain family members returning for holidays from the continent, many towns, coastal resorts and hill villages also mount themed secular events. New music festivals seem to spring to life each season, most of them incorporating an element of traditional Corsican polyphony. Leading the festival stakes is Calvi, whose season is punctuated at regular intervals with large events boasting internationally acclaimed participants as well as the cream of local talent.

Full information on forthcoming events is posted in tourist offices.
Feb (first fortnight) Bastia: Rencontres du Cinéma Meditéranean, Festival of Mediterranean film.
18 March Ajaccio: Notre-Dame de la Miséricorde, Saint's Day religious procession.
April (first week) Bastia: Fête de la Bande Dessinée, Festival of cartoon art.
Good Friday Erbalunga: La Cerca; Sartène: U Catenacciu *(see page 139)*; Calvi: La Granitola. Spiral shaped processions by hooded penitents.
Easter Weekend Calvi: La Passion du Christ, Enactment of the

Crucifixion, with polyphony singing.
3 May Bastia: Fête du Christ Noir *(see page 200)*, Fishermen's patron saint procession through Terra Vecchia.
June (first week) Solenzara: Fiera di u Mare, Various sporting and food events connected to the sea.
2 June Bastia, Ajaccio and Calvi: St-Erasme, Fishermen's festival in Ajaccio harbour.
5 June Col de Bavella: Notre Dame des Neiges, Mass pilgrimage to the Madonna statue on the windswept Col de Bavella.
June (third week) Calvi: Festival du Jazz. Live gigs and jams on the Quai Landry.
June (third weekend) L'Ile Rousse: Festimusica, Folk music performed on an open-air stage in the town centre.
June (third weekend) Corte: San Ghjuva, Polyphony against the backdrop of the citadel.
July Pigna: Festivoce, Celebration of traditional Corsican music.
July (first weekend) Luri: Fiera di u Vinu, Wine and handicraft festival on Cap Corse.
July (end of first week) Bastia: Relève des Gouverneurs, Historical re-enactment.
July (third and fourth week) L'Ile Rousse: Fête du Livre Corse, Literature festival.
15–16 July Montegrosso: Foire de l'Olivier, Olive growers' get-together.
15–16 July Corte: Interlacs, Gruelling fell race around Lakes Nino, Capitello and Melo.
July (last week) St-Florent: Nuits de la Guitarre, International guitar festival.
July–August Olmi-Capella: Rencontres Théâtrales, Theatre festival using natural sets.
August (first week) Erbalunga: Festival de Musique, Eclectic music festival.
August (first week) Lama: Festival du Cinéma rural, Films revolving around the theme of rural life.
August (end of first week) Aregno: Foire de l'Amandier, Almond festival.
August (mid) St-Florent: Porto Latino, Latin music in the Nebbio.
August (third weekend) Sermano: near Corte Violin Festival, Mass

fiddling from around the world.
August Ajaccio: Fêtes Napoléoniennes, Re-enactments to celebrate Napoleon's birthday.
15 August Bastia, Ajaccio and Calvi: L'Assomptio, Son et lumières.
8 September Lavasina: Notre-Dame-de-Lavasina *(see page 206)*, Pilgrimage by candlelight.
8–10 September Casamaccioli: Santa di u Niolu *(see page 91)*, Old agricultural fair and singing competition.
September (around 14–18) Calvi: Rencontres de Chants Polyphonique, The island's largest festival of song.
October (first week) Bastia: British film festival.
October (first fortnight) Bastia: Musicales de Bastia, Live music at venues around town.
October (last week) Calvi: Festiventu, Kites and other wind-related events.
November (mid) Évisa: Fête du Marron, Chestnut gathering, cooking and produce stalls.

Shopping

What to Buy

With the demise of the island's traditional agriculture, the sale of premium Corsican produce to tourists has become an economic lifeline for many villages. Travelling around rural areas, you'll encounter no shortage of roadside signs advertising various *produits corses*, and most towns have at least a couple of Corsican speciality boutiques showcasing fine quality goods.

Food

The stock in trade of such souvenir shops is mostly fresh produce. *charcuterie* – cured meats – comes in a variety of forms and is of a consistently high quality, the pigs having been reard in the woods where they feed on chestnuts and wild roots. Castagniccia, Niolo and Evisa are among the regions renowned for their charcuterie.

An ideal accompaniment for it are the island's wonderful cheeses, made from ewe's milk at altitude in old stone *bergeries*. Using age-old methods, Corsican shepherds produce small quantities, which explains the high cost of the best cheeses, although their pungent strength means a little can go a long way.

Produce derived from the *maquis* – such as dried herbs, flowers and honey – also make great, lightweight presents. Alongside them you'll also see exotic-shaped bottles of powerful *eaux de vie* flavoured with juniper or myrtle – a traditional island *digestif*.

To preserve the reputation of Corsican produce (after a scandal in the 1990s revealed that 70 pecent of pork used in "Corsican" *charcuterie* came from the continent), local farmers formed an organization called Authentica, whose mark assures and local origin. Members' goods are marketed through a chain of shops in: Ajaccio (Délices et Santé, 7 cours Napoléon); Calvi (A Casetta, 16 rue Clemenceau); Porto (Hibiscus A Spusatella, La Marine); Porto-Vecchio (L'Orriu, 5 cours Napoléon); Propriano, (Bocca Fina, rue des Pêcheurs).

Wine

Local wines often carry the aromas of the *maquis* and are for the most part not *vins de gardes* (wines for laying down), which means they travel well and should be drunk within a year or two of being bottled. Names to look out for include: Domaine Comte Péraldi, Clos d'Alzeto, Clos Nicrosi, Clos Gentille, Domaine D'Abbatucci, Domaine Venturi-Pieretti's and Domaine de Gioielli. Many of these are available in large supermarkets for a lot less than you pay in Produits Corses outlets.

Music
Nothing conjours up the mood of the mountains as evocatively as Corsican polyphony, and racks in most towns and resorts stock a selection of CDs and cassettes which make great accompaniment for driving around the island. For tips on what to buy (*see one page box on polyphony music, page 87*).

Handicrafts
The Balagne area of the northwest has become a haven for all kinds of artisans and a route stringing their workshops together was recently inaugurated by the regional development council. Free maps outlining the *Strada di l'Artigiani* (or *Route des Artisans*) are available from tourist offices. A particularly large agglomeration of *ateliers* is to be found at the village of Pigna *(see page 176)*, whose old stone cottages harbour musical box and

flute makers, a lutenist, ceramicist and others. Further west at Lumio *(see page 179)*, on the far side of the bay from Calvi, Christian Moretti has founded a metal workshop where traditional hunting knives are forged from pure Corsican steel. These range from pocket-sized pen-knives to long blades with beautiful olive-wood handles that sell for upwards of €1,000.

Market Etiquette
In a market all goods have to be marked with the price by law. Prices are usually by the kilo or by the *pièce*, that is, each item priced individually. Usually the stall holder *(marchand)* will select the goods for you. Sometimes there is a serve-yourself system – just observe everyone else. If you are choosing cheese, for example, you may be offered a taste to try first; *un goûter*. Here are a few useful words:

bag	**le sac**
basket	**le panier**
flavour	**le parfum**
organic	**biologique**
ripe	**mûr**
tasting	**la dégustation**

Shopping for Lunch
If you want to buy a picnic lunch, remember to buy everything you need before midday. Good delicatessens *(charcuterie)* have delicious ready-prepared dishes, which make picnicking a delight.

Sport

Golf
There is a luxury 18-hole golf course laid out amidst the *maquis* near Bonifacio (Golf Spèrone), as well as nine-hole golf courses at Lucciana near Busha, at Spanu near Lumio and in the Regino valley near Monticello, inland from L'Ile Rousse (both of which are in the Balagne).

Horse Riding
Corsica offers excellent opportunities for horse riding. A chain of *Centres Equestres* have established a range of superb itineraries, ranging from day hacks to isolated beaches, where you can gallop through the shallows, to 14-night traverses of the entire island. The horses, most of which have been raised from traditional Corsican stock well adapted to the island's rocky terrain, are without exception well cared for.
Jacques Abbatucci
"Fil di Rosa", 20150 Serra di Ferro
Tel: 04 95 74 08 08
Fax: 04 95 74 01 07
L'Albadu
Jean Pulicani, ancienne route d'Ajaccio, Corte
Tel: 04 95 46 24 55
Antoine de Rocca Serra
20170 Levie
Tel: 04 95 78 41 90
Fax: 04 95 78 46 03
Arbo Valley
Chez François Vascovali, Saleccia, Monticello, near L'Ile Rousse
Tel: 04 95 60 49 49
Ferme Equestre Baracci
20110 Propriano
Tel: 04 95 76 08 02 or 04 95 76 19 48
A Madunina à Sartène
Sartène
Tel: 04 95 73 42 89

Pierre Milanini
Hameau de Jalicu, 20122 Quenza
Tel: 04 95 78 63 21
L'Ostriconi
Pierre-Jean Costa, Lama, Balagne
Tel: 04 95 48 22 99
Christian et Claude Perrier
Domaine de Croccano, 20100
Sartène
Tel: 04 95 77 11 37
Fax: 04 95 73 42 89
E-mail: christian.perrier@wandoo.fr

Long-distance Walking

Corsica is supremely well set up for long-distance walking, with an extensive network of waymarked trails covering the island's diverse landscapes. The chapter on hiking outlines these routes in more detail and gives guidance on what kinds of accommodation you can expect to find and how to book it. For those wishing to have the advance planning, transport, sleeping and cooking arrangements taken care of, a handful of reliable companies run supported treks with back up and luggage transfer facilities. The level of services they offer varies considerably; some will send along a fully qualified mountain guide to accompany you along the entire route, whereas other will merely provide a written route guide.

Trekking Agencies in the UK
Exodus
9 Weir Road, London SW12 0LT
Tel: 020-8675 5550
Fax: 020-8673 0779
www.exodus.co.uk
Explore Worldwide
Frederick St, Aldershot, Hants
GU11 1LQ
Tel: 01252 760000
Fax: 01252 760001
www.explore.co.uk
HF Holidays
Imperial House, Edgware Rd,
London NW9 5AL
Tel: 020-8905 9556
www.hfholidays.co.uk
Sherpa Expeditions
131a Heston Rd, Hounslow TW5
0RF, England

Tel: 020-8577 2717
Fax: 020-8572 9788
www.sherpa-walking-holidays.co.uk

Trekking Agencies in Corsica
A Muntagnola Quenza
20122 Quenza, Haute-Corse
Tel: 04 95 78 65 19
www.a-muntagnola.com
Camina Mondi
Place de l'Eglise, 20220 Pigna,
Haute-Corse
Tel: 04 95 61 77 36
Fax: 04 95 61 77 36
www.caminamondi.com
Compagnie des Guides et Accompagnateurs de Montagne
20224 Calacuccia, Niolu, Haute-Corse
Tel: 04 95 48 05 22
Fax: 04 95 48 08 80
Couleur Corse
7 Domaine de Loretto, 20000
Ajaccio, Corse-du-Sud
Tel: 04 95 10 52 83
Fax: 04 95 22 24 30
www.couleur-corse.com
Objectif Nature
3 rue Notre Dame de Lourdes,
20200 Bastia
Tel: 04 95 32 54 54
Fax: 04 95 32 57 58
www.ifrance.com/obj-nature
Montagne Corse en Liberté
Le Rond Point, 2 av de la Grande
Armée, 20 000 Ajaccio
Tel: 04 95 20 53 14
Fax: 33 04 95 20 90 60
www.montagne-corse.com

Canyoning

The wilder corners of Corsica's interior valleys could have been purpose-designed for canyoning, an outdoor sport that's a hybrid of climbing and extreme canoeing (without the kayaks). Ropes, harnesses, helmets and abseiling techniques are used to descend particularly steep and impressive sections of gorges via water courses. Apart from gaining you access to some gloriously unspoilt spots, canyoning is also a lot better suited to the Corsican climate than climbing in summer, when the glare

Vallecime
Poggio, 20212 Sermano
Tel: 04 95 48 69 33
Fax: 04 95 48 69 36
www.vallecime.com

Mountain Climbing

Corsica's prime climbing areas are Bavella, in the far south, the chalk seams close to Patrimonio in the Nebbio, the head of the Restonica Valley near Corte, and the awesome granite escarpments around the Refuge de Carrozzu, above Bonifato (inland from Calvi). The only dependable guide published in English is Roger Collomb's *Corsica Mountains* (West Co, UK).

Equipment and leaflets can be hired at the Col de Bavella, where a small German-run climbing school runs guided trips of various levels of difficulty into the famous "Aiguilles".

For longer forays into the mountains, contact one of Corsica's three fully qualified High Mountain Guides: Jean-Paul Quilici, from Quenza (Tel: 04 95 78 64 33); Pierre Griscelli, *gardien* of the Carozzu refuge, Bonifatu, on the GR20 (Tel: 04 95 30 82 51 or 04 95 44 01 95); and Pierre Pietri, leading expert on the Cinto massif (Tel: 04 95 32 62 76).

On the opposite side of the Asco Valley from Pierre Pietri's home village, Moltifao, local climbing enthusiasts recently devised a world-class **Via Ferrata** facility,

and heat radiating from the granite can be an ordeal. Aside from the slight physical risks involved, the only catch is that the best routes are secrets jealously guarded by the few operators who lead canyoning trips on the island. Even if you're an old hand, it pays to join up on a guided trip with a firm such as Corsica Trek in Porto (tel: 04 95 26 82 02 or 04 95 26 21 21, fax 04 95 26 12 49), who offer trips into the Calanche de Piana and Faille de Revinda, between Piana and Cargèse.

which enables you to climb extreme pitches in total safety with the aid of stanchion cables, ramps, fixed ladders and cemented rungs. All the necessary equipment (gloves, helmet, harness, caribiners, lanyards and dynamic ropes) and tickets for the Via Ferrata di a Manicella (and its more rudimentary neighbour, the Via Ferrata di a Scaletta) are available exclusively from Terra Corsa at nearby Ponte Leccia (www.interracorsa.fr).

Diving

Corsica holds no shortage of scuba schools to help you get the most out of superb marine life and underwater scenery lurking just off the coast. Their staff are the best source of advice on where to dive; all sections of the Corsican shore have their strongpoints, but the most diverse subaquatic topography, flora and fauna is to be found along the west coast, particularly the Golfe de Porto, where you can dive close to the UNESCO-listed Scandola Nature Reserve, stronghold of beautiful red gorgonian coral. Corsica's other world-class diving area is around the choppy waters of the Bonifacio Straits, where colonies of huge grouper can be viewed. Visibilty typically fluctuates between 25 metres (82 ft) and 50 metres (164 ft) depending on weather conditions, with water temperatures around the low 20s C (high 60s F) in summer.

Ajaccio region
Valinco
Porto Pollo Plongée
Porto Pollo
Tel/Fax: 04 95 74 07 46
Valinco Plongée
Propriano Marina
Tel: 04 95 76 31 01
U Levante
Propriano Marina
Tel: 04 95 76 23 83

Bonifacio
Atoll
Auberge A Cheda, 2 km (1¼ mile) north of Bonifacio
Tel: 04 95 72 03 83
Fax: 04 95 73 17 72

Barakoud
3 km (2 miles) north of Bonifacio
Tel: 04 95 73 13 02
Kallisté
Bonifacio Marina, near the Elf petrol station
Tel: 04 95 73 53 66

Porto-Vecchio region
Hippocampe
Chiappa, nr Palombaggia
Tel/Fax: 04 95 70 56 54
Kalliste
Palombaggia beach
Tel: 04 95 70 44 59

Porto
Génération Bleue
Porto Marina
Tel/Fax: 04 95 26 24 88
www.generation-bleue.com
Centre de Plongée du Golfe
Porto Marina
Tel: 04 95 26 10 29
www.plongeeporto.com

Calvi and Balagne
Calvi Plongée Citadelle
Thalassa Immersion
2 rue St-Jean, Bastia
Tel: 04 95 31 78 90 or 04 95 65 33 67
École de Plongée de L'Ile Rousse
Port de Commerce
L'Ile Rousse
Tel: 04 95 60 36 85
Fax: 04 95 60 45 21
Club de Plongée Castille
Calvi Marina
Tel: 04 95 65 14 05
Ecole de Plongée Internationale de Calvi
Marina car park
Tel: 04 95 65 42 22

The Nebbio
CESM
Le Roya beach
St-Florent
Tel: 04 95 37 00 61
Fax: 04 95 37 09 60

Bastia and Cap Corse
Thalassa Immersion
2 km (1¼ miles) north
Tel: 04 95 31 78 90
Club Plongée Bastias
Vieux Port

Language

Background

French is Corsica's official language, spoken by all islanders. It tends to be pronounced with a distinctive accent that resembles Ligurian or Tuscan dialects of Italian. Such intonations derive from the indigenous language of the island, Corsican (*Corse* in French), which a recent surveys has shown remains in decline despite attempts to revive it over the past two or three decades through schools and the establishment of a univeristy at Corte *(for more details see feature section on page 83).*

Touring the island, you'll regularly hear Corsican spoken up in the interior hill villages; down on the coast it is less often heard in public and rarely from younger Corsicans. Attempts by visitors to speak the language may not meet with the approving response you might expect. After centuries of government suppression, many locals are defensive about their native tongue, regarding it as a badge of national identity, and do not take well to poor renditions of it from foreigners.

Speakers of Italian will find themselves easily understood; partly as a result of the volume of tourists from across the Ligurian Sea, and partly because of its close affinities with Corsican, Italian is widely understood (even by members of the younger generation) even if it's not always all that fluently spoken. Few Corsicans, on the other hand, speak more than a few rudimentary phrases of English.

Words & Phrases

How much is it? *C'est combien?*
What is your name?
Comment vous appelez-vous?

My name is... *Je m'appelle...*
Do you speak English? *Parlez-vous anglais?*
I am English/American *Je suis anglais/américain*
I don't understand *Je ne comprends pas*
Please speak more slowly *Parlez plus lentement, s'il vous plaît*
Can you help me? *Pouvez-vous m'aider?*
I'm looking for... *Je cherche*
Where is...? *Où est...?*
I'm sorry *Excusez-moi/Pardon*
I don't know *Je ne sais pas*
No problem *Pas de problème*
Have a good day! *Bonne journée!*
That's it *C'est ça*
Here it is *Voici*
There it is *Voilà*
Let's go *On y va/Allons-y*
See you tomorrow *A demain*
See you soon *A bientôt*
Show me the word in the book *Montrez-moi le mot dans le livre*
please *s'il vous plaît*
thank you *merci*
(very much) *(beaucoup)*
you're welcome *de rien*
excuse me *excusez-moi*
hello *bonjour*
OK *d'accord*
goodbye *au revoir*
good evening *bonsoir*
here *ici*
there *là*
today *aujourd'hui*
yesterday *hier*
tomorrow *demain*
now *maintenant*
later *plus tard*
this morning *ce matin*
this afternoon *cet après-midi*
this evening *ce soir*

On Arrival

I want to get off at... *Je voudrais descendre à...*
Is there a bus to Bastia? *Est-ce qu'il ya un bus pour Bastia?*
What street is this? *A quelle rue sommes-nous?*
Which line do I take for...? *Quelle ligne dois-je prendre pour...?*
How far is...? *A quelle distance se trouve...?*
Validate your ticket *Compostez votre billet*

Time

At what time? *A quelle heure?*
When? *Quand?*
What time is it? *Quelle heure est-il?*
● Note that the French generally use the 24-hour clock.

airport *l'aéroport*
customs *la douane*
train station *la gare*
bus station *la gare routière*
bus *l'autobus, le car*
bus stop *l'arrêt*
platform *le quai*
ticket *le billet*
return ticket *aller-retour*
hitchhiking *l'autostop*
toilets *les toilettes*
This is the hotel address *C'est l'adresse de l'hôtel*
I'd like a (single/double) room... *Je voudrais une chambre (pour une/deux personnes)...*
...with shower *avec douche*
...with a bath *avec salle de bain*
...with a view *avec vue*
Does that include breakfast? *Le prix comprend-il le petit déjeuner?*
May I see the room? *Je peux voir la chambre?*
washbasin *le lavabo*
bed *le lit*
key *la clé*
elevator *l'ascenseur*
air conditioned *climatisé*

On the Road

Where is the spare wheel? *Où est la roue de secours?*
Where is the nearest garage? *Où est le garage le plus proche?*
Our car has broken down *Notre voiture est en panne*
I want to have my car repaired *Je veux faire réparer ma voiture*
It's not your right of way *Vous n'avez pas la priorité*
I think I must have put diesel in the car by mistake *Je crois que j'ai mis du gasoil dans la voiture par erreur*
the road to... *la route pour...*
left *gauche*
right *droite*
straight on *tout droit*

far *loin*
near *près d'ici*
opposite *en face*
beside *à côté de*
car park *parking*
over there *là-bas*
at the end *au bout*
on foot *à pied*
by car *en voiture*
town map *le plan*
road map *la carte*
street *la rue*
square *la place*
give way *céder le passage*
dead end *impasse*
no parking *stationnement interdit*
motorway *l'autoroute*
toll *le péage*
speed limit *la limitation de vitesse*
petrol *l'essence*
unleaded *sans plomb*
diesel *le gasoil*
water/oil *l'eau/l'huile*
puncture *un pneu crevé*
bulb *l'ampoule*
wipers *les essuies-glace*

Shopping

Where is the nearest bank (post office)? *Où est la banque/Poste/ PTT la plus proche?*
I'd like to buy *Je voudrais acheter*
How much is it? *C'est combien?*
Do you take credit cards? *Est-ce que vous acceptez les cartes de crédit?*
I'm just looking *Je regarde seulement*
Have you got...? *Avez-vous...?*
I'll take it *Je le prends*
I'll take this one/that one *Je prends celui-ci/celui-là*
What size is it? *C'est de quelle taille?*
Anything else? *Avec ça?*
size (clothes) *la taille*
size (shoes) *la pointure*
cheap *bon marché*
expensive *cher*
enough *assez*
too much *trop*
a piece *un morceau de*
each *la pièce (eg ananas, 15F la pièce)*
bill *la note*
chemist *la pharmacie*
bakery *la boulangerie*
bookshop *la librairie*

library *la bibliothèque*
department store *le grand magasin*
delicatessen *la charcuterie/le traiteur*
fishmonger's *la poissonerie*
grocery *l'alimentation/l'épicerie*
tobacconist *tabac* (can also sell stamps and newspapers)
market *le marché*
supermarket *le supermarché*
junk shop *la brocante*

Sightseeing

town *la ville*
old town *la vieille ville*
abbey *l'abbaye*
cathedral *la cathédrale*
church *l'église*
keep *le donjon*
mansion *l'hôtel*
hospital *l'hôpital*
town hall *l'hôtel de ville/la mairie*
nave *la nef*
stained glass *le vitrail*
staircase *l'escalier*
tower *la tour* (La Tour Eiffel)
walk *le tour*
country house/castle *le château*
Gothic *gothique*
Roman *romain*
Romanesque *roman*
museum *le musée*
art gallery *la galerie*
exhibition *l'exposition*

Emergencies

Help! *Au secours!*
Stop! *Arrêtez!*
Call a doctor *Appelez un médecin*
Call an ambulance *Appelez une ambulance*
Call the police *Appelez la police*
Call the fire brigade *Appelez les pompiers*
Where is the nearest telephone? *Où est le téléphone le plus proche?*
Where is the nearest hospital? *Où est l'hôpital le plus proche?*
I am sick *Je suis malade*
I have lost my passport/purse *J'ai perdu mon passeport/porte-monnaie*

tourist information office *l'office de tourisme/le syndicat d'initiative*
free *gratuit*
open *ouvert*
closed *fermé*
every day *tous les jours*
all year *toute l'année*
all day *toute la journée*
swimming pool *la piscine*
to book *réserver*

Dining Out

Table d'hôte (the "host's table") is one set menu served at a set price. Prix fixe is a fixed price menu, usually very good value. A la carte means dishes from the menu are charged separately.

I am a vegetarian *Je suis végétarien*
I am on a diet *Je suis au régime*
What do you recommend? *Que'est-ce que vous recommandez?*
Do you have local specialities? *Avez-vous des spécialités locales?*
I'd like to order *Je voudrais commander*
That is not what I ordered *Ce n'est pas ce que j'ai commandé*
Is service included? *Est-ce que le service est compris?*
May I have more wine? *Encore du vin, s'il vous plaît?*
Enjoy your meal *Bon appétit!*
breakfast *le petit déjeuner*
lunch *le déjeuner*
dinner *le dîner*
meal *le repas*
first course *l'entrée/les hors d'oeuvre*
main course *le plat principal*
made to order *sur commande*
drink included *boisson comprise*
wine list *la carte des vins*
the bill *l'addition*
fork *la fourchette*
knife *le couteau*
spoon *la cuillère*
plate *l'assiette*
glass *le verre*
napkin *la serviette*
ashtray *le cendrier*

Breakfast and Snacks

baguette long thin loaf
pain bread
petits pains rolls
beurre butter

False Friends

False friends are words that look like English words but mean something different.
le car motorcoach, also railway carriage
le conducteur bus driver
la monnaie change (coins)
l'argent money/silver
ça marche can sometimes mean walk, but is usually used to mean working (the TV, the car etc.) or going well
actuel "present time" (*la situation actuelle* the present situation)
rester to stay
location hiring/renting
personne person or nobody, according to context
le médecin doctor

poivre pepper
sel salt
sucre sugar
confiture jam
oeufs eggs
...à la coque boiled eggs
...au bacon bacon and eggs
...au jambon ham and eggs
...sur le plat fried eggs
...brouillés scrambled eggs
tartine bread with butter
yaourt yoghurt
crêpe pancake
croque-monsieur ham and cheese toasted sandwich
croque-madame with a fried egg on top
galette type of pancake
pan bagna bread roll stuffed with salad Niçoise
quiche tart of eggs and cream with various fillings
quiche lorraine quiche with bacon

First course

An amuse-bouche, amuse-gueule or appetizer is something to "amuse the mouth", served before the first course
anchoiade sauce of olive oil, anchovies and garlic, served with raw vegetables
assiette anglaise cold meats
potage soup

rillettes **rich fatty paste of shredded duck, rabbit or pork**
tapenade **spread of olives and anchovies**
pissaladière **Provençal pizza with onions, olives and anchovies**

Viande Meat

la viande **meat**
bleu **very rare**
saignant **rare**
à point **medium**
bien cuit **well done**
grillé **grilled**
agneau **lamb**
andouille/andouillette **tripe sausage**
bifteck **steak**
boudin **sausage**
boudin noir **black pudding**
boudin blanc **white pudding (chicken or veal)**
blanquette **stew of veal, lamb or chicken with a creamy egg sauce**
boeuf à la mode **beef in red wine with carrots, mushroom and onions**
à la bordelaise **beef with red wine and shallots**
à la Bourguignonne **cooked in red wine, onions and mushrooms**
brochette **kebab**
caille **quail**
canard **duck**
carbonnade **casserole of beef, beer and onions**
carré d'agneau **rack of lamb**
cassoulet **stew of beans, sausages, pork and duck, from southwest France**
cervelle **brains (food)**
châteaubriand **thick steak**
choucroute **Alsace dish of sauerkraut, bacon and sausages**

The Alphabet

Learning the pronunciation of the French alphabet is a good idea. In particular, learn how to spell out your name.
a=ah, **b**=bay, **c**=say, **d**=day **e**=er, **f**=ef, **g**=zhay, **h**=ash. **i**=ee, **j**=zhee, **k**=ka, **l**=el, **m**=em, **n** =en, **o**=oh, **p**=pay, **q**=kew, **r**=ehr, **s**=ess, **t**=tay, **u**=ew, **v**=vay, **w**=dooblah vay, **x**-=eex, **y**=ee grek, **z**=zed

Basic Rules

Even if you speak no French at all, it is worth trying to master a few simple phrases. The fact that you have made an effort is likely to get you a better response. More and more French people like practising their English on visitors, especially waiters in the cafés and restaurants and the younger generation. Pronunciation is the key; they really will not understand if you get it very wrong. Remember to **emphasise each syllable**, but not to pronounce the last consonant of a word as a rule (this includes the plural "s") and always to drop your "h"s. Whether to use "**vous**" or "**tu**" is a vexed question; increasingly the familiar form of "tu" is used by many people. However it is better to be too formal, and use "vous" if in doubt. It is very important to be polite; always address people as **Madame** or **Monsieur**, and address them by their surnames until you are confident first names are acceptable. When entering a shop always say, "Bonjour Monsieur/ Madame," and "Merci, au revoir," when leaving.

confit **duck or goose preserved in its own fat**
contre-filet **cut of sirloin steak**
coq au vin **chicken in red wine**
côte d'agneau **lamb chop**
daube **beef stew with red wine, onions and tomatoes**
dinde **turkey**
entrecôte **beef rib steak**
escargot **snail**
faisan **pheasant**
farci **stuffed**
faux-filet **sirloin**
feuilleté **puff pastry**
foie **liver**
foie de veau **calf's liver**
foie gras **goose or duck liver pâté**
gardiane **rich beef stew with olives and garlic, from the Camargue**
cuisses de grenouille **frog's legs**
grillade **grilled meat**
hachis **minced meat**
jambon **ham**
lapin **rabbit**
lardon **small pieces of bacon, often added to salads**
magret de canard **breast of duck**
médaillon **rolled meat**
moelle **beef bone marrow**
mouton navarin **stew of lamb with onions, carrots and turnips**
oie **goose**
perdrix **partridge**
petit-gris **small snail**
pieds de cochon **pig's trotters**
pintade **guinea fowl**
Pipérade **Basque dish of eggs, ham, peppers, onion**
porc **pork**

pot-au-feu **casserole of beef and vegetables**
poulet **chicken**
poussin **young chicken**
rognons **kidneys**
rôti **roast**
sanglier **wild boar**
saucisse **fresh sausage**
saucisson **salami**
veau **veal**

Poissons Fish

Armoricaine **made with white wine, tomatoes, butter and cognac**
anchois **anchovies**
anguille **eel**
bar (or loup) **sea bass**
barbue **brill**
belon **Brittany oyster**
bigorneau **sea snail**
Bercy **sauce of fish stock, butter, white wine and shallots**
bouillabaisse **fish soup, served with grated cheese, garlic croutons and *rouille*, a spicy sauce**
brandade **salt cod purée**
cabillaud **cod**
calmars **squid**
colin **hake**
coquillage **shellfish**
coquilles Saint-Jacques **scallops**
crevette **shrimp**
daurade **sea bream**
flétan **halibut**
fruits de mer **seafood**
hareng **herring**
homard **lobster**
huître **oyster**

langoustine **large prawn**
limande **lemon sole**
lotte **monkfish**
morue **salt cod**
moule **mussel**
moules marinières **mussels in white wine and onions**
oursin **sea urchin**
raie **skate**
saumon **salmon**
thon **tuna**
truite **trout**

Légumes Vegetables

ail **garlic**
artichaut **artichoke**
asperge **asparagus**
aubergine **eggplant**
avocat **avocado**
bolets **boletus mushrooms**
céleri remoulade **grated celeriac with mayonnaise**
champignon **mushroom**
cèpe **boletus mushroom**
chanterelle **wild mushroom**
cornichon **gherkin**
courgette **zucchini**
chips **potato crisps**
chou **cabbage**
chou-fleur **cauliflower**
concombre **cucumber**
cru **raw**
crudités **raw vegetables**
épinard **spinach**
frites **chips, French fries**
gratin dauphinois **sliced potatoes baked with cream**
haricot **dried bean**
haricots verts **green beans**
lentilles **lentils**
maïs **corn**
mange-tout **snow pea**
mesclun **mixed leaf salad**
navet **turnip**
noix **nut, walnut**
noisette **hazelnut**
oignon **onion**
panais **parsnip**
persil **parsley**
pignon **pine nut**
poireau **leek**
pois **pea**
poivron **bell pepper**
pomme de terre **potato**
radis **radis**
roquette **arugula, rocket**
ratatouille **Provençal vegetable stew of aubergines, courgettes, tomatoes, peppers and olive oil**

riz **rice**
salade Niçoise **egg, tuna, olives, onions and tomato salad**
salade verte **green salad**
truffe **truffle**

Fruits Fruit

ananas **pineapple**
cavaillon **fragrant sweet melon**
cerise **cherry**
citron **lemon**
citron vert **lime**
figue **fig**
fraise **strawberry**
framboise **raspberry**
groseille **redcurrant**
mangue **mango**
mirabelle **yellow plum**
pamplemousse **grapefruit**
pêche **peach**
poire **pear**
pomme **apple**
raisin **grape**
prune **plum**

Sauces Sauces

aioli **garlic mayonnaise**
béarnaise **sauce of egg, butter, wine and herbs**
forestière **with mushrooms and bacon**
hollandaise **egg, butter and lemon sauce**
lyonnaise **with onions**
meunière **fried fish with butter, lemon and parsley sauce**
meurette **red wine sauce**
Mornay **sauce of cream, egg and cheese**
Parmentier **with mashed potatoes**
paysan **rustic style**
pistou **Provençal sauce of basil, garlic and olive oil; vegetable soup with the sauce**
provençale **sauce of tomatoes, garlic and olive oil**
papillotte **cooked in paper**

Puddings Dessert

Belle Hélène **fruit with ice cream and chocolate sauce**
clafoutis **baked pudding of batter and cherries**
coulis **purée of fruit or vegetables**
gâteau **cake**
île flottante **whisked egg whites in custard sauce**
crème anglaise **custard**

pêche melba **peaches with ice cream and raspberry sauce**
tarte tatin **upside down tart of caramelised apples**
crème caramel **caramelised egg custard**
crème Chantilly **whipped cream**
fromage **cheese**
chèvre **goat's cheese**

In the Café

If you sit at the bar (le zinc), drinks will be somewhat cheaper than if you sit at a table. Settle the bill when you leave; the waiter may leave a slip of paper on the table to keep track of the bill. A tip of 10 percent is customary. The French

Numbers

0	zéro
1	un, une
2	deux
3	trois
4	quatre
5	cinq
6	six
7	sept
8	huit
9	neuf
10	dix
11	onze
12	douze
13	treize
14	quatorze
15	quinze
16	seize
17	dix-sept
18	dix-huit
19	dix-neuf
20	vingt
21	vingt-et-un
30	trente
40	quarante
50	cinquante
60	soixante
70	soixante-dix
80	quatre-vingts
90	quatre-vingt-dix
100	cent
1000	mille
1,000,000	un million

● *The number 1 is often written like an upside down V, and the number 7 is crossed.*

enjoy bittersweet aperitifs, which are often diluted with ice and fizzy water.
drinks *les boissons*
coffee *café*
...with milk or cream *...au lait or crème*
...decaffeinated *déca/décaféiné*
...black/espresso *express/noir*
...American filtered coffee *filtre*
tea *thé*
...herb infusion *tisane*
...camomile *verveine*
hot chocolate *chocolat chaud*
milk *lait*
mineral water *eau minérale*
fizzy *gazeux*
non-fizzy *non-gazeux*
fizzy lemonade *limonade*
fresh lemon juice served with sugar *citron pressé*
fresh squeezed orange juice *orange pressée*
full (eg full cream milk) *entier*
fresh or cold *frais, fraîche*
beer *bière*
...bottled *en bouteille*
...on tap *à la pression*
pre-dinner drink *apéritif*
white wine with cassis, black-currant liqueur *kir*
kir with champagne *kir royale*
with ice *avec des glaçons*

On the Telephone

How do I make an outside call?
Comment est-ce que je peux téléphoner à l'exterieur?
I want to make an international (local) call
Je voudrais une communication pour l'étranger (une communication locale)
What is the dialling code? *Quel est l'indicatif?*
I'd like an alarm call for 8 tomorrow morning.
Je voudrais être réveillé à huit heures demain matin
Who's calling?
C'est qui à l'appareil?
Hold on, please
Ne quittez pas s'il vous plaît
The line is busy
La ligne est occupée
I must have dialled the wrong number
J'ai dû faire un faux numéro

neat *sec*
red *rouge*
white *blanc*
rose *rosé*
dry *brut*
sweet *doux*
sparkling wine *crémant*
house wine *vin de maison*
local wine *vin de pays*
Where is this *De quelle région*
wine from? *vient ce vin?*
pitcher *carafe/pichet*
...of water/wine *...d'eau/de vin*
half litre *demi-carafe*
quarter litre *quart*
mixed *panaché*
after dinner drink *digestif*
brandy from Armagnac region of France *Armagnac*
Normandy apple brandy *calvados*
cheers! *santé!*
hangover *gueule de bois*

Days and Months

Days of the week, seasons and months are not capitalised in French.
● **Days of the week**
Monday *lundi*
Tuesday *mardi*
Wednesday *mercredi*
Thursday *jeudi*
Friday *vendredi*
Saturday *samedi*
Sunday *dimanche*
● **Seasons**
spring *le printemps*
summer *l'été*
autumn *l'automne*
winter *l'hiver*
● **Months**
January *janvier*
February *février*
March *mars*
April *avril*
May *mai*
June *juin*
July *juillet*
August *août*
September *septembre*
October *octobre*
November *novembre*
December *décembre*

● **Saying the date**
12th August 2000, *le douze août, deux mille*

Further Reading

General

An Account of Corsica, by James Boswell. In Print Publishing, UK 1999. Descriptions of his journey around the island and visit to Pasquale Paoli.

Columba, by Prosper Mérimée. Paris 1840. Based on the story of the *vendetta* that took place in the village of Fozzano in the Sartenais in 1833.

Corsica: Columbus's Isle, by Joseph Chiari. London 1960. Delves into the possibilities of Columbus actually having been born in Calvi.

The Dream-Hunters of Corsica, by Dorothy Carrington. Weidenfeld and Nicholson, London, 1995. An excellent study of the folk customs of the island by one of the island's distinguished residents.

Granite Island: a Portrait of Corsica, by Dorothy Carrington. Penguin paperback, New York and London, 1984. The classic account of the island's history and culture, woven together with travelogue drawn from more than three decades of living in Corsica.

Journal of a Landscape Painter in Corsica, by Edward Lear. London 1870. Through both his engravings and his writings, Lear was one of the first to portray the splendours of Corsica to the outside world.

The Life and Letters of Sir Gilbert Elliot, by Emma Eleanor Elliot. London 1874. Compiled by the grand-daughter of this aristocratic Scot, who as the Viceroy from 1794–96 acquired a genuine love of the island.

His Majesty of Corsica, by Valerie Pirie. London 1939. Biography of Theodor von Neuhof (King Theodore).

Napoleon, by Vincent Cronin. Fontana/Harper Collins, 2000. The most accessible popular biography in print, delving into Napoleon's family background to elucidate his peronality and career.

Napoleon and his Parents on the Threshold of History, by Dorothy Carrington. London, 1987. The definitive account of the future emperor's early years in and around Ajaccio.

Pasquale Paoli: an Enlightened Hero, by Peter Adam Thresher. London 1970. The most authoritative work on the island's greatest hero.

The Summer King, by Aylmer Vallance. London 1956. Another account of the fortunes of the Westphalian nobleman who wanted to rule Corsica.

The Scented Isle: a parallel between Corsica and the Scottish Highlands, by Joseph Chiari. Glasgow 1945. Comparing Corsica with his native country.

Other Insight Guides

The Insight Guide series covers nearly 200 destinations. These are among the titles on Mediterranean hot spots.

Insight Guide: France. Europe's most diverse nation is captured in 408 full-colour pages. And it's further explored in the Insight Guides to **Alsace**, **Brittany**, **Burgundy**, **The French Riviera**, **Normandy**, **Paris**, **Provence** and **The Loire Valley**.

Insight Guide: Sardinia is another of Insight's island guides.

Other Mediterranean island titles cover **Crete**, **The Greek Islands**, **Cyprus**, **Malta** and **Sicily**.

In Insight's companion *Compact Guide* series, handy-sized books designed as mini-encyclopedias for instant on-the-spot reference, current titles include **Malta**, **The Greek Islands**, **Tuscany**, **Paris** and **Rome**.

The *Insight Pocket Guide* series is written by local hosts. The books, many with full-size fold-out maps, take you on specially worked-out tours which help to make the most of a visit when time is limited. Current titles include **The Aegean Islands**, **Corsica**, **Ibiza**, **Mallorca**, **Malta**, **Rhodes**, **Sardinia** and **Sicily**.

Insight Guide Fleximaps have a laminated finish for ease of use, informative text and detailed cartography. There are Fleximaps to the following destinations: **Corsica**, **the French Riviera** and **Sardinia**.

Feedback

We do our best to ensure the information in our books is as accurate and up-to-date as possible. The books are updated on a regular basis, using local contacts, who painstakingly add, amend and correct as required. However, some mistakes and omissions are inevitable and we are ultimately reliant on our readers to put us in the picture.

We would welcome your feedback on any details related to your experiences using the book "on the road". Maybe we recommended a hotel that you liked (or another that you didn't), as well as interesting new attractions, or facts and figures you have found out about the country itself. The more details you can give us (particularly with regard to addresses, e-mails and telephone numbers), the better.

We will acknowledge all contributions, and we'll offer an Insight Guide to the best letters received.

Please write to us at:
Insight Guides
PO Box 7910
London SE1 1WE
United Kingdom
Or send e-mail to:
insight@apaguide.co.uk

ART & PHOTO CREDITS

David Abram 4/5, 6/7, 57, 59, 250, 253, 254, 255
Anita Back 87, 92, 93
Pete Bennett/Apa back cover centre left, bottom, centre, spine, back flap bottom, front flap bottom, 4BL/R, 17, 21, 30, 31L/R, 36, 37, 41, 42, 58, 60/61, 62/63, 80, 96, 97, 98, 99, 100, 101, 105, 110/111, 115, 117, 118, 123, 126, 128, 130/131, 133, 137, 138, 140/141, 143, 145, 146, 147, 150, 155, 158, 159, 161, 165, 167, 170, 172, 175, 176L/R, 179, 184, 185, 191, 192/193, 194, 204, 208, 210, 211, 212/213, 215, 217, 218, 219, 220, 221, 222, 223, 224, 225L/R, 226, 227, 230
Patricia Bonnin 50, 52, 55, 56, 94, 95, 180
Franz Füss 69, 249, 252
Michel Gotin back cover top, 2/3, 5B, 8/9, 10/11, 67, 74, 79, 83, 90, 91, 125, 127, 157, 197, 198, 200, 235, 239
Clare Griffiths 70, 71, 72, 73, 134, 151, 153, 245, 246, 247
Historia Photo 35, 43, 46, 102, 103
Hartmut Lücke 234, 237, 251
Neill Menneer 1, 12, 119, 120, 122, 136, 168

Musée régional d'Anthropologie de la Corse 25, 27, 48, 84
Musée Fesch 121
Christine Osborne 66, 88/89, 106/107, 190
Frank Rother 29
Alphons Schauseil 3B, 51, 75, 81, 108/109, 173, 238
Jutta Schütz front flap top, 14/15, 16, 20, 22, 23, 24, 26, 28, 32, 33, 38, 39, 44, 49, 53, 54, 114, 142, 154, 156, 169, 177, 195, 201, 209, 240L/R, 256
Francois Schia 65
U. Snowdon back flap top, 243
Janos Stekovics 18, 19, 34, 40, 64, 76, 77, 82, 85, 86, 132, 135, 171, 199, 205, 207, 214, 231, 236, 241
Werner Stuhler 178, 188, 189, 202/203
Topham Picturepoint 162/163
Ken Wright 68, 148/149, 164, 182/183, 187, 228/229

Map Production Laura Morris/Apa Publications

Cartographic Editor **Zoë Goodwin**
Production **Linton Donaldson**
Design Director **Klaus Geisler**
Picture Research **Hilary Genin**

Index

Numbers in italics refer to photographs